全国翻译专业本科系列教材

TEXT ANALYSIS AND APPLICATION: BUSINESS TEXTS
商务文本分析与应用教程

李睿 贺莺 编

清华大学出版社
北京

内 容 简 介

本书共有 10 章,选取了访谈、演讲、报告、社评、新闻等多种文体。所选话题紧密结合时代发展,涉及知识面广,用语生动自然,旨在为学生提供最前沿和最地道的信息输入和语言素材。本书的一个突出特点是通过指导学生利用网络资源来构建基本的商务知识框架,培养学生的自主学习意识、网络搜索能力、理性思维能力和语言逻辑表达能力。

本书适合英语专业和翻译专业学生使用,也适合作为了解外媒对世界和中国经济形势看法及基本商务翻译技巧和知识的参考资料。

本书部分内容配有视频,请点击以下链接进行下载学习(提取码:t9uc):https://pan.baidu.com/s/1ub2FFBB4Tcbk-FPqS66U3w。

版权所有,侵权必究。举报:010-62782989,beiqinquan@tup.tsinghua.edu.cn。

图书在版编目(CIP)数据

商务文本分析与应用教程 / 李睿,贺莺编. —北京:清华大学出版社,2018(2023.8重印)
(全国翻译专业本科系列教材)
ISBN 978-7-302-51240-0

Ⅰ.商… Ⅱ.①李… ②贺… Ⅲ.①商务–英语–翻译–高等学校–教材 Ⅳ.①F7

中国版本图书馆CIP数据核字(2018)第213823号

责任编辑:刘 艳
封面设计:子 一
责任校对:王凤芝
责任印制:刘海龙

出版发行:清华大学出版社
网　　址:http://www.tup.com.cn,http://www.wqbook.com
地　　址:北京清华大学学研大厦A座　　邮　编:100084
社 总 机:010-83470000　　邮　购:010-62786544
投稿与读者服务:010-62776969,c-service@tup.tsinghua.edu.cn
质量反馈:010-62772015,zhiliang@tup.tsinghua.edu.cn

印 装 者:涿州市般润文化传播有限公司
经　　销:全国新华书店
开　　本:170mm×230mm　　印　张:20.75　　字　数:334千字
版　　次:2018年11月第1版　　印　次:2023年8月第5次印刷
定　　价:75.00元

产品编号:075779-01

前 言

"商务文本分析与应用"是西安外国语大学高级翻译学院本科二年级的专业必修课,与翻译专业"文化平行文本分析与应用""时事平行文本分析与应用"形成梯级课程,授课时长为一学期。本课程旨在为学生构建基本的商务知识框架,引导学生使用微观和宏观经济原理反思日常经济现象,培养学生的阅读、理解、思考、书面或口头表达等多项技能,并提高他们的分析理解能力、语言表达能力和调查研究能力,为高年级阶段学习商务笔译课程打好基础。本书提炼具有知识性和趣味性的当代经济和金融方面的话题,选取访谈、演讲、报告、社评、新闻等多种文体,借助互文性理论,指导翻译专业低年级学生对平行文本、可比文本进行观察、分析,形成对商务术语和商务文本中英表达范式差异性的基础认识。

本书共分10章,按照一学期18周、每周6课时计算,每章计划教学时长为一周至两周。本书的编排思路如下:编者首先从每章甄选的主题出发扩散出相关的话题,然后针对各相关话题选择单语文本、平行双语文本或可比文本,目的是使学生从篇章理解、术语学习、商业背景知识构建过渡到各种商务口笔头输出,从理解逐步深入到应用。

在全球化背景下,新世纪对学习双语或多语的中国人的语言交流能力提出了更高的要求,这就需要单语种的传统教学突破自我,运用语言资源管理的整体思维,从受教育者的语言权利和语言发展出发,以"家国情怀"和"民族认同"为基石,增进国际理解,开阔"世界胸怀"。本书英文文章均出自近年来《经济学人》《华尔街时报》《金融时报》《哈佛商业周刊》等欧美国家的主流财经媒体,平行汉语材料包括百科词条、中国主流媒体编译的新闻或报道等。所选话题紧密结合时代发展,涉及知识面广,用语生动自然,旨在为学生提供最前沿和最地道的信息输入和语言素材。每一篇文章后都有类型多样的练习,以扩大学生的国际视野,增强他们的家国情怀。

从本科翻译专业本身的培养目标来看,与学生翻译相关的能力包括语言能力、文本操控能力、了解专题知识的能力、跨文化交流能力。本书改变了传统单语输入的教学方式,首次引入了平行文本和可比文本的概念,从知识素养入手,通过指导学生利用网络资源构建基本的商务知识框架,培养学生的自主学习意识、网络搜索能力、理性思维能力和语言逻辑表达能力。每章练习包含相关商务概念及术语的整理与积累、信息的整合综述以及基于同主题的中英文写作和翻译,通过课内课外的内容及活动设计,让学生在学习过程中学会沟通和合作。

学习翻译需要学生付出艰苦的努力,特别是要善于突破传统的外语学习习惯,找到提高翻译能力的有效方法。感谢我的学生,他们在教材几年的试用中给了我许多灵感和宝贵的反馈意见。感谢清华大学出版社的编辑不辞辛劳地促成了本书的出版。希望本书对所有学习翻译的学生及希望了解一些外媒对世界和中国经济形势看法的同学有所裨益。

本书部分内容配有视频,请点击以下链接进行下载学习(提取码:t9uc):https://pan.baidu.com/s/1ub2FFBB4Tcbk-FPqS66U3w。

编者

2018 年 11 月

Contents

Chapter 1 Marketing Strategies ... 1

Pre-reading Activities ... 2
Part 1: Case Study of KFC ... 2
Part 2: Case Study of Hai Di Lao ... 12
Part 3: Case Study of Disneyland ... 17
Part 4: Case Study of Promotional Strategies ... 22
Business Application ... 30

Chapter 2 Corporate Scandals ... 31

Pre-reading Activities ... 32
Part 1: Volkswagen Emissions Scandal ... 32
Part 2: How United Airlines Handles an Overbooked Flight ... 42
Part 3: Well Fargo's Fake Accounts ... 50
Part 4: Tesco's Accounting Fiasco ... 55
Business Application ... 59

III

Chapter ③ Cars and Oil 61

Pre-reading Activities 62

Part 1: Car Ownership Restrictions 63

Part 2: M&A: Geely and Volvo 73

Part 3: Car Models and Auto Shows 79

Part 4: Oil Pricing Mechanism 82

Business Application 87

Chapter ④ China's Internet Companies 89

Pre-reading Activities 90

Part 1: Case Study of WeChat 91

Part 2: Case Study of Vancl 100

Part 3: Case Study of Alibaba 105

Part 4: Case Study of Jack Ma 109

Business Application 119

Chapter ⑤ China's Property Market 121

Pre-reading Activities 122

Part 1: China's Real Estate Bubble 122

Part 2: Beijing's Property Control Measures 134

Part 3: Property Boom/Bust 144

Part 4: China's Women and Property 148

Business Application 153

Contents

Chapter 6 China's High-Speed Rail 155

Pre-reading Activities 156
Part 1: Trajectory of China's HSR Development 156
Part 2: News Reports on China's HSR 162
Part 3: Industry Implications of High-Speed Rail 169
Part 4: High-Speed Rail in the U.S. 177
Business Application 180

Chapter 7 China's Demographic Economics 187

Pre-reading Activities 188
Part 1: China's Demographic Challenges 189
Part 2: Challenges Facing the Old 203
Part 3: Maternity Tourism 212
Part 4: Controversial Assistant Reproductive Methods 220
Business Application 228

Chapter 8 RMB Exchange Rate 233

Pre-reading Activities 234
Part 1: U.S.' and China's Stance on RMB Valuation 235
Part 2: The Fall of RMB's Value 243
Part 3: RMB's Addition to the IMF's Currency Basket 248
Part 4: President Trump's Stance on RMB 252
Business Application 256

Chapter 9 European Debt Crisis and Brexit 259

Pre-reading Activities 260
Part 1: European Debt Crisis Explained 261
Part 2: Debt Crisis in Greece 267
Part 3: Brexit Explained 275
Part 4: Aftermath of Brexit Referendum 281
Business Application 290

Chapter 10 U.S. Tax Reform 291

Pre-reading Activities 292
Part 1: How to Pay U.S. Individual Taxes 292
Part 2: Why Is Tax Reform Difficult? 300
Part 3: U.S. Tax Reform at a Glance 307
Part 4: Republicans VS. Democrats on Tax Reform 314
Business Application 320

Chapter 1
Marketing Strategies

Overview

Every company wants to succeed in the market, but doing business, much like fighting a battle, involves a set of strategies to stay strong and competitive. What is the recipe for KFC's success in China? Why are so many Chinese people lovers of the hotpot chain Hai Di Lao? Are you willing to pay a high entrance ticket to Disneyland? How do you take advantage of social media sites to promote your brand in China? The chapter, through four case studies, will take you on a business tour and reveal secrets behind some notable corporate successes.

Pre-reading Activities

1. Which company in the world do you admire most? What do you think contribute to its success?

2. What do you think are the essential components of a corporate marketing strategy? Give examples to illustrate your points.

3. Watch the video "The Marketing Mix" from the CAW Business School.

Part 1
Case Study of KFC

Read the following two texts, one in Chinese and one in English, and carry out your reading tasks as directed.

Text 1

KFC China's Recipe for Success

If there were just a few things that China has wholly embraced from the West, it would be their love for Kentucky Fried Chicken, or KFC as it is more commonly known. In 1987, the fast-food operator opened its first outlet near Tiananmen Square in Beijing. Then came 2,000 other outlets, which sprung up across China within the next 20 years—a phenomenal achievement by any standard.

The improbable success of KFC China can be attributed to a few key ingredients: context, people, strategy and execution, so says Warren Liu, a former vice president of

Chapter 1 Marketing Strategies

business development and a member of Tricon Greater China Executive Committee. Tricon was the predecessor to KFC China's parent company YUM! Brands.

In his book *KFC in China: Secret Recipe for Success*, Liu says it was firstly the context in which KFC entered the Chinese market that paved the way for its eventual success. "Strategy is context-dependent; a strategy that works well in a stable and mature market economy would most likely not work well in China, given the diversity of its people, geography, the heritage of a rich and complex culture, and a rapidly and continuously changing business environment since China's economic reforms commenced in 1978," Liu says in his book.

Case in point: When KFC first entered Hong Kong, China in 1973, it quickly grew to 11 restaurants in the following year. But it misjudged the local market and failed to develop a suitable business model. By 1975, all 11 restaurants were forced to close their shutters. Ten years later, KFC came back with a vengeance, eventually franchising its operations to a company called Birdland, which was backed by a group of local investors.

KFC's rocky experience in Asia served as invaluable and relatively inexpensive lessons in preparation for its entry into China in 1987. At a time when joint ventures were the only viable alternative in the late 1980s and early 1990s, KFC China selected local partners with government connections and effectively leveraged their tangible and intangible local resources. Once joint ventures were no longer required by Chinese regulations, and sufficient knowledge and resources had been transferred from the local partners, KFC went direct in order to avoid the paralysis that can result from disagreements between partners.

The "Taiwan Gang"

Another vital ingredient in KFC's secret recipe is its leadership team, specifically its founding leadership team known as the "Taiwan Gang", mainly because most had hailed from Taiwan, China. According to Liu, members of this pioneering team of KFC had accumulated at least 10, if not 15 to 20 years of fast-food industry experience prior to landing in China. Though predominantly Western-educated, being ethnic Chinese, they inherently understood China. Many also came with a background from McDonald's.

That factor led to an intuitive knowledge of the market context, which then put KFC China on track to becoming a successful enterprise. "In order to be successful, especially for foreign companies or non-local companies, a deep understanding and a broad understanding of that market context is critical to success. To the extent that understanding is (even) intuitive. Being intuitive means that you don't have to do the market research, you don't have to have multiple meetings to come to the best solution to a problem or to point to a future strategic direction," Liu told INSEAD Knowledge.

"Those money and time saved are going to add to your probability of success in the long run because in a dynamic and fast-changing market environment, speed becomes a lethal competitive differentiator, the speed with which to come up with the best ideas, to make the optimal decisions, and to execute those decisions once they are made. Over time, speed contributes to the accumulation of a competitive advantage in a fast-paced and rapidly-changing market environment."

Going Local

Intuition led to product localization, which is also a very important part of the success formula. Liu says that KFC China tended to introduce new products more frequently than their competitors in China. Also the fact that KFC has chicken as its core product offering is a very natural advantage that fits this context very well, since most Chinese prefer pork, followed by chicken; whereas beef and mutton lag far behind. So in that light, KFC enjoys a natural product advantage over McDonald's.

That KFC has also done a lot of work to continuously invent and launch new products; products that better fit the Chinese consumers' taste preference have allowed them to keep the competition at bay. It has got a 2:1 ratio over McDonald's in China, whereas outside China it's the other way around.

Although KFC's original recipe is accepted by most Chinese, KFC China did not stop there. The highly localized menu includes congee or Chinese-style porridge for breakfast; Beijing Chicken Roll served with scallion and seafood sauce; Spicy Diced Chicken resembling a popular Sichuan-style dish. Their latest creation is you tiao or Chinese dough

Chapter 1 Marketing Strategies

fritters.

Yet for all its hits, there are already rising brands that are not the KFCs or the Burger Kings or the McDonald's. Liu says that Wei Qian La Mian, also known as Ajisen Ramen, is a Japanese product that has been doing very well in various cities throughout China. So is Zhen Gongfu or Real Kung-fu, a Chinese fast food chain which is showing a lot of promise.

The competition has even gone hi-tech. "I recently heard about a robot developed with subsidy from the Chinese government which is capable of preparing dozens of popular Chinese dishes at high speed, and with excellent taste, based on expert knowledge."

Dawn of a New Era?

This probably explains why KFC China has fired its latest salvo. Liu says: "I think the reason that YUM! Brands is interested in launching and launching aggressively this new brand called East Dawning is for reasons both offensive and defensive in nature...because (they) wanted to fend off potential local Chinese fast-food competitors."

However, Liu thinks KFC China should reposition East Dawning, and move its market focus and resources to outside China; and within China, continue to focus on KFC, Pizza Hut and Pizza Hut Express. After all, he says, KFC China is the indisputable star of YUM! Brands' worldwide growth engine.

That being said, Liu feels that more attention in the future should be paid to the flavour, quality and price performance of new products—not frequency of new product introduction, as this can detract consumer focus away from core products offerings.

He also thinks that the company should develop senior local talent within KFC China to take on top national, regional and even international leadership roles in the next few years.

"While the 'Taiwan Gang' played its historical mission exceptionally well during the first two decades, it's time for the baton to be passed on to the local Chinese—not for any altruistic reasons, but simply because the locals understand this market even better than the 'Taiwan Gang'," he says in his book.

But past achievements do not guarantee future success. So will the "Local Gang" be as good or even better than the "Taiwan Gang"? That, Liu says, remains to be seen. "It all depends on the evolution of that leadership team and the evolution of China, the market, in the future."

Implementation will be key. And in China, successful implementation requires not only sound, localized products, people, systems and processes, but also the flexibility to change direction according to a new government policy, crisis or opportunity.

"Only the most perceptive and swiftest-moving companies will rise to the top, and stay on top," Liu says in his book, although having said that, he still has a lot of faith in his former company. "KFC's leadership position in the Chinese restaurant industry is KFC's to lose."

Text 2

肯德基"土"配方谋变

当洋快餐开始卖油条、豆浆和米饭时,产品已经不是问题,态度才是关键。

2010年6月1日,肯德基在中国内地的第3000家门店在上海开张,同期,全球快餐业霸主麦当劳在中国大陆只有1100多家门店。

从1987年进入中国大陆开始,百胜餐饮集团下属的肯德基品牌在门店数量上就一直领先老对手麦当劳,这让许多人误以为两家连锁餐厅势均力敌,肯德基略占上风。而实际上,从全球市场来看,肯德基连锁餐厅数量比麦当劳少15.6%。在美国本土,肯德基更是被彻底边缘化,完全不是麦当劳、汉堡王和赛百味的对手。

为何肯德基品牌能在中国大陆获得成功?对此,肯德基的回答是"本土化"。

"自1987年来到中国,肯德基一直秉承'立足中国、融入生活'的总策略。"在接受《世界博览》采访时,百胜集团公关部的李薇介绍说,对于一家快餐店来说,首要任务是为消费者提供好吃的食物,否则一切都是空谈。肯德基一直想在全球树立"烹鸡专家"的形象,当家产品有吮指原味鸡、香辣鸡翅、香辣鸡腿汉堡等,但仅凭这些产品坐吃老本是不现实的。

20世纪90年代中期,肯德基中国分部就成立了自己的产品研发团队,至今已发展到 100 多人的规模，他们的主要任务就是开发适合中国人口味的食品。1987 年，北京前门肯德基餐厅里只卖 8 种产品；现在，餐厅里至少有 57 种常规产品可供选择。在过去 20 多年里，肯德基推出的新产品超过 140 种；最近几年，在中国市场更是平均每年推出 20 种新食品。

2002 年，肯德基在广东地区推出第一款中国特色食品——早餐粥。随后，油条、豆浆、蔬菜等菜式不断推出。

肯德基公司解释说，更改产品线的关键在于增加了蔬果类食品，让烹饪方式不再局限于油炸，而是更加多元化，这样能避免被贴上"垃圾食品"的标签。2010 年，肯德基最大的举措是推出了米饭类食品，这可以说是开了"洋快餐"的先河。

除了丰富的本土化菜单以外，肯德基的另一个法宝是管理的本土化。与很多外企喜欢聘请东南亚或在国外长大的华裔经理人做高管不同，肯德基中国公司的核心团队大多来自中国台湾地区，甚至有媒体称其为"台湾帮"。据说这个团队的成员来到大陆之前，大多在快餐行业已经工作了 10~20 年。虽然他们中大多数人受过西方的高等教育，但更了解中国的国情。

肯德基公司向本刊介绍说，1987 年，中国肯德基的员工不到一百人。时隔 24 年，肯德基员工已超过 23 万人，实现了 99.9% 的本土化。肯德基在中国的 16 个分公司总经理中，有 14 个是从公司内部的市场培训提拔上来的，这也充分说明肯德基对员工自身发展的重视。

肯德基在原料供给方面也希望尽量做到本土化。肯德基在中国有 500 多家原料供应商。将一个汉堡拆分开，里面的鸡肉、蔬菜、面包和调味料大多是在中国本土采购的。

即使是在广告中，肯德基都充分考虑到了中国的文化。与崇尚个人主义的美国人不同，中国人更重视集体，特别是自己的家庭，这一点在用餐的时候体现得最明显。中国人不会放弃一切同家人一起吃饭的机会。

在 2008 年奥运会之前，肯德基在中国共播放过 24 条广告，其中有 7 条都在推销"外带全家桶"。这 7 条广告都在强调同家人朋友分享的快乐，可谓"击中中国人感情中最柔软的部分"。

在广告中，肯德基塑造了一群"主角"，也就是理想中的客户群体——一群朝气蓬勃的年轻人，他们乐观开朗，懂得分享。

另外,在 6 条有孩子出镜的广告中,主角是清一色的男孩儿。这不是性别歧视,而是肯德基敏锐地注意到了几千年农业文明的积淀对中国父母们的影响。

肯德基很早就提出"为中国而改变,全力打造'新快餐'"的理念。肯德基的当家人——百胜餐饮集团中国事业部主席兼首席执行官苏敬轼曾经说过,"中国肯德基是中国人的肯德基"。在同麦当劳的竞争中,本土化让肯德基节省了资源和时间,给消费者留下了肯德基总是先行一步的印象。

Summary Writing

1. Complete the following summary of Text 1 in Chinese.

肯德基在中国市场的四大利器	
店面管理结构	香港模式:_____;大陆模式:_____ 模式不同的原因:_____
管理层	特　　点:_____;优　　势:_____
产品	产品做到以_____为主,同时推出_____。
战略执行	推出_____;关注_____; 而非_____;加速_____。

2. Complete the following summary of Text 2 in English.

Localization in KFC
Product: _____ Supply chain: _____ Management: _____ Promotion: _____

Chapter **1** Marketing Strategies

Reading Comprehension

Briefly answer the following questions about the two texts in English.

1) Do you like to dine out or eat at home? What are the main reasons for you to dine out compared with eating at home?
2) What is your favorite restaurant/chain? Why are you attracted to it?
3) What do you know about YUM! Brands, the parent company of KFC?
4) Text 1 is based on an interview conducted by INSEAD Knowledge. What do you know about INSEAD?
5) According to Text 1, KFC used franchising in Hong Kong, China. If you were to start your own restaurant, would you like to start your own brand or choose franchising? What are the advantages and drawbacks of franchising?
6) Summarize the differences and similarities between KFC and McDonald's or between any of your favorite fast food restaurants based on Text 2.

Translation

1. Provide the Chinese equivalents to the following terms and expressions.

1) fast-food operator
2) outlets
3) Greater China
4) vice president
5) parent company
6) franchising
7) joint ventures
8) launch new products
9) product introduction
10) subsidy
11) core product offering

2. Translate the following sentences/paragraphs into Chinese.

1) If there were just a few things that China has wholly embraced from the West, it would be their love for Kentucky Fried Chicken, or KFC as it is more commonly known.

2) "Strategy is context-dependent; a strategy that works well in a stable and mature market economy would most likely not work well in China, given the diversity

of its people, geography, the heritage of a rich and complex culture, and a rapidly and continuously changing business environment since China's economic reforms commenced in 1978," Liu says in his book.

3) "...YUM! Brands is interested in launching and launching aggressively this new brand called East Dawning is for reasons both offensive and defensive in nature...because (they) wanted to fend off potential local Chinese fast-food competitors."

4) "While the 'Taiwan Gang' played its historical mission exceptionally well during the first two decades, it's time for the baton to be passed on to the local Chinese— not for any altruistic reasons, but simply because the locals understand this market even better than the 'Taiwan Gang'," he says in his book.

5) "Only the most perceptive and swiftest-moving companies will rise to the top, and stay on top," Liu says in his book, although having said that, he still has a lot of faith in his former company. "KFC's leadership position in the Chinese restaurant industry is KFC's to lose."

Ⅳ Language Exercises

Replace the expressions in bold in the following sentences/paragraphs without changing their meanings.

1) KFC China's **Recipe for Success**
2) The improbable success of KFC China can be attributed to **a few key ingredients**: context, people, strategy and execution, so says Warren Liu,...
3) ...it was firstly the context in which KFC entered the Chinese market that **paved the way for its eventual success**.
4) **Another vital ingredient** in KFC's secret recipe is its leadership team, specifically its founding leadership team known as the "Taiwan Gang",...
5) ...in a dynamic and fast-changing market environment, speed becomes **a lethal competitive differentiator**, ...

Chapter 1 Marketing Strategies

6) Implementation will be **key**.

7) Intuition led to product localization, which is also a very important part of **the success formula**.

8) By 1975, all 11 restaurants were forced to **close their shutters**. Ten years later, KFC **came back with a vengeance**,...

9) Then came 2,000 other outlets, which **sprung up** across China within the next 20 years...

10) KFC's **rocky experience** in Asia served as invaluable and relatively inexpensive lessons in preparation for its entry into China in 1987.

11) That factor led to an intuitive knowledge of the market context, which then **put KFC China on track to** becoming a successful enterprise.

12) ...KFC China is the indisputable star of YUM! Brands' worldwide **growth engine**.

13) ...KFC went direct in order to avoid the **paralysis** that can result from disagreements between partners.

14) "While the 'Taiwan Gang' played its historical mission exceptionally well during the first two decades, **it's time for the baton to be passed** on to the local Chinese...," he says in his book.

15) That KFC has also done a lot of work to continuously invent and launch new products; products that...has allowed them to **keep the competition at bay**.

16) This probably explains why KFC China has **fired its latest salvo**.

17) "...this new brand called East Dawning is for reasons both **offensive and defensive** in nature...because (they) wanted to **fend off** potential local Chinese fast-food competitors."

11

Part 2
Case Study of Hai Di Lao

Read the following English text and carry out your reading tasks as directed.

Chinese Hot Pot Chain Hai Di Lao Makes Move to U.S.

If P. T. Barnum had ever opened a restaurant, it might look a lot like Hai Di Lao, the popular chain of 75 Chinese eateries planning its first foray into the U.S. market this fall.

Talk about a three-ring circus: Diners pass the time in the waiting area with Internet terminals, board games and kids' toys. They can nibble on unlimited free snacks. Or kick back for a shoeshine, manicure or hand massage.

In the dining room, patrons wearing full-size aprons provided by the restaurant lean together over the boiling caldrons embedded in each table, dropping morsels of uncooked meat, fish, vegetables or tofu in a spicy steaming broth, then dipping them in flavorful sauces. On special holidays, magicians in colorful, traditional masks perform tricks. Patrons order using iPads. Periodically, a server breaks into the restaurant's signature Olympic-style "noodle dance".

Such showmanship, along with service, has set Hai Di Lao apart in China's burgeoning restaurant landscape and has distinguished it from competitors that also sell hot pot, the traditional communal cuisine that originated in Mongolia centuries ago. Spicy versions emerged from the southwestern city of Chongqing and expanded in neighboring Sichuan Province and then across China. Hot pot is particularly popular with groups of young people and families. The act of pulling food from the caldron lends to the chain's name, which in Mandarin means "fishing in the bottom of the sea".

Owner Zhang Yong, who launched Hai Di Lao in Sichuan in 1994 and opened his first international branch in Singapore last year, hopes the touches that established his brand in China will also pave the way for his first U.S. outpost. It is scheduled to open this September in the affluent Los Angeles enclave of Arcadia.

Chapter 1　Marketing Strategies

Only in the past several years have Chinese companies significantly embarked outside the country. But most have centered on sectors like energy and manufacturing. Mr. Zhang is one of the few who have gone after consumers.

In China, every Hai Di Lao employs a handful of "noodle masters", who train an average of four to six months before starting to perform their dance in the middle of the dining room. They stretch foot-long wads of dough into at least 10 feet of slender, ribbonlike noodle by whipping the center out like a jump rope and rippling and swirling it through the air like the ribbons twirled by Olympic rhythmic gymnasts. Often, the dancer flings the dough over customers' heads as they squeal and clap, before folding it with a flourish and dropping it in the broth.

Hot pot itself isn't totally foreign to the U.S. market. Yum! Brand, Inc., which owns KFC and acquired Chinese hot-pot chain Little Sheep in 2011, already has a dozen outlets in the U.S. They are predominantly in areas with high Chinese populations, like Flushing, N.Y. According to the most recent census, Arcadia, Hai Di Lao's new U.S. home, is more than 50% Asian.

The staff doles out a steady stream of hot towels and other niceties: hair elastics to longhaired customers (to prevent hair from falling in food), eyeglass wipes to the bespectacled (all that steam can fog one's vision) and plastic bags to phone-toting eaters to protect mobiles from getting messy. Unlike at many Chinese restaurants, patrons don't have to yell out for menus or checks. In the restrooms, they have access to an array of free perfumes and lotions.

Hai Di Lao's 75 outlets made more than 10% profit on 3.127 billion yuan ($510 million) in revenue in 2012, up 54% from a year earlier, Mr. Zhang said.

The entrepreneur is well aware that not every trick in his playbook will work for the U.S. market. Manicures in restaurants aren't likely to pass muster with U.S. food-safety inspectors. Costs for amenities like hot hand-towel service and dancing wait staff are bound to be higher in the U.S., just as they have been in Singapore.

Some broth flavors, like the sour vegetable fish soup, may not translate, either. Mr. Zhang said he would tweak the menu to fit consumers' tastes, but using chopsticks to eat remains a must.

He also said he would offer individual pots for U.S. customers rather than the group caldrons used in China. The reason, Mr. Zhang said, is that Western dining is more individual. "Whatever they want is what I'll give them," he said.

❶ Reading Comprehension

Briefly answer the following questions about the text in English.

1) Describe the distinctive services of Hai Di Lao based on the text above and then come up with more based on your own dining experience.

2) What is the recipe for Hai Di Lao's success?

3) Do you think the success of Hai Di Lao can be repeated in the U.S.? What services should remain the unchanged and what should be adapted to suit the U.S. market?

❷ Language Exercises

Search the text and the Internet for expressions associated with "火锅".

❸ Translation

1. Translate the following sentences/paragraphs into Chinese.

1) Talk about a three-ring circus: Diners pass the time in the waiting area with Internet terminals, board games and kids' toys. They can nibble on unlimited free snacks. Or kick back for a shoeshine, manicure or hand massage.

2) In the dining room, patrons wearing full-size aprons provided by the restaurant lean together over the boiling caldrons embedded in each table, dropping morsels of uncooked meat, fish, vegetables or tofu in a spicy steaming broth, then dipping them in flavorful sauces.

3) On special holidays, magicians in colorful, traditional masks perform tricks.

Chapter 1 Marketing Strategies

Patrons order using iPads. Periodically, a server breaks into the restaurant's signature Olympic-style "noodle dance".

4) ...hot pot, the traditional communal cuisine that originated in Mongolia centuries ago. Spicy versions emerged from the southwestern city of Chongqing and expanded in neighboring Sichuan Province and then across China. Hot pot is particularly popular with groups of young people and families.

5) In China, every Hai Di Lao employs a handful of "noodle masters", who train an average of four to six months before starting to perform their dance in the middle of the dining room.

6) They stretch foot-long wads of dough into at least 10 feet of slender, ribbonlike noodle by whipping the center out like a jump rope and rippling and swirling it through the air like the ribbons twirled by Olympic rhythmic gymnasts.

7) Often, the dancer flings the dough over customers' heads as they squeal and clap, before folding it with a flourish and dropping it in the broth.

2. **Translate the following sentences/paragraphs into English. Note that you must use expressions you picked from the text to translate the parts in bold.**

   1) 改革开放以来，大量外资企业进入中国；不过随着中国经济的腾飞，越来越多的中国本土企业也开始"走出去"。

   2) 《中国好声音》注重选手的实力而不是外表，因此在中国迅速发展的歌唱类选秀节目中脱颖而出。

   3) 世界酒业巨头帝亚吉欧收购水井坊后，将把其打造成国际品牌。英国是该品牌进入欧洲市场的第一站。

   4) 阿里巴巴绝非仅仅是美国电子商务公司在中国的"仿制品"。实际上，有些公司还曾借鉴过马云的经营理念。

   5) 上月，新西兰乳业公司恒天然集团的部分批次婴儿奶粉质检**不达标**。中国质检总局要求立即召回可能受到污染的产品。

   6) 社交网络上的好友数量**不代表**真正的友情。真正的友谊并不是打开手机、电脑就能找到的，而需要切实付出，祸福与共。

15

IV Research and Discussion

Search the Internet for answers to the following questions and share your findings in class.

1) What are the most important factors that affect your choice of a restaurant? Rate them in terms of importance.

2) China's restaurant industry has been racked by a spate of scandals in recent years. For example, there are reports of some hotpot restaurants using "gutter oil", or recycled cooking oil, as substitute for good ones in their broths. Describe in bilingual terms the food scares you've heard about or experienced personally.

3) What are the effective measures to ensure China's food safety and that restaurants are rule followers?

V Bilingual Debate

The following is an excerpt from a Chinese news report on Hai Di Lao. Take a stance on the following motion "Should Hai Di Lao Be Forgiven for Its Unsanitary Kitchen Practices and Breach of Public Trust?" and state your reasons in both Chinese and English in class.

为什么那么多人选择原谅海底捞？

海底捞的官网上，醒目地挂着两句话——海底捞可能有两种死法：第一种是管理出问题，死亡过程可能持续数月甚至上年；第二种是食品安全出问题，一旦发生，海底捞可能明天就会关门，生死攸关。

然而谁也不曾想到，眼下，身为中国餐饮业标杆、视食品安全如命的海底捞，真的摊上了第二种"生死攸关"的问题。

2017年8月25日上午11:00：《法制晚报》发布了一篇记者暗访报道，称海底捞后厨有老鼠爬进装食品的柜子，扫帚、簸箕、抹布与餐具一同清洗，洗碗机内部肮脏不堪，顾客用过的漏勺被拿来掏下水道……

14:46：海底捞发表致歉信，承认媒体披露的问题属实，表示"感到非常难过和痛心，也十分愧疚"。

Chapter ❶ Marketing Strategies

17:16：海底捞通报了关于这起事件的处理结果，宣布北京劲松店、太阳宫店停业整改。通报大意："这锅我背，这错我改，员工我养"。

18:00 左右："海底捞回应"的消息上了新浪微博热搜第一位，这时的评论风向已经开始改变。

Part ③
Case Study of Disneyland

Read the following English text and carry out your reading tasks as directed.

Of Course Disney Should Use Surge Pricing at Its Theme Parks

The Walt Disney Company is reportedly considering implementing surge pricing at its various theme parks. Admission to Disneyland in Anaheim, CA, for instance, is currently $99 for any day of the week. The rumored pricing plan involves offering Gold ($115), Silver ($105), and Bronze ($99) ticket options that are priced based on anticipated demand. Gold would be good for admission any day of the week; Silver ($105) would be for off-peak weekdays and weekends; Bronze ($99) would get you in on select off-peak weekends.

Implementing demand-based pricing strategies at Disneyland, or any theme park for that matter, simply makes sense. Raising prices during popular times such as Fourth of July weekend capitalizes on higher consumer valuations. Is this gouging? Some observers think so, but if customers are willing to pay more in certain instances, I vote for accepting this "free money".

One refinement I'd consider making to the rumored Disney pricing plan is reducing the lowest Bronze plan price. It's worth investigating whether a significantly lower price can activate "dormant customers" to fill the park on otherwise sparse days. By dormant customers, I mean those who are interested in coming to the theme park, but haven't done so because the price has been too high. By offering deeper discounts on off-peak days, customers who otherwise would not have enjoyed Disneyland could now do so. This would result in growth. Since theme parks are high fixed cost and low variable cost entities, revenue from discount-enticed new customers is virtually all profit...free money. These newly activated dormant customers would also likely show up hungry and snap up souvenirs... more free money.

Using discounts to activate dormant customers can be highly effective. Randy's Car Wash, located across the street from the *Harvard Business Review*'s office, offers a $5.99 wash special on Tuesdays. Shazam: Demand is so strong on some Tuesdays that a police officer has to direct traffic. The upside of discounting for Randy is...free money.

Having a lower price option—as part of a surge pricing strategy—provides a great rebuttal to potential pushback on premium prices: "Yes, we've raised prices on popular days, but you now have the option to visit at a much lower price on certain days." Framing pricing options in this manner makes a price increase more palatable. Instead of forcing a "take it or leave it" decision, customers tend to feel better because they've chosen to pay more: "I had the opportunity to get a lower price, but I decided to pay more because that option was more convenient for me."

There are plenty of other industries—such as restaurants, barbershops, and health clubs—that can also benefit from surge pricing. Surge pricing has typically been used in industries with perishable goods (e.g., hotel rooms), but it can be used any time when demand varies. Should beer prices at the TD Garden be higher at a rowdy Boston Bruins game than when a traveling circus is using the arena? I think so.

Another instance when surge pricing can be used is in cases of fluctuating supply. Restaurants, for example, often charge "market price" for seafood entrees to reflect varying supply conditions. I visit a neighborhood where four gas stations are located in close proximity and compete vigorously on price. However, only one of these stations is open 24 hours. Should the all-night gas station raise prices every evening between 11 p.m. and 6 a.m. when its competitors are closed? Yup, I think so.

Managers are often wary of raising prices during times of high demand because they fear a consumer backlash. It's a fair concern, but it's worth noting that consumers are becoming desensitized to surge pricing—high/low pricing is being used more often in more industries. If well-known companies that are fiercely protective of their brands—such as

Chapter 1 Marketing Strategies

Disney—are contemplating (and using) surge pricing, other companies are probably good to go. And of course, another way to view this strategy is instead of raising prices, you are offering discounts during low-demand periods.

Back in Economics 101, we were taught that every company faces a demand curve for its products and services. The reality is that this demand curve is not static: There are times when demand is higher and other times when it is lower. Surge pricing enables companies to capture additional profit when demand is high and just as importantly, provide discounts to generate growth during off-peak periods.

Reading Tasks

❶ Reading Comprehension

Briefly answer the following questions about the text in English.

1) What does "surge pricing" mean according to the text?
2) Does the author agree with this strategy? What is his line of logic to support his claim?
3) What revisions does he make to Disney's pricing strategy?
4) Can Disney pricing strategies be applied to other industries? Come up with concrete examples to support your points.
5) What other pricing strategies are used in real life besides surge pricing? Give examples to back up your observation.

❷ Translation

1. **Provide the Chinese equivalents to the following terms and expressions.**

   1) off-peak
   2) admission
   3) gouging
   4) perishable goods
   5) economics 101
   6) dormant customers
   7) demand curve

19

2. **Translate the following sentences/paragraphs into Chinese.**

1) Implementing demand-based pricing strategies at Disneyland, or any theme park for that matter, simply makes sense. Raising prices during popular times such as Fourth of July weekend capitalizes on higher consumer valuations.

2) Since theme parks are high fixed cost/low variable cost entities, revenue from discount-enticed new customers is virtually all profit...free money. These newly activated "dormant customers" would also likely show up hungry and snap up souvenirs...more free money.

3) Having a lower price option—as part of a surge pricing strategy—provides a great rebuttal to potential pushback on premium prices...

4) Instead of forcing a "take it or leave it" decision, customers tend to feel better because they've chosen to pay more...

5) Managers are often wary of raising prices during times of high demand because they fear a consumer backlash. It's a fair concern, but it's worth noting that consumers are becoming desensitized to surge pricing—high/low pricing is being used more often in more industries.

Survey

Conduct a survey on Shanghai Disneyland on campus based on the following questions and share your findings in class.

What Do You Think of Shanghai Disneyland?

After more than a decade of planning and five years of construction, Shanghai Disneyland finally opened its door on June 16th, 2016—and already there's been plenty of debate within China. News reports on the theme park have focused on topics ranging from the price of its tickets to the taste of its food. Hit the streets on your campus to find out more about people's views of the resort.

1) Have you heard about Shanghai Disneyland? Do you have any plans to visit the park? With whom? And when? Is surge pricing a decisive factor in deciding when

Chapter 1 Marketing Strategies

you visit the park?

2) What do you think of the admission price of Shanghai Disneyland? What is an appropriate price? And based on what criteria (age/height)?

3) Compared with that of Disneyland in other locations worldwide, do you think the admission price is fair in proportion to China's per capita income?

4) Given the perennial crowds at popular rides at Shanghai Disneyland, do you think the park should charge for fast pass? And if your answer is yes, how much should it be?

5) Some visitors have complained that the food at the park is so expensive and looks totally different from how it's shown in ads, and that rides sometimes malfunction. What do you think about these complaints?

6) How do you think Shanghai Disneyland should adjust their operation to suit Chinese preferences?

IV Research and Discussion

Search the Internet for answers to the following questions and share your findings in class.

In 2016, Disney opened a $5 billion theme park in Shanghai. But Chinese billionaire Wang Jianlin said his parks would leave Disney in the dust. "We will make Disney unprofitable in China within the next decade or two," Wang predicted in an interview on Chinese state television. Wang said he's betting the Chinese cultural themes at his parks would outdraw Mickey Mouse and Snow White, that Shanghai's weather is too rainy in summer and cold in winter for Disney's outdoor attractions and that Disney's building costs will result in tickets that are too pricey for local customers. "Disney really shouldn't have come to China," Wang said, drawing applause from the studio audience. "Our strategy is based on the saying that one tiger is no match for a pack of wolves."

1) Do you agree with Wang Jianlin's observation? Do you think his remarks are fact-based or simply an attempt to gain public attention?

2) Do you think Shanghai Disneyland is competitive enough to beat local rivals?

Where does its competitiveness lie?

3) Do you think China's homegrown theme parks will pose a credible threat to Disney? And why?

Part 4
Case Study of Promotional Strategies

Read the following English text and carry out your reading tasks as directed.

How to Promote Your Brand on China's Social Media

In China there are around 900 million Internet users and 91% of Chinese online users have a social media account, in comparison with U.S. where around 67% of online population have a social media account.

Around 800 million people use mobile devices to access the Internet. Every day, Chinese netizens spend an average of 46 minutes on social media platforms.

Internet users follow an average of eight brands and over 38% of Chinese netizens make purchasing choices based on recommendations that they find and read on social media platforms.

In order to increase your brand presence, it is mandatory to have an active presence on social media platforms.

In China, more than in other countries, Chinese users spend more time online and because of that, companies have to deepen their knowledge about social media networks.

As reported by OgilvyOne, over 55% of Chinese users had participated in online discussions about brands and those discussions are able to directly affect businesses.

Nowadays, the importance of understanding what customers are saying about a brand through social media networks has become the only way to be truly visible and stand out from the crowd.

Chapter 1 Marketing Strategies

Content is the basis of all social media strategies in China. Some of the most important social networks in China are WeChat, Sina Weibo, KOL, Qzone, Little Red Book, Zhihu and Meipai.

WeChat

WeChat is the number one social network. This platform includes texts messages, voice messaging, video, games, e-commerce and mobile payments.

In 2017 WeChat counts 950 millions users and is the first App used in China. WeChat has to be considered by brands seeking to engage consumers directly. The platform allows brands to target ads according to age, gender and region in order to reach more potential customers. One of the most common strategies in WeChat is offering unique content and access to special offers. Through this strategy, brands have a positive impact on consumer loyalty, which helps to increase brand reputation.

When brands are planing its marketing strategies, they should consider these different points:

WeChat content

WeChat is totally different from the Western social network. If you want to reach a lot of Chinese customers, you have to adapt your contents to their needs. Chinese customers look for rich, authentic and relevant contents. They are tired to see the same content. So, for an efficient WeChat campaign, you have to work on your contents. The WeChat content marketing must be consistently good.

Creative posts H5

As Facebook, Twitter, Instagram...etc., on WeChat you can also make a post. This feature allows you to share all your services or products with all your followers. This is a great way to increase your visibility and engage more customers, because they are very interested by innovative and creative posts. You can publish five types of contents such as video, text, audio, picture and picture with text. Actually, many brands incorporate H5 pages into their posts and official accounts, in order to optimize WeChat contents and increase the quality of user experience.

Promotion group

After releasing your content, you have to promote it in your community through some WeChat groups. It's always important to be a member of some groups. You can also create your own group but make sure you have a lot of followers.

Advertising

If you want to succeed starting your business in China, it is essential to have a sensitive and effective presence on social network. It's important to understand the way WeChat works and the subtleties of this mobile application.

The most familiar way for advertising on WeChat is to promote on WeChat Moment. WeChat Moment ads were launched in early 2015. WeChat advertising is the most effective way to increase engagement in China on the nation's number one social media tool.

Sina Weibo

Another popular social platform is the microblogging website called Sina Weibo. This platform is known like the "Chinese Twitter" due to its similar aspect. The same as Twitter, it allows members to post 140 characters including videos, pictures and links.

Sina Weibo has around 550 million users and is ideal for brands in order to get customers' feedback, engage in conversations with members and promote themselves. Brands have to focus their efforts on creating relevant and highly shareable contents.

Weibo, one of Chinese most famous social networks, is the must-know tool for the marketers who want to engage in Chinese digital marketing. However, to advertize on Weibo is not an easy thing due to its various ad options and functions.

There are four types of Weibo advertising:

Banner Advertizements: It's more like a backlink that leads you to the advertizer's homepage when you click it.

Weibo Search Engine Promotion: It's Weibo search bar that provides the hot search list and the ads search keyword will be listed on the top within a tag "promotion".

Fan Headline ("Fanstop"): As a popular option for advertising on Weibo, it will help to promote your account or the content you post on Weibo directly or via other famous

Chapter 1 Marketing Strategies

accounts.

Fan Tunnel: It could help you target a much larger group of Weibo users. It is not hard to understand because it's based on the whole Weibo users.

KOL

The influencer marketing in China is changing, because now new players are taking part in this new trend. You can call them KOL (Key Opinion Leader) or bloggers, and they are the new biggest influencers in China. The performance of KOLs is closely related to their engagement with their followers. They are able to influence a lot of customers' decisions just through their articles, the posts, videos or comments about brands or products.

Qzone

Qzone is one of the most successful social networking websites in China, with more than 600 million users. This platform allows users to write blogs, watch videos, send photos and listen to music.

Qzone is an attractive social network for brands due to its flexibility. Companies can customize pages, integrate multimedia content and applications and also they can create fully customizable microsites.

Through this platform, brands have the chance to create original experiences for their consumers.

Social media has become essential in the Chinese lifestyle. Consumers use these platforms to find and share information and opinions about products and services.

For businesses with presence in China, including social media platforms in their marketing strategies is an effective way to engage with consumers. Social networks are also useful to develop consumer research, launch products, and manage crises.

Little Red Book

Little Red Book is a social e-commerce shopping App based in Shanghai, with the aim to target Chinese women aged between 18 and 35 years old. This platform helps users discover and buy luxury products from overseas, share shopping tips and swap fashion ideas. With more than 15 million active users and sales of 700 million RMB to the end of September, the App has considerably gained the attention of shoppers and investors both at home and abroad.

The site has good partnerships with many U.S., Japanese and Korean brands, including Japanese skincare company SK-II, designers Vivienne Westwood and Anna Sui, and nutrition company GNC. Moreover, Little Red Book also has mini guidebooks for shopping in the U.S., France and other fashion shops.

Zhihu

Launched in December 2010, Zhihu is a Chinese question-and-answer website for Chinese Internet users who want to seek expert insights into various areas. Basically started as an invitation-only Q&A platform for tech-savvy and entrepreneurial minds, it opened registration in 2013 to everyone. Since then, its topics have diversified to cover popular topics from movies, games, and culture, as well as IT and finance.

2016 was an important transition for Zhihu: It was able to monetize through the launch of new services, including institutional accounts, ads, cooperation with book stores, and Zhihu Live.

Meipai

Live streaming is now very popular among young Chinese who view it as an easy way to become famous and make lots of money. Then, there is Meipai, a China's popular short video service operated by the Hong Kong-listed selfie touch-up App Meitu.

Chinese Internet users are attracted to live streaming by the prospects of making lots of money. For example, Papi Jiang, one of China's top online celebrities, made over 50 million yuan ($7.56 million) in 2016 by posting short videos to entertain 25.76 million followers on Weibo.

Chapter **1** Marketing Strategies

Reading Tasks

I Summary Writing

Complete the following summary of the text in Chinese.

如何在中国社交媒体上推广品牌

微信
平台定位：_____
推广方式：1. _____ 2. _____
　　　　　3. _____ 4. _____

新浪微博
平台定位：_____
推广方式：1. _____ 2. _____
　　　　　3. _____ 4. _____

意见领袖
平台定位：_____
推广方式：_____

QQ 空间
平台定位：_____
推广方式：_____

小红书
平台定位：_____
推广方式：_____

知乎
平台定位：_____
推广方式：_____

27

美拍
平台定位：＿＿＿＿＿＿＿＿＿＿＿＿＿＿＿＿＿＿＿＿＿＿＿＿＿＿＿
推广方式：＿＿＿＿＿＿＿＿＿＿＿＿＿＿＿＿＿＿＿＿＿＿＿＿＿＿＿

Research and Discussion

Search the Internet for answers to the following questions and share your findings in class.

1) Do you like to be advertized? Are you easily influenced by promotions when making a purchase decision?

2) What kind of factors do advertizers take into account when designing a promotional campaign?

3) Do you think ads on your personal social media page are an infringement of your privacy?

4) Apart from what is mentioned in this text, what other promotional methods are commonly used to promote a brand?

Translation

Translate the following sentences/paragraphs into Chinese/English.

1) Chinese audiences watching *Transformers* will recognize more than just the alien robots. In the latest blockbuster, household Chinese brand names loom large as part of an unprecedented product placement push. This Chinese branding campaign is the largest so far in any single Hollywood movie, highlighting Chinese companies' determination to go global and also use global marketing techniques to raise their domestic profiles.

2) Amway is different from the more traditional distribution channels in that business is developed through direct selling. Amway has over three million agents worldwide, who deal directly with clients, build up personal relationships and deliver direct to clients' homes. These agents are highly motivated in face of the commission they get in the process, selling to people they know or meet. They can

also introduce others to the business, and so form their own sales network.

3) Xiaomi is ranked the most innovative company in China in 2014 for reinventing the smartphone business model in the world's largest mobile market. Xiaomi released four new smartphones in 2013 and sold almost 19 million units, up more than 150% from 2012. It's staking out a significant piece of the Chinese market with its low-cost, feature-rich devices. One model sold out its initial run—100,000 units—in less than two minutes. Although founder Lei Jun is compared to Steve Jobs, Jun's strategy is hardly the same as Apple's: He sells his phones—in buzz-generating flash sales—at a razor-thin margin and then takes advantage of the longer potential revenue stream from software.

4) 中秋节将至，许多厂家在各大超市的销售点推出了免费试吃活动。

5) 虽然面临着来自其他品牌的竞争，康师傅在中国茶饮料市场中仍然占据着强有力的领导地位。2009年，康师傅茶饮料系列开始在全国开展促销抽奖活动"再来一瓶"，使其茶饮料的销售在整个茶饮料市场遥遥领先。

6) 在实体门店快速发展的同时，"维多利亚的秘密"把大部分收益都投入直邮目录及在线零售中。通过向潜在目标消费者寄送直邮目录，然后用电话定购或传真定购的方式确认客户需求，以信用卡、支票付账或者货到付款的方式达成交易。

7) 劳力士手表最喜欢采用的营销方式就是赞助网球大师杯赛，同时聘请一线明星代言，彰显其成功人士的品牌内涵。

8) 最新的《广告法》修订草案规定，明星代言产品必须自己先使用。如涉及虚假宣传，该明星与发布广告的媒体都要负法律责任。

9) 凉茶品牌王老吉不但在电视台黄金时间推出广告，还不惜重金，连续几年拿下了《中国好声音》的冠名权。

10) 很多美发店为了增加营业额，通常会劝说顾客购买储值卡，这样顾客在下次消费时就能享受折扣了。

11) 新店开业，凡来我店消费者送代金券50元。

12) 为了吸引消费者购买最新的iPhone 5s和5c，苹果推出以旧换新活动。旧手机经过鉴定可以返还一定金额，以便消费者在店内购买最新的产品。

13) 为了吸引更多的回头客,很多商家推出了会员卡,实行以卡积分换礼活动。

14) 很多餐馆与团购网合作,虽然单独一份交易的盈利空间有限,但是架不住量多,最终都实现了盈利的目的。

15) 随着社交媒体的普及,消费者只需扫扫二维码就能关注某品牌,同时获取最新的电子优惠券。事实上,这种类型的社交媒体营销已经成为中国商家最为青睐的推广产品的方式。

16) 借势营销这种营销思路的逻辑很简单,就是找准自身产品的品类特性,抓住潜在用户群体的心理,巧妙地与热点话题融合在一起,并且快速地在微博、微信等社会化媒体平台上发布,因而受到各行各业中小企业的追捧。

Business Application

1. After you read the case studies in this chapter, you probably have had some basic ideas of the components of a good corporate marketing strategy. Growing out the original 4P marketing mix, the extended version of the marketing mix is very influential in designing a good corporate strategy. Watch the video "The Marketing Mix" again from the CAW Business School and try to provide Chinese subtitles for the video.

2. Imagine you were about to start your own business. Work out an English business plan based on the 4P marketing mix and then pitch your ideas to potential investors for funding. Make sure that you meet the following two requirements.

   1) Your business plan must include essential information on:
      · Product (types of services/products; amenities)
      · Place/Location (location; business hours; decoration)
      · People (management/staff; partners; target clients)
      · Promotions (types of promotions; estimated benefits)
      · Pricing (source of start-up capital; budget; service/product price)

   2) The whole plan must be economically logical and viable.

Chapter 2
Corporate Scandals

Overview

Bad news travels fast. The public always have an appetite for a scandal, and many misdeeds on the part of the global business make headlines. Admittedly, scandal, mismanagement and financial shenanigans are facts of business life in any country and once exposed, they cost dearly to shareholders, employees, and management. This chapter selects four notorious business scandals over the past couple of years. Now with the benefit of hindsight, in what way did these companies fail in assuming their social responsibilities and what effective safeguards do you believe can prevent similar mistakes from happening again?

Pre-reading Activities

1. What was the most notorious corporate scandal that you have ever heard of? Who was the wrong doer? What were the consequences of the scandal? How was the scandal handled? Whose interests were hurt the most in that scandal?

2. What responsibilities should a company take for its employees, stakeholders, customers and the whole society?

3. Why do corporate scandals always trigger public outrage?

4. What should be done if a company does not assume its social responsibilities?

5. How is a public company governed in terms of corporate management? Who should be ultimately held responsible in case of a scandal?

Part 1
Volkswagen Emissions Scandal

Read the following two texts, one in English and one in Chinese, and carry out your reading tasks as directed.

Text 1

Volkswagen: The Scandal Explained

What Is Volkswagen Accused of?

It's been dubbed the "diesel dupe". In September, the Environmental Protection

Chapter 2 Corporate Scandals

Agency (EPA) found that many VW cars being sold in America had a "defeat device"—or software—in diesel engines that could detect when they were being tested, changing the performance accordingly to improve results. The German car giant has since admitted cheating emissions tests in the U.S.

VW has had a major push to sell diesel cars in the U.S., backed by a huge marketing campaign trumpeting its cars' low emissions. The EPA's findings cover 482,000 cars in the U.S. only, including the VW-manufactured Audi A3, and the VW models Jetta, Beetle, Golf and Passat. But VW has admitted that about 11 million cars worldwide, including eight million in Europe, are fitted with the so-called "defeat device".

The company has also been accused by the EPA of modifying software on the three-litre diesel engines fitted to some Porsche and Audi as well as VW models. VW has denied the claims, which affect at least 10,000 vehicles.

In November, VW said it had found "irregularities" in tests to measure carbon dioxide emissions levels that could affect about 800,000 cars in Europe, including petrol vehicles. However, in December it said that following investigations, it had established that this only affected about 36,000 of the cars it produces each year.

This "defeat device" sounds like a sophisticated piece of kit. Full details of how it worked are sketchy, although the EPA has said that the engines had computer software that could sense test scenarios by monitoring speed, engine operation, air pressure and even the position of the steering wheel.

When the cars were operating under controlled laboratory conditions—which typically involve putting them on a stationary test rig—the device appears to have put the vehicle into a sort of safety mode in which the engine ran below normal power and performance. Once on the road, the engines switched out of this test mode.

The result? The engines emitted nitrogen oxide pollutants up to 40 times above what is allowed in the U.S.

What Has Been VW's Response?

"We've totally screwed up," said VW America boss Michael Horn, while the group's chief executive at the time, Martin Winterkorn, said his company had "broken the trust of our customers and the public". Mr. Winterkorn resigned as a direct result of the scandal and was replaced by Matthias Mueller, the former boss of Porsche.

"My most urgent task is to win back trust for the Volkswagen Group—by leaving no stone unturned," Mr. Mueller said on taking up his new post.

VW has also launched an internal inquiry. With VW recalling millions of cars worldwide from early next year, it has set aside €6.7 billion (£4.8 billion) to cover costs. That resulted in the company posting its first quarterly loss for the first time in 15 years of €2.5 billion in late October.

But that's unlikely to be the end of the financial impact. The EPA has the power to fine a company up to $37,500 for each vehicle that breaches standards—a maximum fine of about $18 billion.

The costs of possible legal action by car owners and shareholders "cannot be estimated at the current time", VW added.

How Widespread Are VW's Problems?

What started in the U.S. has spread to a growing number of countries. The U.K., Italy, France, South Korea, Canada and, of course, Germany, have opened investigations. Throughout the world, politicians, regulators and environmental groups are questioning the legitimacy of VW's emissions testing.

VW will recall 8.5 million cars in Europe, including 2.4 million in Germany and 1.2 million in the U.K., and 500,000 in the U.S. as a result of the emissions scandal.

No wonder the carmaker's shares have fallen by about a third since the scandal broke.

Will More Heads Roll?

It's still unclear who knew what and when, although VW must have had a chain of management command that approved fitting cheating devices to its engines, so further departures are likely.

Christian Klingler, a management board member and head of sales and marketing, is leaving the company, although VW said this was part of long-term planned structural changes and was not related to recent events.

In 2014, in the U.S., regulators raised concerns about VW emissions levels, but these were dismissed by the company as "technical issues" and "unexpected" real-world conditions. If executives and managers willfully misled officials (or their own VW superiors), it's difficult to see them surviving.

Are Other Carmakers Implicated?

That's for the various regulatory and government inquiries to determine. California's Air Resources Board is now looking into other manufacturers' testing results. Ford, BMW and Renault-Nissan have said they did not use "defeat devices", while other firms have either not commented or simply stated that they comply with the law.

The U.K. trade body for the car industry, the SMMT, said: "The E.U. operates a fundamentally different system to the U.S., with all European tests performed in strict conditions as required by E.U. law and witnessed by a government-appointed independent approval agency."

But it added: "The industry acknowledges that the current test method is outdated and is seeking agreement from the European Commission for a new emissions test that embraces new testing technologies and is more representative of on-road conditions."

It Sounds Like That E.U. Testing Rules Need Tightening Too.

Environmental campaigners have long argued that emissions rules are being flouted. "Diesel cars in Europe operate with worse technology on average than the U.S.," said Jos Dings, from the pressure group Transport & Environment. "Our latest report demonstrated that almost 90% of diesel vehicles didn't meet emission limits when they drive on the road. We are talking about millions of vehicles."

Car analysts at the financial research firm Bernstein agree that European standards are not as strict as those in the U.S. However, the analysts said in a report that there was, therefore, "less need to cheat". So, if other European carmakers' results are suspect, Bernstein says the "consequences are likely to be a change in the test cycle rather than legal action and fines".

It's All Another Blow for the Diesel Market.

Certainly it is. Over the past decade and more, carmakers have poured a fortune into the production of diesel vehicles—with the support of many governments—believing that they are better for the environment. Latest scientific evidence suggests that's not the case, and there are even moves to limit diesel cars in some cities.

Diesel sales were already slowing, so the VW scandal came at a bad time. "The revelations are likely to lead to a sharp fall in demand for diesel engine cars," said Richard Gane, automotive expert at consultants Vendigital.

"In the U.S., the diesel car market currently represents around 1% of all new car sales and this is unlikely to increase in the short to medium term. However, in Europe the impact could be much more significant, leading to a large tranche of the market switching to petrol engine cars virtually overnight."

Text ❷

大众作弊门：为何连名企都变坏？

近日，德国大众汽车尾气排放作弊事件成为全球经济的热门事件。这再次证明，好人做坏事远比坏人做坏事更让人震惊。为什么名企也会变坏？国内的作弊情况又如何？

● **行业造假成风**

此次大众汽车"排气门"不仅导致大众要面临最高180亿美元的天价罚单，更重要的是，让这个世界第一大车企多年来经营出的好形象变得摇摇欲坠。这一切全都是因为一个小小的作弊软件。这款被称为defeat device的软件能够自动在尾气排放检测中动手脚，保证监测能够通过。但实际上，这些汽车在正常使用下的排放量是监测标准的10~40倍。

很多人将此次事件与以往曝光的汽车质量缺陷事件相比较，这实际是一种误区。产品质量存在缺陷会对消费者形成安全隐患，这个问题看似更为严重，但这种质量缺陷往往不是有意造成的，只要厂商在发现缺陷后积极地召回，基本上不

Chapter 2　Corporate Scandals

会面临严厉指责，通常还会被认为是制造商对产品和消费者负责的表现。

但这次"排气门"不同，本质上是一种故意作弊的行为，不仅欺骗监管部门，也欺骗了消费者。不要以为消费者对排气作弊无所谓，欧美很多注重环保的消费者都是奔着"清洁柴油"这种低污染宣传去的。而在环保议题越来越重要的今天，这种故意的污染欺诈会引发多少连锁反应可想而知。所以，大众汽车面临的不仅仅是天价罚款的问题，更重要的还在于失去人心。失去人心多少年都挽救不回来，影响比去年的"断轴门"可能更为恶劣。

这种企业作弊行为在国内也并不少见。在专题《大众汽车为何铤而走险挑战美国法律》中，我们提到过，中国的柴油车环保造假更为严重。这些造假企业不用高明的作弊手段，很轻易地就能拿到"环保标"上路。这些柴油大货车的超量尾气排放成为大气污染的罪魁祸首。

不只是在汽车行业。在消费电子领域，以手机为例，罗永浩曾公开炮轰大部分安卓手机跑分作弊。他指出跑分高的手机都要对跑分软件做出优化，而这种针对性的优化，本质上就是作弊。国产手机在跑分作弊上尤为严重，因为有些厂商直接给跑分软件做战略性投资。比如某款手机测试软件版本从 V5.7.2 升级到 V5.7.3 之后，某款国产手机的得分从 37 306 提升到 49 928。版本不同，跑分差别如此之大，这其中的猫腻不言而喻。如果手机厂商拿作弊的高分做文章，进行优势宣传，既有失公平，又误导了消费者。

在电影领域，"偷票房"的作弊行为也非常普遍，即假如你去看 A 电影，电影院给你一张 B 电影的票，拿着 B 电影的票你可以去看 A 电影，但这样一来，票款算到了 B 电影头上，A 票房就差了。作弊行为本身并不影响消费者的观影感受和对电影的评价，但电影发行方却可以从票房排名中获利。一些片方与影院合作通过偷取其他电影的票房来提升自身的票房积累，让自己的市场反应"一路走高"，给人以获得观众喜爱的假象，从而误导消费者。

在工业生产领域，环评弄虚作假已经司空见惯。本来是有污染风险的企业，却能通过环评审批。诸多污染事故、爆炸事故的发生都与环评作弊脱不了干系。

● 企业业绩驱动

　　国内企业造假、作弊，原因一般都比较好理解。但国外的大企业往往都是百年老店，为何要冒毁掉招牌的巨大风险去参与作弊呢？

　　通过检索以往的信息我们可以发现，大众"排气门"其实只是该行业的冰山一角。尾气排放检测造假绝非仅限于大众汽车一家企业。《金融时报》在一篇报道中指出："通过用胶带封住车门和给轮胎过度充气等手段减少阻力，以便在欧洲燃油效率测试中蒙混过关——这种做法已经如此寻常"；"在美国，福特曾在1997年被曝在货车上安装非法'排放失效装置'——这也是大众现在面临的指控。现代和起亚去年因操纵测试数据被罚款1亿美元。"

　　这种造假服务还有专门的提供商。据《经济学人》爆料，这些测试虽是由国家监管机构监督，但汽车厂商可以委托专业公司进行测试。这些公司为了抢生意，承诺将测试条件"最优化"。报道称，"西班牙一条颇受欢迎的测试车道位于高海拔地区，稀薄的空气降低了气动阻力，而且路面非常光滑，仅此一项就将性能提升了3个百分点"。

　　当大家都选择作弊时，自己不作弊就要吃亏。因为作弊的企业有成本优势，市场中可能出现优质企业竞争不过劣质企业的现象，即会出现"逆淘汰"。优质企业为了避免这种情况的发生，必须造假。由于这种负向激励的存在，市场上大多数企业都在竞相造假。大众汽车的作弊选择很可能也是经不起诱惑的从众行为。而国内一家柴油车制造商在接受采访时就直截了当地表示，如果自己生产符合排放规定的车，而别人在造假，那可能第二天自己的企业就垮掉了。

　　所以，行业里作弊成风，有点像是落入了"囚徒困境"——众多企业默契地选择与行业法规打擦边球。百年老店也有经营压力。大众之所以进行如此广泛而又严重的作弊，原因很可能还在于，名企的日子并不像我们想的那样好过。

　　汽车行业的利润率并不高，成本是汽车工业的命脉。据报道，去年年末，大众汽车集团在内部会议上就宣布，未来三年将削减50亿欧元的开支成本，旨在提升大众乘用车品牌的利润率，从之前的2%左右提高到6%左右。大众汽车CEO马丁·文德恩甚至在会议上敦促高管行动要更加果断，强调汽车行业竞争不断加剧，公司面临着越来越严峻的压力。这种早已存在的危机感是让大众选择错误道路的原因之一。"排气门"显然是这种思路下的产物。

另外，对于职业经理人等企业员工来说，企业业绩比企业信誉更关乎自身利益，因为业绩直接影响到自己的工资和奖金，而企业信誉则可以慢慢透支，或者祈求作弊事件不在自己任上被发现，这是百年老店不得不面对的道德风险。对于大众汽车的管理人员来说，他们近年来的当务之急是不让世界第一大车企的头衔易主，不被丰田公司超过。在这种情况下，"病急乱投医"也就可想而知了。

● 监管水平低下

既然造假如此普遍，为什么监管机构没有发现呢？以大众汽车作弊事件为例，《彭博商业周刊》上发表的《大众汽车见不得人的小秘密》一文为我们提供了答案——多年以来，汽车制造商一直都在利用检测系统的漏洞。原来，按照美国目前的规定，汽车制造商可以自行对本公司生产的汽车进行检测，只要把结果提交给美国国家环境保护署审核即可，而审核其实就是走个形式，几乎无一例外会被通过。

欧美之所以汽车排放审核做得不严，很大原因是客观上的，即严格审核需要的成本和人力资源都很大。但在中国情况又有所不同。还以中国的柴油车为例，环保数据造假几乎是人人都心知肚明的事情。而且《大气污染防治法》中明确规定可以对造成污染的车辆罚款和没收销毁。但从 2002 年全国人大通过以来，这条法律却从未实施过。记者给出的答案是由于"执法主体不明确"，即与柴油车管理相关的三个部门，答案即环保部、工信部和质检总局，看起来似乎都有执法的权力，但各自并不确定自己是否是执法主体。这导致的后果是：一方面，执法部门惰政，相互之间推诿责任；另一方面，即便有部门想要积极执法，也会底气不足。

● 寻租泛滥

即便被认为是公众利益代表的政府官员，其实也是"理性人"，他们也会重视自身利益。因此，政府官员常常会基于自身利益的考虑来行使权力。比如为了获得经济利益，人为地对一些不需要政府干预的领域进行管制，并因此获得收益，这就留下了"寻租"空间。他们还会为了政绩，讨好企业，对企业的造假行为视而不见。监管在这里失灵了。

比如我国的汽车尾气检测造假腐败。《大气污染防治法》规定，机动车船排放污染物不得超过规定的排放量。国务院在《大气污染防治行动计划》中明文要求，对尾气排放不达标的车辆不得发放环保合格标志，不得上路行驶。然而，新华社在对机动车尾气检测造假的调查（《揭秘机动车尾气检测造假腐败》）中发现，排放标准和规定形同虚设，任何车只要花300元就能通过检测，获得绿标。这其中除了验车非法中介在搞鬼外，还有就是环保部门的不尽责。即便凭一张未检测尾气的报告，也能最终获得"环保部监制"的绿色环保合格标志。如此轻易地拿到"环保标"，让人不能不怀疑环保部门和检测中介之间是否存在勾结、包庇的关系。

即便这次大众作弊事件并未涉及中国，但在行业造假普遍、国内竞争环境、监管环境差的情况下，很难保证国外的老牌车企在中国就一定不会出问题。问题是存在的，只是还没到值得重视的程度。正如《金融时报》在《"大众造假门"：作弊竞赛的必然结局》一文中提到的，当作弊成为惯例的时候，监管机构也是睁一只眼闭一只眼。当有一天，有人做得太过分了，丑闻就会产生。

● 结语

行业造假成风，企业业绩驱动，监管水平低下，"寻租"泛滥。无论从哪一方面来看，国内的环境都更为恶劣。对于中国人来说，想办法对付"企业作弊竞赛"是个更大的课题。

❶ Summary Writing

Complete the following summary of Text 1 in Chinese.

大众排气门始末

1) 大众到底干了什么：_____
2) 大众对此如何回应：_____
3) 排气门涉及多少车辆：_____

Chapter 2 Corporate Scandals

4) 大众公司还有谁会因此离职：＿＿＿＿＿＿＿＿＿＿＿＿＿＿＿＿
5) 其他车厂有没有类似的小动作：＿＿＿＿＿＿＿＿＿＿＿＿＿＿＿＿
6) 大众排气门对柴油车市场产生了怎样的影响：＿＿＿＿＿＿＿＿＿＿

❶ Reading Comprehension

Briefly answer the following questions about the two texts in English.

1) Who started the investigation into VW? And what triggered the investigation? Is the investigation conducted elsewhere? Is there any probe in China? And why?
2) How does this "diesel dupe" work?
3) What are the penalties VW faces in the U.S.? Whom should they pay penalties to?
4) Why are people concerned about diesel cars? What are the advantages and drawbacks of diesel cars compared with petrol engine cars? Do diesel cars really cause less harm to the environment as is claimed by VW?
5) What specifically drive VW to design and fit some cars with the cheating device?
6) What is "prisoner's dilemma"? Do you agree with the analogy drawn in Text 2?
7) With all the talks about global warming and climate change, people have started to care more about the environment and air quality. Yet VW, as the world's biggest carmaker, has dared to commit such blatant cheating for years. What is your response when you heard of the scandal?

❷ Translation

Provide the English equivalents to the following terms and expressions.

1) 逆淘汰
2) 病急乱投医
3) 打擦边球
4) 跑分
5) 偷票房
6) "寻租"

IV Research and Discussion

Search the Internet for answers to the following questions and share your findings in class.

1) In what way do you think VW fails in performing its corporate social responsibilities?
2) Penalties are meted out when there is already substantial harm. What are the safeguards that can prevent such scandal from happening in the first place?
3) Can you list some of cheating committed by other companies?
4) Do you agree with the viewpoints presented in the Chinese passage? Who should play an oversight role?

Part 2

How United Airlines Handles an Overbooked Flight

Read the following English text and carry out your reading tasks as directed.

The United Fiasco: What We Know Now

It's been an ugly few days for United Airlines.

A passenger was dragged, bloodied and screaming, up the aisle and off a plane by authorities at Chicago O'Hare International Airport on Sunday when he refused to give up his seat on a United (UAL) flight to Louisville, Kentucky. The airline needed to free up seats to transport commuting crew members.

The story didn't end there.

On Monday, passenger videos of the incident started to go viral. United CEO Oscar Munoz made matters worse by issuing a widely-ridiculed apology for "having to re-accommodate...customers". He later doubled down in a letter to employees, defending the airline's actions and describing the passenger as "disruptive and belligerent".

Chapter 2 Corporate Scandals

The company's response dominated headlines on Tuesday. United's stock dropped about 4% in the morning. Munoz finally issued a full-throated apology around 3 p.m., calling the event "truly horrific".

The dust hasn't settled yet. But here's what we know now.

The Incident Is under Investigation.

Munoz, in the statement he put out on Tuesday, has pledged a full review by April 30 "to fix what's broken so this never happens again".

"I want you to know that we take full responsibility and we will work to make it right," he said in a statement. "I promise you we will do better."

The company is now looking into how it moves crews and deals with oversold flights, as well as how it works with airport authorities and local law enforcement, he said.

The U.S. Department of Transportation has also said it's reviewing the episode.

Lawyers for the passenger, since identified as Dr. David Dao, said he was still being treated in a Chicago hospital Tuesday afternoon.

It's Been a Total PR Disaster.

Public relations experts were shocked by how United dealt with the fallout. They say Munoz should have quickly offered an unreserved apology. It took him three tries to get there.

Rupert Younger, a PR expert and director of the Oxford University Center for Corporate Reputation, said that Munoz's initial response was a major disappointment.

"The apology by the CEO was, at best, lukewarm or, at worst, trying to dismiss the incident," Younger said.

On Tuesday, #NewUnitedAirlinesMottos was a top trend on Twitter, with users suggesting slogans such as "not enough seating, prepare for a beating". It was also the top trending topic on Chinese social networking platform Weibo, attracting more than 100 million views.

Even the White House weighed in by Tuesday afternoon.

"It was an unfortunate incident," Press Secretary Sean Spicer told reporters. "Clearly, when you watch the video, it is troubling to see how that was handled."

The Company Has Lost $250 Million in Market Value.

Early Tuesday, United shares dropped 4%, wiping out $1 billion of market value.

The company's stock recovered before the close, slipping just over 1% by the end of the day. But the drop still cost the company $250 million of its market value.

It's hard to judge if the imbroglio will hit United's brand in the long run. But it's certainly not a good thing.

The company has been trying to revamp its image after ranking near the bottom of airline customer satisfaction indexes for several years. It's in the process of updating its fleet, and last year added free snacks, premium coffee and better WiFi—as well as upgraded airport lounges.

Rival Airlines Are Trying to Cash In.

United's competitors are watching all this unfold with glee. They have trolled the airline, hoping to capitalize on its blunders.

Royal Jordanian ribbed United with a tweet. "We are here to keep you #united," it said. "Dragging is strictly prohibited." The words were accompanied by an image of a no smoking symbol.

Emirates also got in on the action. In a video, it referenced United CEO Oscar Munoz's putdown of its Middle Eastern competitors last month. He told the airline trade publication *ATW*: "Those airlines aren't airlines. They're international branding vehicles for their countries."

Emirates responded Tuesday with a video.

"Well Mr. Munoz, according to TripAdvisor, the world's largest travel site, not only are we a real airline...we are the best airline," the company said. It ended with a message taking a jab at United's own slogan: "Fly the friendly skies...this time for real."

Chapter 2 Corporate Scandals

Reading Tasks

❶ Summary Writing

Complete the following summary of the text in Chinese.

> 美联航暴力赶客事件进展
>
> 1. _____
> 2. _____
> 3. _____
> 4. _____

❷ Research and Discussion

Search the Internet for answers to the following questions and share your findings in class.

1) What is overbooking? What is its business rationale? Is it used in other industries? Do you think overbooking should be allowed?

2) Are involuntary bumps from flights, as Dr. David Dao experienced in this horrible incident, common and frequent in the airline industry?

3) What are passengers entitled to when they get bumped from a flight? How to avoid being bumped from a flight, and what you're entitled to if you are?

4) How do airlines decide which passengers to bump? What are the industry norms?

5) Since the beating incident, United Airlines has amended its policies on how to bump passengers. What is the change? Do you think it's good?

Language Exercises

1. **Replace the expressions in bold in the following sentences/paragraphs without changing their meanings.**

    1) United CEO Oscar Munoz made matters worse by issuing **a widely-ridiculed apology** for "having to **re-accommodate...customers**".

    2) He later **doubled down** in a letter to employees, defending the airline's actions and describing the passenger as **"disruptive and belligerent"**.

    3) Munoz finally **issued a full-throated apology** around 3 p.m., calling the event "truly horrific".

    4) "The apology by the CEO was, at best, **lukewarm** or, at worst, trying to **dismiss the incident**," Younger said.

    5) Even the White House **weighed in** by Tuesday afternoon.

    6) The company's stock **recovered** before the close, **slipping** just over 1% by the end of the day.

    7) The company has been trying to **revamp its image** after **ranking near the bottom** of airline customer satisfaction indexes for several years.

    8) United's competitors are **watching all this unfold with glee**. They have **trolled** the airline, hoping to **capitalize on its blunders**.

    9) Emirates also **got in on the action**.

    10) On Tuesday, #NewUnitedAirlinesMottos was **a top trend** on Twitter, with users suggesting slogans such as "not enough seating, prepare for a beating".

    11) It was also **the top trending topic** on Chinese social networking platform Weibo, attracting more than 100 million views.

2. **Fill in the blanks in the following sentences/paragraphs with expressions you find from the text.**

    1) The violent removal of a United Airlines passenger from his seat on an overbooked flight Sunday has been a _____ （公关失败）for the company and _____ （热门视频）as far away as China.

Chapter 2 Corporate Scandals

2) The incident on a flight from Chicago to Louisville triggered _____ （纷纷谴责） against United, fueled by videos of the confrontation and what was seen as a tone-deaf response from the airline, whose initial explanations ignored the violence on one of its planes and stated simply that one customer had "refused to leave". Soon after, United's CEO Munoz stated, "I apologize for having to re-accommodate these customers."

3) United Airlines incident has catalyzed discussion around corporate accountability and ethical consumerism. Consumers, especially in the age of social media, possess the ability to _____ （实施联合抵制） products that violate the basic tenets of social justice and equality.

4) Dr. David Dao has _____ （与……和解） with United Airlines for the injuries he received in his April 9th ordeal, which was captured on video and viewed worldwide.

IV Translation

1. Translate the following paragraphs into English.

超售属于国际惯例，因为有些人买了机票可能会改签或不去乘机，如果完全按照实际座位数来售票，就会造成座位空置，资源浪费。所以，一般来说，航空公司会超售一点，以保证客座率。

如果出现超员的情况，中国的做法是与乘客进行协商，给予乘客相应的补偿，多数旅客还是比较配合的。协商是以乘客自愿为原则，不会采取抽签的方式，否则会引起矛盾。

如果没有乘客愿意下机，也肯定不会出现硬把人拖下飞机的情况。该业内人士说，美联航这种硬把旅客拖下飞机的做法有点极端，这种情况在国际上的其他航空公司也比较少见。

2. **Below are reportedly three statements posted online from United Airlines CEO Oscar Munoz on United Express Flight 3411 after the beating incident took place. The tone and wording have changed over the turn of the events. Translate them into Chinese with the appropriate stylistic nuances.**

1) The first statement:

Dear Team,

Like you, I was upset to see and hear about what happened last night aboard United Express Flight 3411 headed from Chicago to Louisville. While the facts and circumstances are still evolving, especially with respect to why this customer defied Chicago Aviation Security Officers the way he did, to give you a clearer picture of what transpired, I've included below a recap from the preliminary reports filed by our employees.

As you will read, this situation was unfortunately compounded when one of the passengers we politely asked to deplane refused and it became necessary to contact Aviation Security Officers to help. Our employees followed established procedures for dealing with situations and while I deeply regret this situation arose I also emphatically stand behind all of you and I want to commend you for continuing to go above and beyond to ensure we fly right.

I do, however, believe there are lessons we can learn from this experience, and we are taking a close look at the circumstances surrounding this incident.

Treating our customers and each other with respect and dignity is at the core of who we are, and we must always remember this no matter how challenging the situation is.

Oscar Munoz,
CEO, United Airlines

2) The second statement:

This is an upsetting event to all of us here at United. I apologize for having to re-accommodate these customers. Our team is moving with a sense of urgency to work with the authorities and conduct our own detailed review of what happened.

We are also reaching out to this passenger to talk directly to him and further address

Chapter 2 Corporate Scandals

and resolve this situation.

Oscar Munoz,

CEO, United Airlines

3) The third statement:

The truly horrific event that occurred on this flight has elicited many responses from all of us: outrage, anger and disappointment. I share all of those sentiments, and one above all: my deepest apologies for what happened. Like you, I continue to be disturbed by what happened on this flight and I deeply apologize to the customer forcibly removed and to all the customers aboard. No one should ever be mistreated this way.

I want you to know that we take full responsibility and we will work to make it right.

It's never too late to do the right thing. I have committed to our customers and our employees that we are going to fix what's broken so this never happens again. This will include a thorough review of crew movement, our policies for incentivizing volunteers in these situations, how we handle oversold situations and an examination of how we partner with airport authorities and local law enforcement. We'll communicate the results of our review by April 30th.

I promise you we will do better.

Sincerely,

Oscar

3. **Read the following Internet memes lashing out at the United Airlines. Find out the sarcasm and humor of each meme and comment on their Chinese translations based on criteria of accuracy, fluency and adequacy.**

   1) We will seat you, beat you, and blame you for our overbookings.
      我们给你座位，然后揍你，因为我们的超售而责怪你。
   2) If you can't seat them, beat them.
      如果不能提供座位，那就揍他们。
   3) Come for the seating, stay for the beating.
      找个座位，等着被打。
   4) Board as a doctor; Leave as a patient.

登机前是个医生，离开时成了一个病人。

5) Not enough seating? Time for a beating!

没有足够的座位了？是时候去打一场了！

6) You can beat our prices! But we can sure beat our passengers!

你可以打败我们的价格！但我们可以打我们的乘客！

7) Even terrorists are afraid to fly our airline.

即使是恐怖分子都不敢选择我们的航线。

8) We treat you like we treat your luggage.

我们对待你就像我们对待你的行李一样。

9) You may have patients, but we don't have patience.

你有病，但我没药。

10) We don't ask you. We choose you.

我们没有在请求你，我们选择了你。

Part 3
Well Fargo's Fake Accounts

Read the following English text and carry out your reading tasks as directed.

Misbehaving Bankers

People respond to incentives. When bankers at Wells Fargo were paid to sign customers up for more and more products, that's exactly what they did. To a fault. Over around five years, starting in 2011, up to 1.5 million deposit accounts and 565,000 credit-card accounts may have been opened without clients' permission; unwanted debit cards were issued; fake e-mail addresses were created to enroll people for online banking.

The gain to Wells was tiny. America's second-biggest deposit-taker and biggest mortgage-lender, which earned $5.6 billion in the second quarter, has so far refunded $2.6 million in charges for overdrafts, failing to maintain minimum balances on unwanted

Chapter 2 Corporate Scandals

accounts and so on. The punishment, at first blush, is small too. At $185 million, the fines announced by regulators on September 8th are loose change next to the ten-digit penalties coughed up by banks since the financial crisis. But the damage done to Wells' reputation, on both Main Street and Wall Street, is harder to gauge.

Wells emerged strongly from the financial crisis, spreading across America from its western base after buying stricken Wachovia, once the country's fourth-largest bank, in 2008. Its watchword was "cross-selling"—prodding customers into taking extra services, to tie them more tightly to the bank. "Eight is great", staff were told. They got pretty close: In the second quarter households with current (checking) accounts had on average 6.27 products. The bank is not abandoning cross-selling. It said it erred on the side of caution in totting up the number of dodgy accounts. But it said on September 13th that it would cease to set staff targets for product sales.

What went wrong? According to the bosses, a few rotten apples in a retail bank employing 100,000: It sacked 5,300 people over the five years. John Shrewsberry, the chief financial officer, has said those at fault were poor performers, "making bad choices to hang on to their job". Of the sacked staff, one-tenth were branch managers or above. They do not include the head of the retail bank, Carrie Tolstedt. Wells said in July that Ms. Tolstedt, who was paid $9.1 million in cash and shares last year, would retire at the end of 2016, after 27 years' service. John Stumpf, the chief executive, piled on the praise.

The bank's embarrassment is not about to end. Federal prosecutors have reportedly begun investigations. Mr. Stumpf has been summoned to appear before the Senate Banking Committee on September 20th. With elections looming, senators will doubtless queue up to give him a good shoeing in front of the cameras.

The stock market has already kicked the share price: This week Wells lost its place as America's biggest bank by market capitalization to JPMorgan Chase. Investors may worry that less pushy selling may dampen earnings—or that the scandal will cost Wells customers. But people stick with their banks, even after bigger blunders than this. Mr. Shrewsberry said this week that Wells had been braced for a flood of calls, e-mails and social-media traffic but "we've had very low volumes". Inertia can be a bank's best friend.

Summary Writing

Complete the following summary of the text in Chinese.

富国银行身败名裂

原因：_____
过程：_____
影响：_____

Research and Discussion

1. The following are some typical retail banking services offered by an American bank. Search the Internet for their Chinese equivalents and compare the differences between products of the same type in class.

   1) checking accounts
   2) savings accounts
   3) certificates of deposit
   4) mortgages on residential and investment properties
   5) automobile financing
   6) credit cards
   7) standing orders
   8) foreign currency and remittance services
   9) personal insurance agency service
   10) wealth management products
   11) money market accounts
   12) brokerage accounts

2. **Search the Internet for answers to the following questions and share your findings in class.**

   1) What is cross-selling? What are its benefits and drawbacks? Is it used in other industries? Have you ever been cross-sold things? What is your response when you realize you have been tricked into buying things you actually don't need?

   2) According to the passage, fake accounts were opened because lower ranking employees were forced to meet targets set by higher-ups. In this sense, Wells Fargo is characterized by a corporate culture of obedience. What are its benefits and drawbacks? What is your favorite style of corporate culture? Which company has the corporate culture that you appreciate most?

   3) According to the passage, Carrie Tolstedt and John Stumpf, as top executives of Wells Fargo, managed to walk away from the scandal with handsome compensation and severance packages, while ordinary bank employees were mercilessly sacked. This kind of protection, in the business world, is called "golden parachute". Can you list some other cases in which top executives are protected? Do you think it is a fair practice? What do you believe are the rightful treatments for ordinary employees and executives?

Language Exercises

Replace the expressions in bold in the following sentences/paragraphs without changing their meanings.

1) When bankers at Wells Fargo were paid to **sign customers up** for more and more products, that's exactly what they did. To a fault.

2) America's second-biggest deposit-taker and biggest mortgage-lender, which earned $5.6 billion in the second quarter, has so far **refunded $2.6 million in charges for overdrafts**, failing to **maintain minimum balances on unwanted accounts** and so on.

3) The punishment, **at first blush**, is small too. At $185 million, the fines announced by regulators on September 8th are **loose change** next to the ten-digit penalties

coughed up by banks since the financial crisis.

4) **Its watchword** was "cross-selling"—prodding customers into taking extra services, to **tie them more tightly to** the bank.

5) It says it **erred on the side of caution** in **totting up** the number of dodgy accounts.

6) What went wrong? According to the bosses, **a few rotten apples** in a retail bank employing 100,000: It sacked 5,300 people over the five years.

7) Mr. Stumpf has been summoned to appear before the Senate Banking Committee on September 20th. **With elections looming**, senators will doubtless queue up to **give him a good shoeing** in front of the cameras.

8) But people **stick with** their banks, even after bigger blunders than this.

9) Mr. Shrewsberry said this week that Wells had been **braced for a flood of calls, e-mails and social-media traffic** but "we've had very low volumes".

10) **Inertia** can be a bank's best friend.

IV Translation

Translate the following paragraphs into English.

富国银行最重要的优势是"交叉销售"。简言之，就是尽量说服客户多使用富国银行的服务，如银行账户、信用卡、按揭贷款、投资理财等。从银行角度出发，这当然是再理想不过的了，一个客户使用6种银行服务，就等于在他/她身上赚了6笔钱。

富国银行的规矩就是销售业绩直接与个人的业绩挂钩。员工如果完不成当天的任务，就需要留下来加班。要么继续打电话推销完成指标，要么就需要准备下一天如何追上指标的计划。

从2013年起，媒体开始报道富国银行的客户有时会莫名其妙多出一些从未申请过的服务，例如多了一个活期账户，多了一张信用卡什么的。银行开始调查，而消费者金融保护局也开始介入。

最终的调查结果惊人：在销售目标和薪酬激励的驱动下，富国银行雇员未经客户允许而私自开设超过153万个借记卡和信用卡账户，甚至将部分客户资金转移到这些未经授权的新账户,造成客户原有账户因资金不足或透支而被迫缴纳费用达 200 万美元以上。

此外,富国银行雇员还未经客户允许就发行和激活借记卡,伪造邮箱地址为客户开通其并不知情的网上银行业务。消费者金融保护局还表示,通过分析发现,富国银行的员工还在客户不知情或未征得其同意的情况下,提交申请了 565,443 个信用卡账户。许多客户并未授权开通信用卡,但在自己名下却产生了信用卡年费、利息及其他费用。

Part 4
Tesco's Accounting Fiasco

Read the following English text and carry out your reading tasks as directed.

Tesco's Accounting Problems, Not So Funny
Booking Revenues, Like Comedy, Is All about Timing.

It is too soon to say whether the accounting misstatement at Tesco was cock-up or conspiracy. The source of the discrepancy is already clear; however, it is as old as book-keeping itself: the premature recognition of revenue.

Suppliers make payments to supermarkets that meet certain sales targets for their products, run promotions or place the goods in eye-catching places, such as at the end of aisles. Tesco managers appear to have been too ambitious in forecasting these "rebates". They may also have underreported the costs of stolen and out-of-date produce.

In a study of accounting scandals at American companies by the Committee of Sponsoring Organizations, a business-ethics body, the misrecording of revenues was to blame in 60% of cases. Manipulation generally falls into one of two categories. In the first, involving "timing differences", the revenue is genuine but, say, sales at the start of a quarter are booked as having been struck in the previous one. The flipside of this is "cookie jar" accounting: pushing today's revenue into tomorrow so it can be dipped into to shore up weak quarters.

In the second, more serious category, the sales are fake: Often, a related party poses as a customer to generate phony invoices. Examples include Gowex, a Spanish technology firm that folded earlier this year, and Satyam Computer of India, whose boss compared the escalation of the $1.5 billion fraud to riding a tiger that was ever harder to dismount without being eaten.

Working out how many revenues to book and when to book can be a matter of fine judgment. It is especially tricky in long-term contracts, such as in construction, or when the sale of goods is bundled with a service agreement, as with photocopiers. In a sign of how complex an area is, only this year—after more than a decade of talks—did European and American standard-setters agree on a common approach to revenue recognition.

The complexity of Tesco's promotional deals with suppliers may also have left much room for discretion, and honest mistakes, as well as deliberate distortions. But the risks around accounting for such payments are hardly new. The auditors of several big retailers have amplified their warnings in recent years as rebates have taken up more space on balance-sheets. In its most recent report, in May, Tesco's auditor, PwC, warned of the "risk of manipulation".

If Tesco's books turn out to have been deliberately cooked, it would be the biggest fraud of its type in retailing since the scandal at U.S. Food Service in 2000–2003. Several executives were fined or jailed for creating bogus rebates to boost profits and bonuses—complete with secret side agreements, in which suppliers agreed not to collect the exaggerated rebates. The Dutch parent company, Royal Ahold, settled with shareholders for $1.1 billion. Even if there was no fraudulent intent and the problems stem from a misunderstanding of the rules rather than knowing misapplication, the apparent scale of the error suggests that, at the very least, Tesco's internal controls need a thorough overhaul.

Chapter 2 Corporate Scandals

Reading Tasks

❶ Reading Comprehension

Briefly answer the following questions about the text in English.

1) What went wrong for Tesco?
2) What are the common ways for a supermarket to earn money?
3) What is rebate income? Why do suppliers make payments to Tesco?
4) When and how is commercial income recognized?
5) What are the differences between the two types of financial manipulation?
6) Is PwC, Tesco's auditor, responsible for failing to spot the manipulation?
7) What type of financial manipulation does Tesco commit? What are the consequences Tesco's management faces?

❷ Research and Discussion

Search the Internet for answers to the following questions and share your findings in class.

1) What is accounting? Is it only about book-keeping? What does accounting involve?
2) What is the role of an auditor? Is it a person or a company? Who are some of the world's most famous auditors? Have they ever been implicated or have they suffered demise if their clients commit financial fraud?
3) What is internal control? What are its relevant components? What significance does it have on accounting?

❸ Language Exercises

1. Replace the expressions in bold in the following sentences/paragraphs without changing their meanings.

1) It is too soon to say whether the accounting misstatement at Tesco was cock-up or

conspiracy. The source of the **discrepancy** is already clear; however, it is as old as book-keeping itself: the premature recognition of revenue.

2) The complexity of Tesco's promotional deals with suppliers may also **have left much room for discretion**, and honest mistakes, as well as deliberate distortion.

3) If Tesco's books turn out to have been deliberately **cooked**, it would be the biggest fraud of its type in retailing since the scandal at U.S. Food Service in 2000–2003.

4) Several executives were fined or jailed for creating bogus rebates to boost profits and bonuses—**complete with** secret **side agreements**, in which suppliers agreed not to collect the exaggerated rebates.

2. **Translate the following sentences/paragraphs into Chinese.**
   1) Booking Revenues, Like Comedy, Is All about Timing.
   2) It is too soon to say whether the accounting misstatement at Tesco was cock-up or conspiracy. The source of the discrepancy is already clear; however, it is as old as book-keeping itself: the premature recognition of revenue.
   3) Manipulation generally falls into one of two categories. In the first, involving "timing differences", the revenue is genuine but, say, sales at the start of a quarter are booked as having been struck in the previous one. The flipside of this is "cookie jar" accounting: Pushing today's revenue into tomorrow so it can be dipped into to shore up weak quarters.
   4) The complexity of Tesco's promotional deals with suppliers may also have left much room for discretion, and honest mistakes, as well as deliberate distortions. But the risks around accounting for such payments are hardly new.
   5) Even if there was no fraudulent intent and the problems stem from a misunderstanding of the rules rather than knowing misapplication, the apparent scale of the error suggests that, at the very least, Tesco's internal controls need a thorough overhaul.

Chapter 2　Corporate Scandals

Business Application

1. After you read the above case studies, you might be appalled by the audacity of the culprits, and shocked by the penalties they face. You might be curious to know more business scandals and further the concepts of corporate social responsibilities and corporate governance. Search the Internet for better understanding of the two concepts and answer the following questions.

   1) What is your definition of corporate social responsibility? How to measure its fulfillment?
   2) Who will stand to lose if a company fails to take its social responsibilities?
   3) Who is to supervise companies for their social responsibilities?
   4) Inside a company, what kind of corporate structure can ensure that a company takes its social responsibility?

2. Every year *Fortune* runs a list of the world's notorious business scandals. For example, in 2016, the top five corporate scandals are:

   - Wells Fargo's Fake Accounts
   - Roger Ailes' Sexual-Harassment Scandal
   - Mylan's Epipen Price Gouging Scandal
   - Samsung Battery Recall
   - The Panama Papers

   And the five biggest corporate scandals of 2015 are:

   - The Volkswagen Emissions Scandal
   - FIFA Corruption Scandal
   - Toshiba Accounting Scandal
   - Valeant's Secret Division
   - Turing Pharmceuticals and Martin Shkreli

   Search the Internet for a corporate scandal and write a bilingual report of the details and lessons to be drawn in terms of social responsibilities and corporate governance.

Chapter 3
Cars and Oil

Overview

With the rise of China's economy, car ownership becomes more widespread and carmakers are doing all they can to woo China's emerging middle class. What will happen as China becomes a country on wheels? Will domestic carmakers grow strong enough to challenge their foreign peers? Why are auto shows held in major Chinese cities every year? And we will shift our discussion to oil, an energy source so essential in modern economy that it earns the nickname "black gold". How is oil made? Who controls oil prices? How are oil prices felt in different countries? What impact will the fluctuations of oil prices have on ordinary people? This chapter will shed light on these questions.

Pre-reading Activities

1. What are the world's top automakers by region? What brands do they own?

2. What domestic car makers do you know are getting increasingly influential in China?

3. What do you know about Ford, Volvo and Geely?

4. What are the world's three best-selling premium auto brands for mass-market?

5. Provide Chinese equivalences to the following terms and describe their differences.

oil	fossil fuel	(non)renewable resources
alternative resources	biogas	petroleum
gas/gasoline	natural gas	crude oil
coal	methane	kerosene
diesel	shale gas	

6. Watch the video "How Crude Oil Turns into Gasoline" from Khan's Academy and complete the following flow-chart of oil making process.

   How Crude Oil Turns into Gasoline?

   Step 1 _____ Step 2 _____ Step 3 _____ (_____ + _____)

   Step 4 _____ Step 5 _____

   *1 barrel = 42 gallons

Chapter ③ Cars and Oil

Part ①

Car Ownership Restrictions

Read the following two texts, one in English and one in Chinese, and carry out your reading tasks as directed.

In China, Congestion and Pollution Rules Spur Big Car Purchases

As more Chinese cities propose license-plate lotteries and other ways of limiting the number of cars on the road, consumers are responding by buying more expensive automobiles with bigger engines.

In Shanghai, one of four major Chinese cities with policies designed to reduce car purchases to ease pollution and traffic congestion, between 9,000 and 10,000 plates are auctioned monthly, fetching an average of 82,000 yuan ($13,400) so far this year.

That steep fee helped convince David Fu, a 26-year-old bank corporate finance manager, to buy an Audi A4 in June for 300,000 yuan after looking at a dozen lower-cost models including those made by Volkswagen AG and China's home-grown carmakers.

"Putting the pricey plate on a more expensive car makes sense," said Mr. Fu. As scarcer plates raise the cost of owning a car, shoppers can rationalize paying more for their car and believe the restrictions may limit them from trading up later, say auto dealers and analysts.

In addition to Shanghai, Beijing, Guangzhou and Guiyang now have policies aimed at reducing car purchases and as many as eight other cities are likely to follow, say industry executives. The result is first-time car buyers are skipping less expensive models, usually Chinese brands.

63

"More and more first-time buyers are buying big cars such as sport-utility vehicles and premium cars," said Yan Jinghui, vice president of Beijing Asian Games Village Automobile Market, a car retail space in Beijing's northern suburb that is home to around 200 car dealerships.

Data from the semiofficial China Association of Automobile Manufacturers (CAAM) show in Beijing the average price per car has surged 88% since 2011 and the market share of cars with an engine size of larger than 1.6 liters has grown 17% over the same period.

CAAM has estimated that the likely car-purchase restrictive policies in the eight cities could slash nationwide car sales by 400,000 units a year at least, or 2% of the total sales of 2012.

Shijiazhuang, one of China's most polluted cities, has proposed limiting the number of new vehicle licenses to 100,000 a year from 2013, equivalent to about 60% of added vehicles in the city in 2011, according to estimates by brokerage house CLSA.

Authorities in the eastern city of Hangzhou in June proposed imposing high license-plate fees on households planning to buy second cars, adding they were prepared to allow the license-plate fee to surpass car prices. Hangzhou has more than one million cars on its roads of the major districts, or one car for every three citizens, according to official sources.

Foreign carmakers shrug off these moves. Martin Kuehl, a spokesman for Audi AG, said the restrictions are encouraging trade-ups. "Would you want to put a 100,000 yuan plate on a 50,000 yuan car?" he asked. Bob Socia, China president at General Motors Co., said even if all 25 cities with severe congestion were to implement restrictions in 2015, the hit to the company's car sales would be just between 2% and 3%.

In contrast, Chinese automakers are concerned that license-plate auctions would severely impact their sales. A Shanghai-like auction in Hangzhou would lift plate prices to the level of neighboring Shanghai—about 82,000 yuan, said Victor Yang, spokesman for Hangzhou-based Zhejiang Geely Holding Group. Geely models are largely priced between 80,000 yuan and 120,000 yuan.

China is already the world's largest market for automobiles, with total sales rising 4.3% to 19.3 million units in 2012. CAAM has forecast that new car sales could reach 30

Chapter ③ Cars and Oil

million units by 2020.

But Hou Yankun, head of Asia auto research at UBS Securities, said that congestion could eventually put a brake on growth of China's car market. "In theory, new car sales in China could grow 20% a year for another decade because of the lower level of private vehicle ownership," he said. "But China's road conditions can't afford such a growth rate. I think China's car sales growth will likely be flat from 2015 or 2016—and such a period could last for a decade."

Every kilometer of road in China has about 200 cars, as many as in Los Angeles, which has some of the worst traffic in the U.S., according to UBS research.

"When traffic in more and more cities becomes as awful as in Beijing, measures that curb car sales will be inevitable," Mr. Hou said. The average speed of car traffic in China's capital is short of 15 kilometers, or 9.3 miles, an hour, about the speed of easy bicycling, and there are 13 other mainland cities in which the average speed of car traffic is lower than 20 kilometers, he added.

Binyam Reja, the World Bank's transport sector coordinator for China, described China's recent moves to reduce congestion and pollution by limiting car ownership as a "good first step". However, in the long run "more comprehensive" policies are needed, he said. This included going beyond the current regulations to include charging people who bring cars to downtown areas during peak hours.

"Because someone owns a car doesn't mean they have to use it," Mr. Reja said.

Text ❷

欧美亚等世界各国城市治堵妙招盘点

城市道路拥堵是汽车社会发展过程中一个不可避免又必须解决的问题，欧美日等发达国家已经积累了丰富的城市治堵经验，而国内骤然而至的限购政策显然并非治堵良策，无法根治城市拥堵的痼疾。他山之石，可以攻玉，了解其他国家的治堵方法或许有助于我们找到城市管理的帕累托最优改进方法。

● 纽约：智能交通有效疏堵

美国是一个智能交通系统大国，智能交通在美国的应用已达80%以上，其相关产品也位居世界前列。智能交通系统是由一系列用于运输网络管理的先进技术及为出行者提供的服务所组成的，目的是使管理者、运营者及出行者能进行有效的信息交流，相互间更为协调，从而做出更为智能化的决策。而纽约作为美国第一大都市，其每日人流量都相当大，发达的智能交通系统让纽约的拥堵情况大大缓解。

这套系统拥有86台闭路电视，负责对全市五个区的主干道交通状况进行监控。纽约市6 600个交通信号灯和4 000个用于测定车流量的环形探测器都由该系统进行管理。装上的大型电子显示屏可以及时跟踪曼哈顿岛上所有交通信号灯的动态变化。一旦某一路段发生交通事故或出现拥堵状况，计算机就会立即发出指令，对附近地区的信号灯重新进行编程。闭路电视也会马上对准现场，为工作人员处理事故和交通拥堵提供实时信息。

● 洛杉矶：大力发展低成本公共交通系统

作为美国第二大城市，洛杉矶的交通有两个鲜明的特点：一是多中心的城市空间结构，市中心的重要性相对较低；二是私人汽车交通在洛杉矶城市交通中占绝对主导地位，公共交通仅占总出行量的3.4%。

为应对城市拥堵，洛杉矶制定了长期交通规划：一是大力发展低成本的快速公共交通系统，停止发展地铁。地铁造价太高，造价低廉的快速公共交通比普通公共交通节省20%左右的出行时间。二是积极建设共乘车道来提高高速公路的通行能力，停止建造新的高速公路。共乘车道只能允许两个人以上共乘的汽车使用。三是开发应用智能交通系统，提高交通系统管理水平。同传统的交通信号控制技术相比，自动车辆监测和控制系统的应用使出行者出行时间、交叉口耽误时间和交叉口不必要的停车时间平均分别减少了12%、32%和30%。

● 巴黎：长期实行公交优先

在20世纪70年代初，由于私家车急剧发展，巴黎的城市交通几近瘫痪。于是，法国政府开始下大力气重点优先发展公共交通。如今，巴黎设置了480

多条全天或部分时间禁止其他车辆使用的公共汽车专用道。对于小汽车，巴黎市政府规定，每逢空气流通不畅的无风日，则采用分单双号车牌形式来限制轿车进城。

巴黎的驾校以考试严格闻名，在上路之前就培养驾驶员良好的责任感和安全意识。巴黎还以"轻微违章不影响交通者不罚，交通高峰期尽量不罚"为原则，避免造成交通拥堵；而对于严重超速和违章停车等容易造成堵塞的驾驶员，则进行严打。

巴黎公路交通标识设置也堪称一流，几乎每个交叉路口都设有指示近、中、远目的地的醒目路标，确保司机不会因为找路分散注意力而引发事故。城市快速路和高速公路上还有电子显示牌，循环显示交通信息，帮助司机提前做好选择，以减少拥堵。

为解决交通拥堵的问题以及减少城市温室气体的排放量，巴黎政府2007年夏天引进了"自行车城市"计划，在市内新建1 450个自行车租赁站，为市民提供廉价的自行车租赁服务，以更多的优惠政策鼓励"自行车自由骑"。

此外，巴黎的出租车大多需要提前预约，街上很少见到挥手打车的情形，这样便减少了出租车的空驶率，也减少了因为出租车随意停车载客而造成拥堵的可能性。

● 伦敦：进入市中心需另交税

针对拥堵问题，伦敦的首要解决方案就是大力发展公共交通。伦敦市内的地铁网络非常发达，共有11条线路，运营里程达400公里，并且在大伦敦城市圈还拥有300公里的市郊铁路。这可以使在中心区上班的75%的人群在上班高峰期间通过铁路网络抵达目的地，节省了在路上拥堵的时间。

另外，伦敦市政当局从2003年2月17日开始，对进入市中心8平方英里范围内的车辆，从早晨7点到下午6点半征收5英镑的"进城费"。随后在2005年，这一费用被调高至8英镑。而从2011年1月开始，交通拥堵费将上涨到10英镑。收费后，取得了显著的效果。伦敦交通局在2008年发布的"交通拥堵费"政策评估报告显示，这一政策使伦敦市中心的交通流量减少了21%；与收费前相比，每天进入伦敦市中心的车辆减少了约7万辆。而提高燃油税也是英国限制汽车使用的重要措施之一。

此外，为缓解早晨上班高峰期的交通拥堵状况，英国政府还准备采取措施，限制家长每天用私家车接送孩子上学。在英国，许多家长都用私家车送孩子上下学，有些学生的家距学校只有1公里左右，也要父母开车接送。不久前的统计显示，每逢学校放假，英国主要街道高峰期的堵车数量就减少五分之一。有关专家指出，家长用私家车接送孩子是造成高峰期交通拥堵的原因之一。

● 斯德哥尔摩：全面覆盖的租用自行车系统

瑞典的斯德哥尔摩经过多年的规划和建设，如今已经拥有一套简易又便宜的租用自行车系统。这项为缓解交通压力和节约能源实行的措施，在瑞典受到人们的广泛欢迎。

在斯德哥尔摩，推广自行车以缓解交通压力的措施得以迅速推行的主要原因是，它确实让人们感觉到了出行的便捷。租赁自行车的网店遍布全城，市民和游客可以在全城任何一个网点存取，非常方便。此外，市政部门重视自行车道的建设，也为推广自行车出行提供了条件。斯德哥尔摩的街道基本都留有一米多宽的自行车道，标志明显，并且规定，在自行车道上，自行车享有优先行驶权，连行人都得让着骑车人。

据悉，瑞典政府2007年宣布，将在以后20年里加大对自行车交通的投入，以减少人们对汽车的依赖。瑞典的公路交通局、铁路交通局和经济与地区发展署每年将增加5亿瑞典克朗的投入，用于实施各种发展自行车交通的措施，如修建更多的自行车专用道，改建公共交通工具以使人们能携带自行车乘坐公共汽车和火车，增设安全的自行车停车场等。

● 香港：完善公共交通，合理规划交通建设

香港人口700多万，面积约1 100平方公里。跟内地许多大中城市相比，土地分散、人口密集的程度都有过之而无不及，但就是这个想象中应该是"拥堵不堪"的城市却是以井然有序的道路交通闻名于世。

首先是香港的城市大公交非常发达，香港几乎所有的繁华路面交界附近都盘踞一到四个地铁站，香港人倡导的"公交优先"并不是要全面控制私家车，而是

引导私家车在不阻碍城区交通的情况下继续使用，不要让私家车增加城市的拥堵程度。私家车会在深夜或假期出游才开，平时上下班大多数人会选择公共交通。其次是香港的交通线路规划非常科学、人性化，空中、地面交通完美结合，打造了一个立体的交通世界。再者，香港完善的交通管理，以及司机、行人极高的交通素质也是该城市"畅通无堵"的重要原因。

另外，在香港市区内停车的代价非常大，一个小时少则二三十元，最贵的要超过100元。正因为很多人停不起车，自然就不会把车开进市区，这样就减少了市区内的交通拥堵。

● 东京：立体交通覆盖城市

日本是一个交通网络高度发达的国家。城市高速公路、城市道路、地铁、电气铁道、新干线、新交通系统组成了日本市际交通与市内交通的整体化网络与便捷的换乘交通枢纽。日本交通的最重要特色是地面、地上和空中组成的立体交通网。地面网主要是城市一般道路，地下网全部是地铁和电车等公共交通，而空中网则是由新干线、高速公路和电车组成。东京是立体交通网络的典型代表。

20世纪60年代，在日本经济高速发展的同时，东京也产生了严重的交通拥堵问题。为此，东京市政府下决心大力发展城市轨道立体交通系统。如今，整个东京已经被一张巨大的轨道立体交通网所覆盖，总里程达2 355公里。交通系统每天运送旅客2 000多万人次，承担了东京全部客运量的86%。

巨大的立体交通网所设立的站点多，但不重复繁乱。站点分布和不同交通工具的换乘非常合理科学，站点的高效化利用使得人口密度大的东京的拥堵情况大为改善。东京都中心区的交通枢纽站，不管是市内地铁换乘市内电车，还是由市内电车、地铁换乘城郊电车或新干线，大都在站内就可实现。

● 首尔：经济杠杆缓解交通难

韩国首都首尔的市区拥堵程度曾经不亚于北京，在韩国政府双管齐下的治理后，已经明显好转。

第一就是用政策调控。1996年年底，韩国首都将汽油税提高了一倍，并征收道路使用费。在拥堵最严重的时段对市中心的两条主干道车征收拥堵费,每辆车收 2 000 韩元,但又规定,如果一辆车内乘员超过 3 人,就可免交费。同时,提升城市公共停车场的收费价格,商业中心和办公楼附带的停车位数量也被削减。这一规定出台后,汽车通行量减少了 9%,其中小轿车减少了 53%,通行速度提高了一倍。

第二是建设公共交通,具体来说有开辟公交专用道、建地铁、拆掉高架桥建立快速公交线路等,现在首尔的公共交通系统已经是世界级的了。

● 新加坡:市区收费及购车需竞买拥车权

新加坡是世界上人口密度最高的国家之一,而新加坡道路面积约占国土面积的 12%,机动车总数目前有近百万辆。然而新加坡的快速路及市中心道路上基本实现无堵车现象。做到这一点的关键在于新加坡实行车辆数年度配额和拥车证这两项措施。

车辆数年度配额制度实施于 1990 年。新加坡政府每年根据道路网络新增容量制定全国本年度小汽车增量的配额。配额确定后,每月举行公开招标,由公众竞买"拥车权"。中标者买得拥车证后才可购买新车,而且拥车证的价格是非常昂贵的。这有效控制了市区的车流量及车辆总体数量。

此外,新加坡还有一个独特的电子道路收费系统。由于城市空间极其有限,当地政府早从 1975 年就开始实施市区道路收费。安装在汽车前端的短波无线电发射器可与电子收费系统进行信息交换,然后在车主的信用卡里直接扣款。根据不同的车型和时段,收费大概在 0.5 新元到 3 新元(约 1 美元)之间,以保证市内车辆能达到 35~65 公里左右的时速。有数据显示,电子道路收费系统使新加坡市中心的车流量减少了 13%,高峰时段平均车速提高了 20%。

Chapter 3　Cars and Oil

Reading Tasks

I Summary Writing

1. Complete the following summary of Text 1 in English.

Car Ownership Restrictions				
Cities	Shanghai	Shijiazhuang	Hangzhou	Beijing
Policies to Restrict Car Ownership				
Impact				

2. Complete the following summary of Text 2 in English.

How Do World's Mega Cities Tackle Congestion

New York: _____　　Los Angeles: _____
Paris: _____　　London: _____
Stockholm: _____　　Hong Kong: _____
Tokyo: _____　　Singapore: _____
Seoul: _____

II Reading Comprehension

Briefly answer the following questions about the two texts in English.

1) How does car licence plate lottery work in Beijing in Text 1?
2) How does car licence plate auction work in Shanghai in Text 1?
3) Compare the advantages, drawbacks and loopholes of car license plate lottery in Beijing and license plate auction in Shanghai. What do you think is the most equitable and effective measure among the four mentioned in Text 1?
4) What other restrictive measures do you know are taken in China to limit vehicle

traffic on roads?

5) What do you think is the most applicable and effective measure to tackle congestion among those mentioned in Text 2?

6) What is "帕累托最优" in Text 2? Define the term in your own words and if necessary, use some examples to support your points.

III Translation

Provide the English equivalents to the following terms and expressions.

1) 车牌
2) 自主品牌
3) 经销商
4) 排量
5) 限购
6) 换车
7) 路况
8) 私家车保有量
9) 拥堵
10) 摇号
11) 智能交通
12) 立体交通
13) 共乘车道
14) 公交专用道
15) 单双号限行
16) 电子道路收费系统

IV Research and Discussion

Search the Internet for answers to the following questions and share your findings in class.

1) If you were the mayor of a big city such as Xi'an, taking lessons from the experience of the world's mega cities in tackling congestion, what would you do to deal with the gridlocks?

2) As China reels from some of the most polluted winters in recent years, what do you think is the main culprit behind the dismal air pollution? And what is the cure?

3) What kind of car do you plan to buy as your first car taking into account what is happening in China right now? How much is your budget? What model and what make is your dream car?

Chapter 3 Cars and Oil

Part 2
M&A: Geely and Volvo

Read the following English text and carry out your reading tasks as directed.

Geely Buys Volvo

An Obscure Chinese Carmaker Buys a Famous but Ailing Swedish One.

If opposites attract, Ford's sale of Volvo to a Chinese upstart, Geely, for $1.8 billion ought to be a marriage made in heaven. Sweden's Volvo is the epitome of good middle-class taste; its slightly dull but hugely safe and practical cars were, in better days, the default choice on many a suburban driveway in America and Europe. Geely, on the other hand, is barely known outside China, partly because its range of mainly cheap, small cars is not yet capable of meeting the rich world's more stringent safety and environmental regulations. But it is ambitious.

The deal, which was signed on March 28th, brings to an end protracted negotiations by Ford to sell the last of the European premium brands it acquired in a spell of expansionary hubris starting at the end of the 1980s. Having disposed of Aston Martin and Jaguar Land Rover, Alan Mulally, the chief executive brought in from Boeing in 2006, was determined to offload Volvo too, which lost $1.3 billion last year and sold only 335,000 cars. Although Volvo this year appears to have turned a corner and is operating at "sustainable levels", Mr. Mulally's thus far successful "One Ford" strategy involves concentrating all the firm's financial and managerial resources on reviving the Blue Oval.

For Geely, acquiring Volvo is both an extraordinary statement of intent and a huge gamble. The deal could help Geely realize the dream of its founder, Li Shufu, the self-styled Henry Ford of China, to become a big international car maker. Even though Ford has done its best to ring-fence its intellectual property, Volvo has plenty of its own, especially in the critical area of safety, to which Geely will have access and which will lend credibility to its cars as its range expands in both scope and scale. It will also learn from Volvo about how to run a global supply chain and an international dealer network.

But Mr. Li believes that Volvo will benefit too. Most important, it will realize its potential in China, the world's biggest and fastest-growing vehicle market. Fifteen years ago Volvo outsold Audi in China, but these days the German premium brand's sales in the country dwarf Volvo's, which were only 22,000 cars last year. He also thinks that away from Ford and the Premier Automotive Group that used to house its upmarket brands, Volvo will have freedom to go into market segments that were previously closed to it because they were occupied by models from Jaguar, Land Rover or Ford itself.

Volvo may still struggle to become a genuine competitor for Audi, BMW and Mercedes, which define and dominate the premium end of the market, but Geely should give it a big presence in China. Volvo's main production sites will continue to be in Sweden and Belgium, but Geely has plans for two factories and an engine assembly plant in China. These, combined with Geely's clout in distribution, could help Volvo nearly double its sales to 600,000 by 2015, Mr. Li believes.

But what should really ensure Volvo's future success in China is the government's commitment to it. Although Geely is that rare thing, a privately owned Chinese car maker, it could not have raised the money needed to buy Volvo (along with the $900 million it is planning to inject in working capital) without the support of state-owned banks and provincial governments' investment funds. The presence at the signing ceremony in Gothenburg of Li Yizhong, the Minister of Industry and Technology, was significant: Geely is buying Volvo, but so too is China.

Nonetheless, doubts linger. The record of cross-border carmaking mergers is atrocious. Geely intends to allow Volvo to operate with a high degree of autonomy, but cultural clashes are almost certain. Within China, there are worries that Geely lacks the expertise to take on the management of a famous but ailing foreign company—a concern of which Mr. Li is well aware. Ford, for its part, insists that Geely has what it takes to be a worthy steward of Volvo. Lewis Booth, Ford's chief financial officer, is said to have taken a shine to Mr. Li, seeing in him a real passion for the car business. At a time when relationships between China and other international companies are under severe strain, the future of a

Chapter 3 Cars and Oil

small Swedish car firm is not the only thing at stake.

Reading Comprehension

Briefly answer the following questions about the text in English.

1) How do Geely and Volvo impress you respectively?
2) Why did Ford decide to sell Volvo?
3) What does Geely want to gain in buying Volvo?
4) What is Beijing's attitude towards the deal?
5) What is the synergy, if any, in the deal?
6) What challenges lie ahead for both Geely and Volvo?

Translation

Proofread the following two Chinese translations of the text and work in groups to make necessary revisions and elaborate on your reasons for changes in class.

版本一：

吉利收购沃尔沃

不起眼的中国汽车制造商收购了在困境中的瑞典豪华汽车品牌

如果福特和吉利因相异而相互吸引，福特将沃尔沃以18亿美元出售给中国后起之秀吉利应该是个天合之作。瑞典的沃尔沃是中等偏上阶级喜好的缩影；在许多美国和欧洲郊区车道上行驶的话，没有比选择略显迟钝但具有强大的安全性和实用性的沃尔沃更好。相反，吉利鲜被海外知晓，部分原因是它主要生产价格低廉的小型车系列，尚无能力满足世界上越来越严格的安全和环保法规。但是吉利充满雄心壮志。

3月28号签署的这笔交易结束了旷日持久的谈判，福特出售了它最后一个欧洲顶级汽车品牌，这是自20世纪80年代末开始因自我膨胀而傲慢收购的品牌。舍弃了阿斯顿马丁、捷豹、路虎之后，2006年从波音调过来的总裁艾伦·穆拉里也决心把去年损失13亿美元、销量仅为335 000辆的沃尔沃舍弃。尽管沃尔沃今年出现转机并能在稳定的水平中运行，但目前为止穆拉里的"一个福特"战略集中在振兴所有与蓝色椭圆系列业务相关的财务和管理资源。

对于吉利来说，收购沃尔沃既需要下特别大的决心，也是一场大赌博。这份协议将有助于吉利实现其创始人李书福自封为中国的亨利·福特成为大的国际汽车生产商的梦想。尽管福特已经尽最大的努力去圈定他的知识产权，但是吉利将获得沃尔沃拥有的许多属于自己在安全这一关键领域的知识产权，借沃尔沃的信誉在规模和范围上扩大自己的影响。吉利还能从沃尔沃那里学到如何运行全球供应链和国际销售网络。

但是李书福认为沃尔沃也将受益。更重要的是，这将实现沃尔沃在中国这个世界最大、发展最快的汽车市场中的潜力。15年前沃尔沃在中国的销量超过奥迪，但这些日子德国高档品牌在中国的销量使去年仅销售22 000辆车的沃尔沃相形见绌。他也相信脱离福特和这个曾经禁锢其高档品牌的Premier汽车集团，沃尔沃能够自由地进入因被捷豹、路虎、福特本身占据的车型而曾被关闭的部分市场。

沃尔沃将坚持奋斗成为定义和主宰高端品牌市场的奥迪、宝马、奔驰的真正竞争对手，但吉利应该让沃尔沃在中国有一个大的保有量。沃尔沃的主要生产基地将继续在瑞典和比利时，但是吉利计划再投资两个工厂和一个发动机装配厂。李先生认为，结合吉利的区域影响力，这将帮助沃尔沃在2015年销量翻一番，到600,000辆。

但真正保证沃尔沃未来在中国的成功在于政府的承诺。吉利是中国罕见的私有汽车制造商，没有国有银行和省政府投资支持，它不能筹集到收购沃尔沃的资金（9亿美元加上计划中注入的流动资金）。工业和信息化部长李毅中出席了在歌德堡的签字仪式并表示：吉利收购沃尔沃，也就是中国收购沃尔沃。

然而，心存疑虑的是跨境汽车制造的合并记录简直糟糕透顶。吉利打算让沃尔沃在一个高度自治的环境下运营，但是文化冲突几乎是肯定的。李先生清楚地知道在中国有人担心吉利缺乏管理在困境中的著名外国企业的经验。福特坚信吉利已经具备成为沃尔沃东家的所有条件。福特首席财政官刘易斯·布思非常赞赏李先生，在他身上看到对汽车产业真正的激情。此时，中国与其他国际公司的关系压力重重，一个瑞典小汽车公司的未来并不是唯一受到威胁的。

版本二：

吉利收购沃尔沃

鲜为人知的中国汽车制造商收购了显赫而衰败的瑞典巨头

福特以 18 亿美元将旗下沃尔沃出售给中国新生代汽车制造商吉利，如果异性相吸适用于此，这应该被视为完美的联姻。瑞典的沃尔沃被视作中产阶级的品位之选；它的设计略显沉闷，但具备良好的安全性及实用性，这保证了它在景气的时代是欧美乡间高速公路上的首选。另一方面，吉利在中国以外籍籍无名，或许是因为它所生产的小型廉价车还不足以达到发达国家严格的安全和环境检测标准。严酷的现状也不能挫伤吉利的勃勃雄心。

自 20 世纪 80 年代末起福特的欧洲生产线就处于风雨飘摇之中，而这份签署于 3 月 28 号的沃尔沃转卖协议，终于让福特处理掉在欧洲最后一个子公司。在作别了阿斯顿马丁、陆虎揽胜后，2006 年从波音转投福特的 CEO，Alan Mulally 觉得到了和沃尔沃说再见的时候。沃尔沃在上一年亏损 13 亿美元，仅仅售出 33.5 万辆轿车。尽管今年以来销量复苏回稳，Mulally 先生还是决定弃卒保车。这一策略目前为止大获成功，就是要一门心思集全集团人力财力来重塑蓝色巨人昔日辉煌。

对吉利而言，收购福特既出人意表又是巨大的赌博。中国的亨利·福特，吉利创始人李书福，可以借此将吉利打造为世界性的汽车制造商。尽管福特尽一切可能防止自己的知识产权外流，但沃尔沃有自己的一套尤擅安全的专业技术。吉利通过收购无疑让自有品牌的车辆也隐隐打上了高安全的标签。吉利还将借鉴沃尔沃的经验来铺设全球范围的供应商和零售点。

李书福认为收购对沃尔沃也有好处。最重要的是给沃尔沃挖掘了中国市场。中国有着世界最大、上升速度最快的汽车需求量，15 年前沃尔沃在中国比奥迪更畅销，但现在形式远远逆转了，去年瑞典厂商只在中国卖出 22,000 辆轿车。李也认为脱离福特给沃尔沃带来了更广阔的发展前景。之前因为发展方向和捷豹、陆虎或福特已有车型重叠而不得不放弃的构思也可以重拾起来。

沃尔沃尚不可一举对奥迪、宝马、奔驰构成真正威胁，那些品牌已经是中国高档车领域的代名词和统治者。但吉利会给沃尔沃在中国巨大的出镜率。沃尔沃主要生产线仍将留守瑞典、比利时，但吉利计划将其两个工厂和引擎组装线迁至中国。

李书福坚信融合吉利的品牌优势后，沃尔沃在2015年前将卖出接近现状一倍多的车，达到60万辆一年。

但要保证吉利将来在中国一帆风顺，必须得有中国政府的默许。吉利是中国少数的完全不借助国有银行贷款或省级政府注资完成收购融资的企业（并还计划独立集资9亿美元注入生产线）。但在Gothenburg签约仪式上一同出现的工信部部长李毅中再明显不过地昭示了，买下沃尔沃的不仅仅是吉利，而是整个中国。

前路还是疑云重重。跨国的汽车厂商合并总是龃龉不断。吉利倾向于鼓励沃尔沃主攻高端市场，但在这个过程中文化的摩擦不可避免。中国担心吉利缺乏管理拥有辉煌品牌但正走下坡路公司的能力。而福特坚持吉利是值得沃尔沃托付的选择。福特CFO Lewis Booth就看好李书福，称他是对汽车工业真正有热情的人。现在正是中国与海外公司关系日趋紧张的时刻，赌桌上的筹码可不仅是小小的瑞典公司那么简单。

Research and Discussion

Search the Internet for answers to the following questions and share your findings in class.

1) Compare the differences between organic growth and growth through mergers and acquisitions.

Organic Growth	Mergers and Acquisitions

2) Why do people also hope 1+1 >2 in a M&A deal?

3) Does an M&A deal need the regulatory approval to go through?

4) The text is about why Geely, an obscure Chinese start-up, successfully merged with Volve, a famous Swedish company. How do other Chinese companies fare in their cross-border M&A efforts?

5) What are the possible impacts of an M&A deal on the following groups of people? Use real examples to illustrate your points and write down your findings.

① If you are a consumer...

② If you work in the company that goes through the M&A...

③ If you are a competitor of the new company...

④ If you are the industry regulator...

Part ③ Car Models and Auto Shows

Read the following English text and carry out your reading tasks as directed.

Car Babes Banned? China Wants Eyes on Cars, Not Models at Auto Show

The China auto show is a big deal in China, as the organizers like to remind you. It's the biggest show in Asia, and one of the largest auto shows in the world. The superlatives tend to set your expectations for some serious car gawking when you plan on attending.

What you discover, perhaps even more than China's fascination with cars, is why many of the nearly 1 million attendees pay $13 to get in: the models. No, not the kind with fenders. We're talking about supermodels in dresses, evening gowns, short skirts, T-shirts, and the occasional tube top.

Sure, at the auto shows in Detroit or New York, you'll see plenty of models—but they're usually hugging a Lamborghini or elevated on stage. In China's auto show the models are, well...everywhere—standing next to countless Chinese cars throughout massive new exhibition halls, not just the ones on stage. And their apparent willingness to stare into camera lenses encourages the mostly male attendees to take as many pictures as possible. Nearly every model is hounded from the moment the doors open at 9 a.m. until they close at 8 p.m.

But when China's biggest auto show opens in Shanghai this year, the only models on display will be the ones with four wheels.

Gone, show organizers hope, will be the scantily-clad "car babes" that in previous years have posed provocatively on car hoods and sashayed through the aisles to draw crowds to the 9-day event. The focus, instead, will be the latest offerings from an array of global car manufacturers, which—models or not—are pulling out all the stops to compete for Chinese customers in what since 2009 has been the world's largest car market.

Reading Tasks

I Research and Discussion

Search the Internet for answers to the following questions and share your findings in class.

1) What are the major differences between American auto shows and China's auto shows?
2) What are the purposes for Chinese cities to hold auto shows?
3) Have you ever been to an auto show? What attract you to an auto show?
4) Who bears the cost of holding an auto show and who are the biggest beneficiaries of an auto show?

II Translation

Translate the following sentences/paragraphs into Chinese.

1) The superlatives tend to set your expectations for some serious car gawking when you plan on attending.
2) What you discover, perhaps even more than China's fascination with cars, is why many of the nearly 1 million attendees pay $13 to get in: the models. No, not the kind with fenders. their apparent willingness to stare into camera lenses encourages the mostly male attendees to take as many pictures as possible.

3) Nearly every model is hounded from the moment the doors open at 9 a.m. until they close at 8 p.m.

4) Gone, show organizers hope, will be the scantily-clad "car babes" that in previous years have posed provocatively on car hoods and sashayed through the aisles to draw crowds to the 9-day event.

5) The focus, instead, will be the latest offerings from an array of global car manufacturers, which—models or not—are pulling out all the stops to compete for Chinese customers in what since 2009 has been the world's largest car market.

Bilingual Debate

The following is an excerpt from a Chinese news report following Shanghai's ban on car babes at auto shows. Take a stance on the following topic "Should Car Models Be Banned at Auto Shows in China?" and state your reasons in both Chinese and English in class.

上海车展取消车模　车模扮乞丐乞讨抗议

上海车展的车模今年以新方式呈现自己,不在展馆内,而在……路边乞讨。正在进行的上海车展因为取消车模一度引发全民热议。只见车,不见模,更没有了乍泄的春光,车展不再用车模来吸引眼球。早在车展开幕那几天,就有车模扛着牌子出现在现场抗议,而据"央视微博客户端"26日晚消息,一大波美女车模打扮成乞丐,在上海徐家汇街头乞讨,以抗议车展拒绝车模导致自己失业。

车模扮乞丐抗议的做法,网友看法不一。

@王君超:女丐帮?怀疑是行为艺术人士的炒作。

@股海股海我来啦:各个行业都会发生变化,没有一专多能的本领难以生存。建议她们去炒股。

@青衫客007:举牌、端碗、扶棍,变弱势群体了。

@奥鹏胡珊珊:美女丐帮,挺个性的。不过,不求转变,等别人"施舍"总是无法赢得掌声。

Part 4
Oil Pricing Mechanism

Read the following English text and carry out your reading tasks as directed.

Oil Pricing Mechanism Explained

What Costs Make Up the Price of Gas at the Pump?

1. Crude oil: Crude oil is the raw material used in the production of gasoline. The price of a barrel of crude oil varies on a daily basis. A one-dollar-per-barrel change in price translates to a five-cent change in gasoline prices, according to EIA. A 2011 study by American Petroleum Institute determined that the cost of crude oil comprises approximately 69 percent of the total cost of gasoline.

2. Refining: Refining is the cost of converting crude oil into gasoline. Refining accounts for approximately 7 percent of gasoline prices. Refining cost may be increased in areas that impose stricter refining regulations, such as the West Coast and California. Refining cost may also be affected by natural disasters in areas of high refining capacity. For example, this did happen when Hurricane Katrina hit the Gulf Coast.

3. Distribution and marketing: Distribution and marketing costs are included in gasoline prices. According to EIA, these costs account for approximately 10 percent of the price of gasoline. These costs include transportation, operating expenses and advertizement.

4. Taxes: Taxes account for approximately 14 percent of the price of gasoline. The federal motor gasoline tax is 18.4 cents per gallon. There are also state taxes imposed on gasoline. State tax varies from state to state and include sales tax and road taxes. Combined federal, state and local taxes can be as high as 70 cents per gallon.

Pain at the Pump

Pump Pain Index, also known as pain at the pump, is measured by the percentage of average daily income needed to buy a gallon of fuel. Bloomberg publishes a ranking of countries listed by gas price and pain at the pump.

Chapter 3 Cars and Oil

Top Five Factors Affecting Oil Prices in 2015

The big question is what oil prices will do in 2015. Oil prices are unsustainably low right now—many high-cost oil producers and oil-producing regions are currently operating in the red. That may work in the short term, but over the medium and long term, companies will be forced out of the market, precipitating a price rise. The big question is when they will rise, and by how much.

So, what does that mean for oil prices in 2015? It is anybody's guess, but here are the top five variables that will determine the trajectory of oil prices over the next 12 months, in no particular order.

1. China's economy. China is the second largest consumer of oil in the world and surpassed the United States as the largest importer of liquid fuels in late 2013. What is more important for oil prices is how much China's consumption will increase in the coming years. According to the EIA, China is expected to burn through 3 million more barrels per day in 2020 compared to 2012, accounting for about one-quarter of global demand growth over that timeframe. Although there is much uncertainty, China just wrapped up a disappointing fourth quarter, capping off its slowest annual growth in over a quarter century. It is not at all obvious that China will be able to halt its sliding growth rate, but the trajectory of China's economy will significantly impact oil prices in 2015.

2. American shale. By the end of 2014, the U.S. was producing more than 9 million barrels of oil per day, an 80 percent increase from 2007. That output went a long way to creating a glut of oil, which helped send oil prices to the dumps in 2014. Having collectively shot themselves in the foot, the big question is how affected U.S. drillers will be by sub-$60 WTI. Rig counts continue to fall, spending is being slashed, but output has so far been stable. Whether the industry can maintain output given today's prices or production begins to fall will have an enormous impact on international supplies, and as a result, prices.

3. Elasticity of demand. The cure for low prices is low prices. Will oil selling at fire sale prices spur renewed demand? In the U.S., gasoline prices are now below $2.40 per gallon, more than 35 percent down from mid-2014. That has led to an uptick in gasoline consumption. In the waning days of 2014, the U.S. consumed gasoline at the highest daily rate since 2007. Low

prices could spark higher demand, which in turn could send oil prices back up.

4. OPEC's next move. OPEC deserves a lot of credit (or blame) for the remarkable downturn in oil prices last year. The mere fact that oil prices crashed after the cartel's November meeting demonstrates just how influential they are over price swings. For now OPEC—or more accurately, Saudi Arabia—has stood firm in its insistence not to cut production quotas. Whether that remains true through 2015 is up in the air.

5. Geopolitical flashpoints. In the not too distant past, a small supply disruption would send oil prices skyward. In early 2014, for example, violence in Libya blocked oil exports, contributing to a rise in oil prices. In Iraq, terrorists overran parts of the country and oil prices shot up on fears of supply outages. But since then, geopolitical flashpoints have had much less of an effect on the price of crude. During the last few weeks of 2014, violence flared up again in Libya. But after a brief increase in prices, the markets shrugged off the event. Nevertheless, history has demonstrated time and again that geopolitical crises are some of the most powerful short-term movers of oil prices.

Reading Tasks

❶ Summary writing

Complete the following summary of the text in Chinese.

油价的构成环节及占比
1. _____ 2. _____   3. _____ 4. _____

加油痛苦指数
衡量标准: _____

Chapter ③ Cars and Oil

> **2015 年影响油价变动的五大因素**
>
> 因素一：_____
> 因素二：_____
> 因素三：_____
> 因素四：_____
> 因素五：_____

II Reading Comprehension

Briefly answer the following question about the text in English.

What factors determine oil price? What do you think is the most important factor?

III Research and Discussion

Search the Internet for answers to the following questions and share your findings in class.

1) What will be the impacts of high oil prices on your life even if you don't own a car?

2) What is OPEC? What is its relationship with oil prices? What are some of the major events in the history of OPEC? Share your findings with the help of the passages and the Internet resources.

   In the 1960s: _____
   In the 1970s: _____
   In the 1980s: _____
   In the 1990s: _____
   In the 21st century: _____

3) What are some of the world's major oil makers by region? Do they come from OPEC countries?

4) How does China's oil pricing mechanism work?

5) Do these factors still hold true and have ramifications today?

IV Translation

1. **Translate the following sentences/paragraphs into Chinese.**

   1) Still think filling up is expensive? Imagine shelling out $9.26 a gallon, the price in Norway. Indianans and Pakistanis put in a full day's work to afford a single gallon.

   2) Of course, not all gas tanks are created equally. Even at low prices, American's unparalleled thirst for gas takes a toll on budgets.

   3) Amid an unprecedented North American oil boom, gasoline prices fell worldwide by an average 7.2 percent in the last six months.

   4) Saudi Arabia is OPEC's biggest oil producer and heavily subsidizes its unchanging price of gasoline. Saudis rank among the greatest gas guzzlers in the world but devote the smallest shares of their incomes to buying it.

   5) Norway's high gasoline prices are an electric car maker's dream.

   6) China regulates the price of retail gasoline and diesel fuel to curb inflation. With low average wages, the country ranks among the worst for gas affordability, despite a gas price that's lower than the global average.

2. **Proofread the following chart made by news.163.com based on the Bloomberg ranking of the Pump Pain Index and make revisions in case of any wrong or inadequate information.**

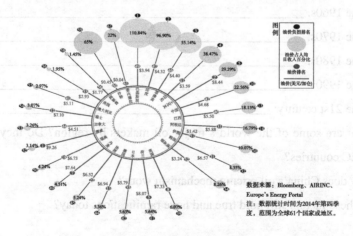

图 3-1　全球油价负担排名

Chapter 3 Cars and Oil

Business Application

1. Driving and car ownership is now widely accessible to average Chinese. What are the most common car types of purchase? Compile them in a vocabulary list.

2. Provide the English equivalents to a car's major parts.

    1) 挡风玻璃雨刮　　　　　　2) 方向盘
    3) 离合器　　　　　　　　　4) 油门
    5) （全景）天窗　　　　　　6) 前车盖
    7) 后视镜　　　　　　　　　8) 后备厢
    9) 脚刹　　　　　　　　　　10) 档位
    11) 转向灯　　　　　　　　　12) 远光灯 / 近光灯
    13) 换胎（千斤顶）　　　　　14) 油箱
    15) 底盘　　　　　　　　　　16) 保险杠

3. Provide English equivalents to the following Chinese expressions on driving and a context for these expressions.

    1) 驾驶手动挡（自动挡）　　2) 变道 / 并道
    3) 倒车　　　　　　　　　　4) 超车
    5) 按汽车喇叭　　　　　　　6) 拼车
    7) 系上安全带　　　　　　　8) 停车
    9) 加油　　　　　　　　　　10) 打车软件
    11) 闯红灯　　　　　　　　　12) 酒驾（醉驾）
    13) 肇事逃逸　　　　　　　　14) 酒精测试
    15) 代驾　　　　　　　　　　16) 理赔
    17) 划车　　　　　　　　　　18) 追尾
    19) 被摄像头监控超速　　　　20) 乱穿马路 / 人行道
    21) 吊销执照　　　　　　　　22) 更换执照
    23) 自驾游　　　　　　　　　24) 碰瓷

25) 人行横道   26) 十字路口
27) 丁字路口   28) 天桥
29) 地道   30) 汽车展厅
31) 4S 店   32) 道路坑洼

4. What are the most common types of car accidents and problems? Compile them in a vocabulary list.

5. What are the most common expressions associated with car insurance? Compile them in a vocabulary list.

6. The current car industry is undergoing some profound changes due to climate change concerns. Suppose you were a car industry analyst, dust clean your crystal ball and offer your wildest predictions on the changes that are about to take place in the industry for the coming years. Write down your predictions in the form of a bilingual report and use real evidence to back your claim.

Chapter 4
China's Internet Companies
Overview

China's mobile Internet market is booming, with the world's largest number of Internet users and mobile phone users. China's Internet companies are also taking note and responding with great gusto. Some of them rolled out services that specially cater to Chinese people; some chose to list in U.S. stock exchange. Leading groups include Tencent and Alibaba. What set them apart from the rest? Through a selection of reports on China's Internet companies, you can feel the strong pulse of vigor of China's Internet market.

Pre-reading Activities

1. What is (are) your favorite Chinese website(s)? And why? How much time do you spend online every day? What do you usually do online?

2. How do you characterize yourself as an Internet user?

3. Can you list popular expressions to describe your Internet using habits? Provide examples in both English and Chinese.

4. Compare your shopping behaviors with those of your parents or grandparents and summarize as many differences as possible by filling in the following table. Think about how their differences are capitalized on by today's Internet companies.

Features of Old-generation Chinese Consumers	Features of Modern Young Chinese Consumers
E.g.: Old generation Chinese are more conservative and prefer to save than to spend their hard-earned money.	E.g.: The young people tend to live at the moment and are more of an impulsive kind for things they like.

5. Watch the video "Chairman Ma" by CBS program *60 Minutes*.

Chapter 4 China's Internet Companies

Part 1
Case Study of WeChat

Read the following two texts, one in English and one in Chinese, and carry out your reading tasks as directed.

WeChat's World

Like most professionals on the mainland, Yu Hui uses WeChat rather than e-mail to conduct much of her business. The App offers everything from free video calls and instant group chats to news updates and easy sharing of large multimedia files. She also uses her smartphone camera to scan the WeChat QR (or quick response) codes of people she meets far more often these days than she exchanges business cards. Yu Hui's husband uses the App to shop online, to pay for goods at physical stores, settle utility bills and split dinner tabs with friends, just with a few taps. He can easily book and pay for taxis, dumpling deliveries, theater tickets, hospital appointments and foreign holidays, all without ever leaving the WeChat universe.

In a way, WeChat is there "at every point of people's daily contact with the world, from morning until night". It is this status as a hub for all Internet activities, and as a platform through which users find their way to other services, that inspires Silicon Valley firms, including Facebook, to monitor WeChat closely.

Among all its services, it is perhaps its promise of a cashless economy that impresses onlookers the most. Thanks to WeChat, Chinese consumers can navigate their day without once spending banknotes or pulling out plastic. It is the best example yet of how China is shaping the future of the mobile Internet for consumers everywhere.

That is only fitting, for China makes and puts to good use more smartphones than any other country. More Chinese reach the Internet via their mobiles than in America. Many leapt from the pre-web era straight to the mobile Internet, skipping the personal computer altogether. About half of all sales over the Internet in China take place via mobile phones, against roughly a third of total sales in America. In other words, the conditions were all there for WeChat to take wing: new technologies, business models built around mobile phones, and above all, customers eager to experiment.

The service, which is known on the mainland as Weixin, began five years ago as an innovation from Tencent, a Chinese online-gaming and social-media firm. By now, over 700m people use it, and it is one of the world's most popular messaging Apps. More than a third of all the time spent by mainlanders on the mobile Internet is spent on WeChat. A typical user returns to it ten times a day or more.

WeChat has worked hard to make sure that its product is enjoyable to use. Shaking the phone has proven a popular way to make new friends who are also users. Waving it at a television allows the App to recognize the current programme and viewers to interact. A successful stunt during last year's celebration of Chinese New Year's Eve saw CCTV, the official state broadcaster, offer millions of dollars in cash rewards to WeChat users who shook their phones on cue.

Most importantly, over half of WeChat users have been persuaded to link their bank cards to the App. That is a notable achievement given that China is a distrustful society and the Internet is a free-for-all of cybercrime, malware and scams. Yet, using its trusted brand, and putting to work robust identity and password authentication, Tencent was able to win over the public. In contrast, Western products such as Snapchat and WhatsApp have yet to persuade consumers to entrust them with their financial details.

How did Tencent take WeChat so far ahead of its rivals? The answer lies partly in the peculiarities of the local market. Unlike most Westerners, many Chinese possessed multiple mobile devices, and they quickly took to an App that offered them an easy way to integrate them all into a single digital identity. In America, messaging Apps had a potent competitor in the form of basic mobile-phone plans, which bundled in SMS messaging. But text messages were costly in China, so consumers eagerly adopted the free messaging App. And

Chapter 4 China's Internet Companies

e-mail never took off on the mainland the way it has around the world, mainly because the Internet came late; that left an opening for messaging Apps.

But the bigger explanation for WeChat's rise is Tencent's ability to innovate. Many Chinese grew up using QQ, a PC-based messaging platform offered by Tencent that still has over 800 million registered users. QQ was a copy of ICQ, a pioneering Israeli messaging service. But then the Chinese imitator learned to think for itself. Spotting the coming rise of the mobile Internet, Tencent challenged several internal teams to design and develop a smartphone-only messaging App. When Tencent launched the new App, it made it easy for QQ's users to transfer their contacts over to the new App.

Another stroke of brilliance came two years ago when the service launched a "red packet" campaign in which WeChat users were able to send digital money to friends and family to celebrate Chinese New Year rather than sending cash in a red envelope, as is customary. It was clever of the firm to turn dutiful gift-giving into an exciting game. It also encouraged users to bind together into groups to send money, often in randomized amounts (if you send 3,000 yuan to 30 friends, they may not get 100 yuan each; WeChat decides how much). That, in turn, led to explosive growth in group chats. This year, over 400 million users (both as individuals and in groups) sent 32 billion packets of digital cash during the celebration.

The enthusiasm with which WeChat users have adopted the platform makes them valuable to Tencent in ways that rivals can only dream of. After years of patient investment, its parent now earns a large and rising profit from WeChat. While other free messaging Apps struggle to bring in much money, WeChat earned about $1.8 billion in revenues last year.

E-commerce is another driver of the business model. The firm earns fees when consumers shop at one of the more than 10 million merchants (including some celebrities) that have official accounts on the App. Once users attach their bank cards to WeChat Wallet, they typically go on shopping sprees involving far more transactions per month than, for instance, Americans make on plastic. Three years ago, very few people bought things using

WeChat, but now roughly a third of its users are making regular e-commerce purchases directly though the App. A virtuous circle is operating: As more merchants and brands set up official accounts, it becomes a buzzier and more appealing bazaar.

Users' dependence on the portal means a treasure-trove of insights into their preferences and peccadilloes. That, in turn, makes WeChat much more valuable to advertizers keen to target consumers as precisely as possible. There are few firms better placed to take advantage of the rise of social mobile advertising than WeChat. When BMW, a German carmaker, launched the first-ever ad to appear on the WeChat Moments page of selected users, there followed nothing like pique at the commercial intrusion, but rather an uproar from people demanding to know why they had not received the ad. Even though Tencent has deliberately trodden carefully in introducing targeted ads on users' Moments pages, its official corporate accounts enjoy billions of impressions each day.

Indeed, WeChat has already proved itself in the teeth of competition. It has withstood numerous attempts by Alibaba, a formidable local rival, to knock it and its creations off their perch. WeChat has flourished for simple, commercial reasons: It solves problems for its users, and it delights them with new and unexpected offerings. That will change the mobile Internet for everyone.

Text ❷

微信如何在中国取得成功

无论是微信自己公布的数据还是第三方权威机构的数据，在所有的移动下载中，微信都是排名第一，月活跃用户超过6亿人。也就是说，中国有一半以上的人都在使用微信，这个比例在东南沿海会更高。所以在社交领域里，微信是无可争议的老大，但是为什么在国外，微信的活跃人数就不行了呢？

虽然微信在日本、马来西亚、泰国、中国台湾等国家和地区占据着社交市场的主导地位，同时在印尼、新加坡、缅甸、中国香港等国家和地区也有一定的市场份额，但微信的表现还主要集中在中国大陆市场，其活跃用户的快速增长也主要集中在国内市场。纵观全球市场，微信的劲敌还有Facebook。据分析公司研究，2016年4月，Android平台上最热门的社交应用是Facebook，它在109个国家拔得头筹，Facebook Messenger位居第二，微信只能屈居第三。那么，明明在国内发展极具活力的微信，为何在日本、马来西亚、中国台湾等亚洲市场不及Line，在全球市场不及Facebook？

● 不符合海外用户的使用习惯

中国人喜欢一个App可以实现所有功能，所以微信不仅仅是一个社交App，它还集成了购物、出行等一系列与我们生活息息相关的功能。但是国外用户偏向于功能单一的应用，一个应用只做一件事。Facebook发展了这么多年，但是直至今天，它也只是一个分享心情、图片、短文的应用。虽然它曾经也推出过类似微博的私信功能，但是不久之后就把这项功能独立出来，做成了一个叫Facebook Messenger的独立应用。

● Facebook先占领市场，微信难以弯道超车

微信诞生于2011年，而Facebook诞生于2004年，在微信诞生时Facebook已经发展了7个年头。当微信进入海外市场的时候，海外用户已经习惯这些已有应用的使用习惯，而与之配套的信用卡、公交卡等也无法实现绑定。

微信之所以能在中国取得巨大的成功，是因为QQ已经积攒了十年的数据信息，对中国用户非常了解，并且迅速从一个聊天软件变成了一个集所有功能于一身的移动平台。我们能在微信订外卖、租车、缴话费、买机票，看各种自己感兴趣的东西，甚至玩游戏。国际版的微信并没有这么多功能，也没有根据外国人的需求去调整产品。我们忍不住为微信在国际化扩张中的失误而感到可惜，但是这也是无法避免的事情。如果微信想要具备各种强大的功能，复制其在中国的成就，就意味着腾讯要和全世界的企业沟通谈判，建立合作。而这么做需要的精力和成本大到难以想象。

Reading Tasks

❶ Summary Writing

Complete the following summary of Text 1 in English.

> **Reasons for WeChat's Success in China**
>
> 1. _____ 2. _____
> 3. _____ 4. _____

❷ Reading Comprehension

Briefly answer the following questions about the two texts in English.

1) Are you a WeChat user? What do you usually do on WeChat? Describe all the distinctive services of WeChat based on Text 1 and on your own experience.

2) What is target advertising in Text 1? Give examples of target advertising in your own words.

3) Why can't WeChat achieve the same level of success in overseas market according to Text 2? Do you agree with this observation?

❸ Language Exercises

Replace the expressions in bold in the following sentences/paragraphs without changing their meanings.

1) It is this status as **a hub for all Internet activities**, and as a platform through which users find their way to other services,...

2) Thanks to WeChat, Chinese consumers can **navigate their day** without once spending banknotes or **pulling out plastic**.

3) That is only fitting, for China makes and **puts to good use** more smartphones than any other country.

Chapter 4 China's Internet Companies

4) In other words, the conditions were all there for WeChat to **take wing**: new technologies, business models built around mobile phones, and above all, customers eager to experiment.

5) Unlike most Westerners, many Chinese possessed multiple mobile devices, and they quickly **took to** an App that offered them an easy way to integrate them all into a single digital identity.

6) In America, messaging Apps had **a potent competitor** in the form of basic mobile-phone plans, which **bundled in** SMS messaging.

7) And e-mail never took off on the mainland the way it has around the world, mainly because the Internet came late; that **left an opening for** messaging Apps.

8) Another **stroke of brilliance** came two years ago when the service launched a "red packet" campaign in which WeChat users were able to send digital money to friends and family to celebrate Chinese New Year rather than sending cash in a red envelope, as is customary.

9) Once users attach their bank cards to WeChat Wallet, they typically **go on shopping sprees** involving far more transactions per month than, for instance, Americans make on plastic.

10) **A virtuous circle** is operating: As more merchants and brands set up official accounts, it becomes a buzzier and more appealing bazaar.

11) Users' dependence on the portal means **a treasure-trove of insights** into their **preferences and peccadilloes**.

IV Translation

1. Provide the Chinese equivalents to the following terms and expressions.

   1) online-gaming and social-media   2) messaging Apps
   3) basic mobile-phone plans   4) SMS messaging
   5) text message   6) cybercrime
   7) malware   8) scams

9) mobile Internet 10) official accounts
11) targeted advertising 12) impressions
13) portal

2. **Translate the following sentences/paragraphs into Chinese.**

   1) Waving it at a television allows the App to recognize the current programme and viewers to interact. A successful stunt during last year's celebration of Chinese New Year's Eve saw CCTV, the official state broadcaster, offer millions of dollars in cash rewards to WeChat users who shook their phones on cue.

   2) Most importantly, over half of WeChat users have been persuaded to link their bank cards to the App. That is a notable achievement given that China is a distrustful society and the Internet is a free-for-all of cybercrime, malware and scams.

   3) When BMW, a German carmaker, launched the first-ever ad to appear on the WeChat Moments page of selected users, there followed nothing like pique at the commercial intrusion, but rather an uproar from people demanding to know why they had not received the ad. Even though Tencent has deliberately trodden carefully in introducing targeted ads on users' Moments pages, its official corporate accounts enjoy billions of impressions each day.

   4) Indeed, WeChat has already proved itself in the teeth of competition. Many Chinese champions have succeeded only because the government has blocked foreign entrants. Here, too, Tencent breaks the mould. It has withstood numerous attempts by Alibaba, a formidable local rival, to knock it and its creations off their perch.

3. **Translate the following dialogue into English.**
   A: 最近微信朋友圈怎么都没见你更新了呀？
   B: 哎，我已经不玩朋友圈很久了。那里已经不再是一个纯粹和朋友交流感情的地方了。
   A: 怎么这么说呀？我觉得朋友圈还是很有意思的呢。

Chapter 4　China's Internet Companies

B: 我不知道你的朋友圈怎么样，反正我的朋友圈已经被无数微商刷屏了。

A: 微商哦，最近确实很火，以前通过淘宝天猫做生意，现在有个微信 App 就可以做生意了。

B: 可不是吗？各种海外代购，比如奶粉、尿不湿、化妆品、品牌包包等。

A: 这也是一条致富路啊！你的朋友都很有商业头脑啊。

B: 哎，谁说不是呢？他们是致富了，可是我的朋友圈却不再单纯了。所以，我是不是应该收他们广告费呀！

A: 哈哈，其实你也可以把不喜欢的微商屏蔽呀，选择不看他们的朋友圈，就不会觉得勉强了。

B: 好主意！可是，除了形形色色的微商，还有各种各样秀自拍的，都希望趁机成为"网红"。

A: 哈哈哈，有几个网红朋友也不错啊，最近网红都很受欢迎哦。

B: 我知道，从之前的"凤姐""芙蓉姐姐"因为颠覆了大家的审美而成名，到现在各种攀升"天王嫂"的网红，都是锥子脸的标配。

A: 可不是嘛，各种各样的人通过网络都红了起来，真是不得不惊叹于网络的神奇力量！

D: 没错，科技的力量固然推动了社会发展，可是我多么希望可以回到原来单纯美好的朋友圈呀！

Ⅴ Research and Discussion

Search the Internet for answers to the following questions and share your findings in class.

1) WeChat merchants are really popular these days. What do you think of WeChat merchants? Do you think their posts are an infringement on your privacy? What do you do when your friends are WeChat merchants? Should they be banned?

2) Do you have any privacy concerns when you use WeChat? Do you think WeChat is in control of too much of your personal information and once lost, may post considerable security hazard?

3) What do you know about Tencent, the parent company of WeChat? Do you use any of its products? Do these products provide user satisfaction?

Part 2 Case Study of Vancl

Read the following English text and carry out your reading tasks as directed.

Vancl Plans to Raise $1 Billion in Chinese Internet IPO

Chinese online retailer Vancl has hired five banks to manage what could become China's largest Internet initial public offering to date.

The company plans to raise $750 million–$1 billion in a U.S. listing in the fourth quarter, people familiar with the situation said.

It picked Citigroup, Goldman Sachs, Credit Suisse, Morgan Stanley and China International Capital Corp this week to manage the offering.

According to iResearch, the Internet research firm, Vancl was China's largest clothing retailer with a transaction volume of RMB1.85 billion ($285 million) last year and ranks the fifth among online retailers overall behind Taobao Mall, 360buy, Joyo Amazon and Dangdang.

The listing plan is part of a wave of Chinese Internet offerings, backed by feverish demand from investors keen to own a piece of the country's fast-growing sector.

But some recent stock drops for high-profile listings and growing doubts about accounting practices at Chinese listing candidates have fuelled fears that demand might be overshooting.

Earlier this month, Renren, China's largest social networking service, priced its IPO at the top of an already raised range.

The shares jumped almost 30 percent on the first day of trading but have fallen since

Chapter 4   China's Internet Companies

and closed at $12.26 on Wednesday, below its offering price of $14.

The IPO of Jiayuan.com, China's largest online dating service, flopped shortly after the Renren listing.

Thirteen Chinese companies have raised a total of $1.87 billion in U.S. IPOs so far this year, according to Dealogic, following 42 Chinese U.S. listings last year that raised $4.1 billion.

Investor confidence is particularly strong in the e-commerce segment.

Dangdang, China's largest book retailer, raised $272 million on the New York Stock Exchange last December.

Other Chinese e-commerce listings are believed to be at least one year away.

Bankers say they expect Taobao, owned by the Alibaba Group and by far the country's largest online retailer, to go public next year, but the company has denied any such plans.

For Taobao to list, Jack Ma, the founder of Alibaba Group, would also have to settle his dispute with Yahoo, the single largest shareholder in the group since Yahoo sold its China service to Alibaba.

360buy, China's second-largest online retailer by transaction volume, has said it hopes to raise at least $2 billion in a U.S. listing, but doesn't expect this to happen until 2013.

Reading Tasks

❶ Research and Discussion

Search the Internet for answers to the following questions and share your findings in class.

1) What is "上市"? Why does a company want to "上市"? What are the benefits and disadvantages associated with "上市"?
2) What are the procedures a company has to go through to be listed?
3) What are the common types of stakeholders of a listed company?

4) Why do China's Internet companies want to list at American Stock Exchanges?

5) What are the common types of corporate listings?

Language Exercises

The expressions in bold in the following sentences are all related to "上市". Search the Internet for more expressions and account for their differences in usage.

1) Vancl, a start-up that intends to **go public** soon, is satisfying both consumers' desire for instant gratification and their growing brand-consciousness (or dislike of pirated goods).

2) The company plans to raise $750 million–$1 billion in a U.S. **listing** in the fourth quarter, people familiar with the situation said.

3) The **IPO** of Jiayuan.com, China's largest online dating service, flopped shortly after the Renren **listing**.

4) Bankers say they expect Taobao, owned by the Alibaba Group and by far the country's largest online retailer, to **go public** next year.

5) For Taobao to **list**, Jack Ma, the founder of Alibaba Group, would also have to settle his dispute with Yahoo, the single largest shareholder in the group since Yahoo sold its China service to Alibaba.

Translation

1. **Provide the Chinese equivalents to the following terms and expressions.**

   1) sessions
   2) trading
   3) outperform(underperform) the market
   4) jitters
   5) trading volume (turnover)
   6) mark
   7) rally
   8) confidence/sentiment
   9) flop

Chapter 4 China's Internet Companies

2. Proofread the following Chinese translation of the text provided by in-house translators of *Financial Times* and make revisions in case of any wrong or inadequate parts.

凡客计划在美上市筹资 10 亿美元

中国在线零售商凡客诚品（Vancl）已聘请了 5 家银行负责其首次公开发行（IPO）事宜，这可能成为迄今为止中国规模最大的互联网企业 IPO。

知情人士表示，凡客诚品计划今年第四季度在美国上市，筹资 7.5 亿~10 亿美元。

凡客诚品本周选择了花旗集团（Citigroup）、高盛（Goldman Sachs）、瑞信（Credit Suisse）、摩根士丹利（Morgan Stanley）和中金公司（CICC）来管理其上市事宜。

互联网研究机构艾瑞咨询集团（iResearch）的数据显示，凡客诚品是中国最大的服装零售商，去年交易规模达到 18.5 亿元人民币（合 2.85 亿美元），在所有在线零售商中排名第五，排在淘宝商城（Taobao Mall）、京东商城（360buy.com）、亚马逊卓越网（Joyo Amazon）和当当网（Dangdang）之后。

凡客诚品的上市计划是中国互联网企业上市热潮的一部分。而驱动这股热潮的，则是，迫切希望在中国快速增长领域分一杯羹的投资者的狂热需求。

但最近一些高调上市企业的股价下跌，以及人们对于待上市中国企业的会计行为日益增长的疑虑，引发了需求可能过热的担忧。

本月早些时候，中国最大的网络社交服务企业人人网（Renren），将其 IPO 价格定在了调高后的询价区间的最高端。

人人网上市首日股价飙升近 30%，但此后开始下跌。该股周三收盘价为 12.26 美元，低于 14 美元的发行价。

在人人网上市后不久，中国最大的在线婚恋交友网站世纪佳缘（Jiayuan.com）的 IPO 也经历了一些坎坷。

Dealogic 的数据显示，今年迄今为止，有 13 家中国公司在美国上市，总计筹资 18.7 亿美元；而去年有 42 家中国公司在美上市，筹资 41 亿美元。

投资者尤其看好电子商务领域。

中国最大的图书零售商当当网（Dangdang）去年 12 月在美国证交所（NYSE）上市，筹资 2.72 亿美元。

人们认为，其他中国电子商务企业至少要在一年之后才会上市。

银行家们预计阿里巴巴集团（Alibaba Group）旗下的淘宝网将于明年上市，但该公司否认有此类计划。淘宝网是迄今为止中国最大的在线零售商。

淘宝网要想上市，阿里巴巴创始人马云（Jack Ma）还必须解决自己与雅虎（Yahoo）之间的纠纷。自雅虎将其中国业务出售给阿里巴巴以来，雅虎就成为阿里巴巴最大的单一股东。

中国第二大交易规模的在线零售商京东商城表示，公司希望在美国上市并至少筹资20亿美元，但预计在2013年之前不会上市。

3. **Translate the following sentences/paragraphs into Chinese/English.**

1) The Hang Seng Index finished 236.10 ahead at 17 333.61 in moderate turnover of HK$9.8 billion.

2) The Nasdap composite had gained 22.01 at 4 228.36.

3) By midday, the Dow Jones Industrial Average was down 23.12 at 11 064.35, while the S&P 500 index was 6.53 lower at 1 474.73.

4) The stock fell 4.3 percent at 44.10 after touching a session low of 43.70.

5) Shares of Internet Security Systems rose intraday, but finished weaker, off 26 cents, or 1.9%, to 13.25.

6) The Nasdap, which breached the 2000 mark earlier, was up 11.91 at 1 988, 33.

7) The current correction in the property sector helps fuel the rally.

8) Ever since the stock market nosedive in March, investors have had the jitters. They fear Wall Street's generous bull may transform into a vicious bear.

9) U.S. stock posted morning gains as positive sentiment returned to the market after several companies provided cheerful outlooks and consumer confidence data topped expectations.

10) Volkswagen's shares surged as much as 53 percent yesterday, extending recent strong gains. However, the shares then succumbed to gravity in late trading to close 2 percent down.

11) The Chinese authorities on Thursday said they would scrap the stamp duty on

Chapter ④ China's Internet Companies

stock purchases and will use its own funds to purchase to buy shares, including banking shares, which have been pummelled over the year. Investors applauded these moves and shares climbed 9.5 percent to 2,075.091, with many of the stocks increasing their daily 10 per cent limit, led by financial companies.

12) 数据显示，上半年中小板上市的 110 家公司中 47 家破发，而主板上市的 11 家公司中，竟有 10 家破发。

13) 日经指数 18 日以低盘 16 883 点开出后，指数跌幅一路扩大、盘势一度大跌超过 280 点，终场跌了 1.25%，收在 16 724.81 点。

14) 相较于日股的愁云惨雾，美国股市自 2 月 11 日触底之后，一路反弹，上周五（18 日）站上今年以来新高，市场转趋正面。

Part ③ Case Study of Alibaba

Read the following English text and carry out your reading tasks as directed.

E-commerce in China: The Alibaba Phenomenon

On its way to becoming the world's biggest economy, China is passing another landmark. Its e-commerce market is overtaking America's. And one giant firm dominates the market: Alibaba, by some measures already the world's largest e-commerce company. Last year two of Alibaba's portals together handled 1.1 trillion yuan ($170 billion) in sales, more than eBay and Amazon combined. Alibaba is on track to become the world's first e-commerce firm to handle $1 trillion a year in transactions. Yet despite such extraordinary success, many people outside China have barely noticed the rise of this privately held behemoth.

That is about to change. The firm's founder, a former English teacher called Jack Ma, has just announced that he will hand over the chief-executive job to a trusted insider, Jonathan Lu, in May. Soon afterwards, the firm is expected to announce details of its initial public offering (IPO), sure to be the most trumpeted since Facebook's listing last year—and possibly even bigger, too. Facebook's IPO valued the company at $104 billion (its market capitalization has since slipped back to $63 billion). Estimates of the likely valuation of Alibaba range from $55 billion to more than $120 billion.

The IPO will turn global attention to Alibaba's remarkable rise. And there are other reasons to watch the company closely. One is its future growth potential: If it avoids a Facebook-like fumble, in a few years it could be among the world's most valuable companies (the current global leader, Apple, now worth around $420 billion, was only valued at $90 billion in 2009). Another is that, as Alibaba expands and moves into new markets, it has the capacity to change China.

Alibaba's story so far has been one of canny innovation and a clear focus on how to win competitive advantage in China. "Ebay may be a shark in the ocean," Mr. Ma once said, "but I am a crocodile in the Yangzi river. If we fight in the ocean, we lose; but if we fight in the river, we win." The crocodile of the Yangzi, as he became known, started the company in 1999 with Alibaba.com, a business-to-business portal connecting small Chinese manufacturers with buyers overseas. Its next invention, Taobao, a consumer-to-consumer portal not unlike eBay, features nearly a billion products and is one of the 20 most-visited websites globally. Tmall, a newish business-to-consumer portal that is a bit like Amazon, helps global brands such as Disney and Levi's reach China's middle classes.

Alibaba could grow even faster. By 2020 China's e-commerce market is forecast to be bigger than the existing markets in America, Britain, Japan, Germany and France combined. And although it is not about to challenge Amazon in America, Alibaba is expanding globally by capturing the spending of Chinese overseas and by moving into emerging economies. In this the firm is helped by Alipay, its novel online-payments system that relies on escrow (releasing money to sellers only once their buyers are happy with the goods received). This builds trust in societies where the rule of law is weak.

Perhaps Alibaba's greatest untapped resource is its customer data. Its sites account for over 60% of the parcels delivered in China. It knows more than anyone about the spending habits and creditworthiness of the Chinese middle class, plus millions of Chinese

Chapter 4 China's Internet Companies

merchants. Ali Finance is already a big microlender to small firms; it now plans to expand lending to ordinary consumers. In effect, it is helping liberalize Chinese finance. China's big state banks, which channel cheap capital to state-owned enterprises, have long neglected everyone else. The firm is using its online platforms to deliver insurance products too, and more such innovations are on the way.

Alibaba thus sits at the heart of "bamboo capitalism"—the sprawling tangle of private-sector firms that are more efficient than China's state-owned enterprises. Some 6 million vendors are listed with its sites. The firm's efforts are boosting productivity in China's woefully inefficient retail and logistics sectors. And, more than any other company, it is speeding up the country's much-needed shift away from an investment-heavy model of growth towards one that is driven by consumption.

Reading Tasks

❶ Reading Comprehension

Briefly answer the following questions about the text in English.

1) What is market valuation? How to calculate market valuation? What are the popular expressions associated with market valuation?
2) What are the common types of E-commerce?
3) What is escrow payment? How does Alipay work?
4) What is Alipay's significance in China's market?
5) What is micro-lending?
6) How doe Ali Finance work?
7) Why, according to the passage, can Ali Finance liberate China's financial sector?
8) Can you name some of the other financial innovations of Alibaba?
9) What is "bamboo capitalism"?
10) What are the expressions associated with "经济转型"?

Language Exercises

Replace the expressions in bold in the following sentences/paragraphs without changing their meanings.

1) Last year two of Alibaba's portals together **handled** 1.1 trillion yuan ($170 billion) in sales, more than eBay and Amazon combined.

2) Yet despite such extraordinary success, many people outside China have barely noticed the rise of this **privately held behemoth**.

3) Soon afterwards, the firm is expected to announce details of its initial public offering (IPO), sure to be the most **trumpeted** since Facebook's listing last year—and possibly even bigger, too.

4) Alibaba's **story** so far has been one of **canny innovation** and a clear focus on how to win competitive advantage in China.

Translation

1. **Provide the Chinese equivalents to the following terms and expressions.**

   1) business-to-business portal
   2) consumer-to-consumer portal
   3) business-to-consumer portal
   4) escrow
   5) rule of law
   6) creditworthiness
   7) State banks
   8) state-owned enterprises

2. **Translate the following sentences/paragraphs into Chinese.**

   1) Facebook's IPO valued the company at $104 billion (its market capitalization has since slipped back to $63 billion).

   2) Estimates of the likely valuation of Alibaba range from $55 billion to more than $120 billion...if it avoids a Facebook-like fumble, in a few years it could be among the world's most valuable companies (the current global leader, Apple, now worth around $420 billion, was only valued at $90 billion in 2009).

   3) ...it is helping liberalize Chinese finance. China's big state banks, which channel cheap capital to state-owned enterprises, have long neglected everyone else.

Chapter ④ China's Internet Companies

4) Alibaba thus sits at the heart of "bamboo capitalism"—the sprawling tangle of private-sector firms that are more efficient than China's state-owned enterprises.
5) ...it is speeding up the country's much-needed shift away from an investment-heavy model of growth towards one that is driven by consumption.

Ⅳ Research and Discussion

Search the Internet for answers to the following questions and share your findings in class.

1) In addition to what is mentioned in the passage about Alibaba's e-commerce success, what are other areas of business that Alibaba has ventured into based on your knowledge? Use evidence to support your claim.
2) Alibaba is born and grows up in China's market. Does Alibaba have any global ambitions? Search for any news reports related to its global endeavors.
3) Alibaba, Baidu and Tencent are widely regarded as the three pillars in China's Internet market. Do they have any direct competition? If so, in what areas? Use evidence to back up your claim.

Part ④ Case Study of Jack Ma

Read the following English text and carry out your reading tasks as directed.

Chairman Ma: Is Jack Ma the Most Bizarre Billionaire Ever?

When he floated the giant online shopping company he founded on Wall Street for $22 billion, Alibaba's Jack Ma was catapulted into the public eye in the West.

But, while investors in America were getting their first glimpse of Ma, 50, a study of him in China reveals a larger-than-life figure who performs karaoke on stage for thousands of his employees.

Ma, who founded Alibaba from a tiny flat in China in 1999, showed some of his personality to investors as the company floated, declaring on the trading floor of the New York Stock Exchange that his hero was Forrest Gump.

But back on Chinese soil the man behind the Internet giant, which, dwarfs Facebook and Amazon with its $230 billion valuation and has reportedly made him, China's richest man, live an even more bizarre lifestyle.

New footage of the billionaire on home soil, taken by CBS program *60 Minutes* over the past year, shows Ma appearing on stage in glam rock gear in front of massive crowds, as well as conducting mass wedding celebrations for more than 700 of his employees.

According to Ma himself—who seemed bemused to discover this is not typical CEO behavior—it is all to boost the happiness of his employees, who adore him and crowd round for photos at every opportunity.

At one point, the businessman is pictured in outlandish punk rock gear, including a leather jacket, sunglasses, nose jewelry, a white wig and a red mohawk-style headdress serenading a huge crowd to celebrate a company anniversary.

After entering the stage to the theme tune from Disney's *Lion King* movie, he is later heard singing *You Are So Beautiful*—to rapturous applause.

Ma, who saw the Internet for the first time in 1995, and returned to China determined to make it a viable business there, has made his company the biggest online retailer on earth, and himself one of China's richest men.

It is a far cry from his humble beginnings: He grew up in rural Hangzhou without enough to eat, and failed in two college entrance exams.

Before he came up with the idea to found Alibaba, he taught English, but was rejected for more than a dozen other jobs, including a post at KFC.

The online retailer smashed records with its offering—the largest in U.S. history—and is now as valuable as Facebook after its first day on Wall Street.

The e-commerce powerhouse, which sells anything from fat suits to live animals, was valued more than Amazon and eBay at $168 billion, and sent tremors through the market as

Chapter 4   China's Internet Companies

it floated stocks priced at $68 per share on the first day.

Shares quickly jumped to $98 once trading finally launched at 11.53 a.m.—after a delayed start due to an overwhelming influx of orders.

Now, the firm is worth $230 billion—more than Facebook—as stocks closed at $93, up 38 percent.

The following is the script of *Chairman Ma* which aired on Sept. 28, 2014.

By now you've probably heard of Alibaba, the Chinese Internet giant that's able to reach millions upon millions of previously unreachable Chinese consumers. The company went public this month on the New York Stock Exchange and became one of the most valuable in the world and Alibaba is just getting started.

Everything about the Alibaba story is unconventional. Beginning with its founder, Jack Ma, who gained global celebrity status these past 10 days, as his image became ubiquitous on business news channels and media outlets across America. We got to know Jack Ma before the onslaught, beginning over a year ago in China, where he talked with us about his relationship with the Chinese government, and his unorthodox business philosophy, which surprisingly, gives shareholders almost no say over how he runs the company.

Jack Ma: If you want to invest in us, we believe customer number one, employee number two, shareholder number three. If they don't want to buy that, that's fine. If they regret, they can sell us.

Lara Logan: In the U.S., the shareholder is usually first.

Jack Ma: Yeah. And I think they were wrong. The shareholder, good. I respect them. But they're the third. Because you've take care of the customer, take care of the employees, shareholder will be taken care of.

Ma's unconventional view didn't stop Wall Street from pouring $25 billion into his company now listed on the New York Stock Exchange as "BABA". It's an Internet shopping behemoth, a collection of online marketplaces where buyers and sellers connect to do business. Most of the company's money comes from advertising and small transaction fees. On its most popular website, Taobao, users talk to each other, barter and engage in a way that doesn't happen on American e-commerce websites and Alibaba says there are close to a billion products for sale.

Lara Logan: If I'm buying a house, I can do everything from finding an architect to buying doorknobs to furnishing the entire thing from start to finish. What else?

Jack Ma: Yeah. You can buy anything, as long as it's legal. Anything.

Lara Logan: Five, six years ago, you weren't even making a profit. In fact, in 2002, you made $1 in profit. And today you make how much?

Jack Ma: Billions.

Lara Logan: Billions of dollars.

Jack Ma: Yeah. Yeah.

It's now the biggest e-commerce firm in the world, dwarfing the combined sales of Amazon and eBay. And Alibaba has helped create hundreds of millions of Internet consumers, a whole new social class in China, people who never had access to modern commerce before Jack Ma came along.

Lara Logan: And now you have 500 million registered users?

Jack Ma: Yes, yes. It's only, only like a little bit more than 40 percent of China population and we need more. We have over 100 million people visiting the site, shopping every day. Coming. And it's just the beginning.

When Jack Ma dreamed up Alibaba in 1999, the online world looked nothing like it does today. The most popular search engine was Yahoo, not Google. There were no iPods, iPhones or iPads. Only four out of 10 American homes had Internet connections. And the World Wide Web barely reached all the way to China, where retail stores were rare outside the big cities. For most of the country, there was no such thing as package delivery or credit cards. The only way to buy anything was face-to-face and in cash.

Jack Ma: When we started the e-commerce nobody believed that China would have e-commerce because people believed in "guang-shi", face-to-face, and all kinds of network in traditional ways. There's no trust system in China.

He had to overcome centuries of tradition by showing Chinese buyers and sellers that they could trust Alibaba with their money in this new virtual world. He did it by guaranteeing the transactions and creating his own payment system, an escrow account

Chapter 4 China's Internet Companies

where Alibaba holds the buyers' money until the goods are delivered.

Jack Ma: Every day we finish more than 30 million transactions. And that means that there, you are buying things from somebody you have never seen. You are giving products to the person you have never met. And there are some guys you never know that he's going to take your products to that place, to that person. I want to tell the people that the trust is there.

Lara Logan: Because it's all about trust.

Jack Ma: It's all about the trust.

Now anyone, rich or poor, with access to the Internet and something to sell, can connect with hundreds of millions of potential customers on one of Ma's websites. Ordinary people in China, who never had a way to do business with each other before, today have a stake in the online world. That idea was revolutionary. It created millions of jobs and made Jack Ma a hero to millions of Chinese.

Lara Logan: So this is your old stomping ground, right?

Jack Ma: Yeah.

We met Jack Ma in Hangzhou, an ancient city in southeastern China famous for its beauty. This is where he grew up poor in the 1960s, when the country was cut off from the West. Then in 1972, Richard Nixon came to Jack's hometown. It was the first visit by a U.S. president to China and the city became a mecca for foreign tourists. Through them, 12-year-old Jack got his first glimpse of a world beyond China.

Jack Ma: The name Jack was given by an American tourist.

He told us how he taught himself English, walking up to foreigners and offering free tours in exchange for free lessons. Unlike many successful Chinese entrepreneurs, Jack Ma never studied in the U.S. He also had no status, money or connections. The only other way to get ahead in China was education and he failed the college entrance exam twice.

"I never touch keyboard before. I never using computer before. And I say, 'What is Internet?'"

Jack Ma: My parents do not want me to take examinations again.

Lara Logan: Because they didn't want you to fail again.

Jack Ma: They believed I would fail again.

Lara Logan: How did that affect you?

Jack Ma: That's a good question. Nobody ever asked me how that affected me before. It really affected me a lot. I failed for the first time, and then I looked for jobs. I went to interview jobs for about 10 or 15 times and was all rejected by people.

Lara Logan: Why did everyone reject you?

Jack Ma: I was not the standard, that normal people like...

Lara Logan: Because you were small?

Jack Ma: Normal. I was small.

Lara Logan: And skinny?

Jack Ma: Skinny, not handsome and, terrible, the way I talk. And they probably just don't like it.

Ma made it into college on his third try and became an English teacher. With no computing or engineering background, he's an unlikely tech titan but he says he was captivated by the Internet from the moment he first saw it in 1995 when he came to the U.S. as a translator.

Jack Ma: I never touch keyboard before. I never use computer before. And I say, "What is Internet?" He say, "Jack, you know, search whatever you want on the Internet." I say, "How can I search? What does search mean?" He said, "Just type." I say, "I don't want to type. Computers so expensive in China, I don't want to destroy it." He said, "It's not a bomb. Just type." So, I typed the first word called "beer". At that time, very slow, come on the American beer, Japan beer and the German beer but not China beers. So, I was curious. And I type, "China." No China. No data. Came back to Hangzhou with $1 in my pocket, scared, worried. And I came back and I said, "I want to do something called Internet."

"I tell the government, if people have no jobs, you are in trouble. Government will be in trouble. My job is to help more people have jobs."

His first two ventures failed. Four years later, he convinced some friends and former students, most of whom had never used the Internet, to invest in him and his vision for Alibaba. With just over $50,000 in seed money, the company was born. Today, it is valued

Chapter 4 China's Internet Companies

at $231 billion and is headquartered in Hangzhou on a sprawling state-of-the-art campus that rivals any in Silicon Valley. Ma's personal fortune makes him the richest man in China and one of the most influential. It's impossible to run a business on Alibaba's scale without official blessing.

Lara Logan: You were quoted saying, "When you have millions of small companies using your site and billions of dollars in transactions every day, the government cares." So what do they care about?

Jack Ma: They care that I can stabilize the country. I tell the government, if people have no jobs, you are in trouble. Government will be in trouble. My job is to help more people have jobs.

Lara Logan: So usually when people succeed in China, they either have connections, political connections, or they come from a wealthy family. You had neither.

Jack Ma: No.

Lara Logan: And you've done this without interference from the government?

Jack Ma: Well, I never got one cent from the government. I never got one cent from China's banks. So I'm very independent.

That was true when Alibaba began and most of its capital still comes from abroad. But more recently, some of its smaller investors have included institutions with ties to China's ruling elite. Alibaba has also benefited from Chinese government policies that make it difficult for foreign competitors to operate there. Ma explained how he walked a fine line with Beijing.

Jack Ma: I have a very strict talk to my teams. Never, ever do business with government. In love with them. Don't marry them. So, we never do projects for government. If they come to us and say, "Jack, can you help with this?" Good, I will introduce friends to you who are interested in doing that. Or if you wanted me to do it, I will do it free for you. Just next time don't come to me again. Don't. Because of that, we keep very good love-relationship with the government.

When we pressed Ma, he acknowledged there are times he has to bow to Chinese authorities, though he was surprisingly frank about a subject that is also sensitive among U.S. Internet companies, including Google, Facebook and Yahoo.

Lara Logan: You gather more information on Chinese citizens than anyone else in the country.

Jack Ma: You mean me.

Lara Logan: Yes.

Jack Ma: Yeah.

Lara Logan: So when the Chinese government comes knocking on your door asking for that information, how do you handle that? What do you do?

Jack Ma: Okay. We have a very strict process working with the government. If they want to do it, it's related with the national security, we'll work together. Any country, any citizen, anywhere, you have to work. I believe Google has to if the national security of the U.S.A. Facebook has to do it. Alibaba would definitely have to do it.

What worries some investors is the possibility that China could take control of the company and all of its assets at any time. And then there's Alibaba's unusual corporate structure, which puts all the power in the hands of Jack Ma and a small group of insiders.

[Arnold Schwarzenegger: First of all, I want you to put on this.]

But there's another side of him that's little known outside of China, where he's a celebrity. A cult of Ma reaches across the country and inspires almost fanatical loyalty among his employees and their families, who record his speeches and quote his sayings.

Here, he is dressed as a punk rocker performing for an enthusiastic audience of 20,000 Alibaba workers at a company anniversary celebration.

[Jack Ma (singing): You are so beautiful to me.]

The Chairman Ma show is now playing here in the U.S., bringing with it the potential of hundreds of millions of Chinese consumers for products made in America.

Lara Logan: So this is not Jack Ma's American invasion. This is not Google, Amazon, eBay, be afraid.

Jack Ma: We come to help, not invade. For example, bring the U.S. small bus business to China, this is something that we can do better, because we have 100 million buyers today, every day. We don't know, three years, 300 million?

Chapter 4 China's Internet Companies

Reading Tasks

I Reading Comprehension

Briefly answer the following questions about the text in English.

1) Compared with most CEOs, what is so different about Jack Ma?
2) Why is there a cult of Jack Ma in China? What do you think is so inspiring about Jack Ma?
3) Why does the program use "Chairman Ma" as the title?
4) When the host asks Jack Ma "You gather more information on Chinese citizens than anyone else in the country", what sort of information does she refer to?
5) In the sentence "The Chairman Ma show is now playing here in the U.S., ...", what does "Chairman Ma show" mean?

II Language Exercises

Replace the expressions in bold in the following sentences/paragraphs without changing their meanings.

1) When he **floated** the giant online shopping company he founded on Wall Street for $22 billion, Alibaba's Jack Ma **was catapulted into the public eye** in the West.
2) But, while investors in America were getting their first glimpse of Ma, 50, a study of him in China reveals **a larger-than-life figure** who performs karaoke on stage for thousands of his employees.
3) After entering the stage to the theme tune from Disney's Lion King movie, he is later heard singing *You Are So Beautiful*—**to rapturous applause**.
4) It is **a far cry from his humble beginnings**: He grew up in rural Hangzhou **without** enough to eat, and failed in two college entrance exams.
5) The online retailer **smashed records** with its offering—the largest in U.S. history—and is now as valuable as Facebook after its first day on Wall Street.
6) The e-commerce **powerhouse**, which sells anything from fat suits to live animals,

was valued more than Amazon and eBay at $168 billion, and **sent tremors through the market** as it floated stocks priced at $68 per share on the first day.

7) ...his image became **ubiquitous** on business news channels and media outlets across America.

8) We got to know Jack Ma before the **onslaught**, beginning over a year ago in China, where he talked with us about his relationship with the Chinese government, and his unorthodox business philosophy, which surprisingly, **gives shareholders almost no say** over how he runs the company.

9) So this is your old stomping ground...

10) With just over $50,000 in **seed money,** the company was born.

11) Ma explained how he **walked a fine line with** Beijing.

12) When we **pressed** Ma, he acknowledged there are times he has to **bow to** Chinese authorities.

Ⅲ Translation

Translate the following paragraph into English.

  马云是中国最大的电商阿里巴巴的创始人，也是一个特立独行的企业家。他的成功不是偶然的。首先，他的经营理念独树一帜：在阿里巴巴，股东没有管理发言权，客户第一位，员工第二位，股东第三位。其次，阿里巴巴的企业结构非同一般：企业的所有权力集中在马云自己和少数几个共同创业者手中，但员工依然对他疯狂崇拜，马云语录在公司内部广泛传播；在每年的公司年会上，马云会亲自表演；马云还会出席员工的集体婚礼。第三，马云创立了颠覆性的产品：他所创立的电商平台让国人步入互联网交易时代，让老百姓有了就业渠道；创立的第三方支付系统让从未谋面的陌生人可以放心交易。而最让人称道的是马云白手起家、一鸣惊人：他曾高考失利两次、没有留过洋、没有关系、没有家庭背景、没有专业背景；而是靠一帮朋友、一点积蓄，一跃成为中国身家最大、最有影响力的企业家。

Chapter ❹ China's Internet Companies

Ⓥ Research and Discussion

Name a business leader that you admire most and share with the class the reasons for your admiration in English.

Business Application

1. Given the burgeoning of China's Internet landscape, pick a Chinese Internet company and analyze its business model and profit streams in the form of a bilingual report.

2. Search on job-hunting sites such as zhaopin.com to find out the job types, requirements, qualifications and preparations you need to make if you want to work for a Chinese Internet company. Do they offer any translation/interpreting related posts? What preparations should you make in order to work in these companies? Share your finding in the form of a survey report in bilingual terms in class.

Chapter 5
China's Property Market

Overview

Chinese people are obsessed with property investment. Average people would pull together their family resources to get a roof over their heads. Property market is also intimately tied to the overall economy. China's authorities, in the past, have rolled out different measures to cool or revive the market. What are these methods and what are their intended purposes? What are the ramifications of the boom and downturn of the property market? Do Chinese women, in particular, have a stake in a piece of property? By answering these questions, this chapter sets out to take the pulse on China's red-hot property market.

Pre-reading Activities

1. Can you list some popular investment options for Chinese? Why do so many people choose to invest in the property market?

2. What is the trajectory of China's property prices in the last ten years? Give concrete examples, for instance, the property prices in your hometown, to illustrate your points.

3. What do you know about Beijing's efforts to cool off/revive the housing market? Do the changes in property prices reflect the changes in government controlling measures?

4. Watch the video "China's Real Estate Bubble" by CBS program *60 Minutes*.

Part 1
China's Real Estate Bubble

Read the following two texts, one in English and one in Chinese, and carry out your reading tasks as directed.

China's Real Estate Bubble

The following script is from "China's Real Estate Bubble" which originally aired on March 3, 2013, and was rebroadcast on August 3, 2014. Lesley Stahl is the correspondent, and Shachar Bar-On is the producer.

Chapter 5 China's Property Market

For three decades, China had been nothing short of a financial miracle—becoming the world's second largest economy. But now, many in the financial world are looking nervously at China.

That's because one sector Chinese authorities concentrated on was real estate and construction. And as we first reported in March last year, that may have created the largest housing bubble in human history. If you go to China, it's easy to see why there's all the talk of a bubble. We discovered that the most populated nation on Earth is building houses, districts and cities with no one in them.

Lesley Stahl: So this is Zhengzhou. And we are on the major highway, or the major road. And it's rush hour.

Gillem Tulloch: Yeah!

Lesley Stahl: And it's almost empty.

Gillem Tulloch is a Hong Kong-based financial analyst who was one of the first to draw attention to the housing bubble in China. He's showing us around the new eastern district of Zhengzhou, one of the most populated provinces in China—not that you'd know it. We found what they call a "ghost city" of new towers with no residents, desolate condos and vacant subdivisions uninhabited for miles, and miles, and miles, and miles of empty apartments.

Lesley Stahl: Why are they empty? I've heard that they have actually been sold.

Gillem Tulloch: They've all been sold. They've all been sold.

Lesley Stahl: They've all been sold? They're owned.

Gillem Tulloch: Absolutely.

They're owned by people in China's emerging middle class, who now have enough money to invest but few ways to do it. They're not allowed to invest abroad, banks offer paltry returns, and the stock market is a rollercoaster. But 16 years ago, the government changed its policy and allowed people to buy their own homes and the flood gates opened.

Gillem Tulloch: So what they do is invest in property because property prices have always gone up by more than inflation.

Lesley Stahl: And do they believe it will always go up?

Gillem Tulloch: Yeah, just like they believed in the U.S.

Actually, property values have doubled and tripled and more—so people in the middle class have sunk every last penny into buying five, even 10 apartments, fueling a building bonanza unprecedented in human history. No nation has ever built so much so fast.

Lesley Stahl: How important is real estate to the Chinese economy? Is it central?

Gillem Tulloch: Yes. It's the main driver of growth and has been that for the last few years. Some estimates have it as high as 20 or 30 percent of the whole economy.

Lesley Stahl: But they're not just building housing. They're building cities.

Gillem Tulloch: Yes. That's right.

Lesley Stahl: Giant cities being built with people not coming to live here.

Gillem Tulloch: Yes. I think they're building somewhere between 12 and 24 new cities every single year.

Unlike our market-driven economy, in China it's the government that has spent some $2 trillion to get these cities built—as a way of keeping the economy growing. The assumption is "if you build it, they'll come". But no one's coming.

Lesley Stahl: Wow. This is really completely, totally empty and it goes up—

Gillem took us to this shopping mall that's been standing vacant for three years.

Lesley Stahl: Can I find this all over China?

Gillem Tulloch: Yes, you can. They've simply built too much infrastructure too quickly.

Lesley Stahl: But I see KFC behind you. I see Starbucks over there. I see some other very recognizable American franchises coming here. Does that mean they have faith that this is going to ignite?

Gillem Tulloch: No. Just to get potential buyers the impression of what it might look like if they moved in.

Lesley Stahl: They're not real? So I see KFC didn't—

Gillem Tulloch: They haven't—

Lesley Stahl: Buy this space or rent this space?

Gillem Tulloch: No, they haven't.

Chapter 5 China's Property Market

Lesley Stahl: Starbucks?

Gillem Tulloch: No.

Lesley Stahl: They just put the sign up?

Gillem Tulloch: That's right.

It's all make-believe—non-existent supply for non-existent demand.

Lesley Stahl: Look at that. Swarovski. Piaget. They're hoping for high end too.

Gillem Tulloch: H&M. Zara.

Lesley Stahl: And it's all Potemkin.

Gillem Tulloch: Yeah.

It's surreal and it's everywhere. Like the city of Ordos in Mongolia built for a million people who didn't show up. And now, you are not in England. You're in Thames town—a development near Shanghai built like an English village.

Gillem Tulloch: And it was finished, I think, around five or six years. And it must have cost close to a billion U.S. dollars. And you'll see, it's still standing there empty.

Lesley Stahl: Well, I heard that there is some industry there or some business, one business there.

Gillem Tulloch: Marriage.

Lesley Stahl: Wedding pictures!

And what's more uplifting than a wedding—or 10? You can see these empty developments on the edge of almost every city in China.

Lesley Stahl: What about the idea that China is urbanizing? People are flooding into cities by the hundreds of millions. And this is really a smart move: build the housing to accommodate the urbanization process.

Gillem Tulloch: Well, so people are being moved into the cities. But that doesn't necessarily mean that they can afford these apartments which, you know, cost $100,000 or whatever. I mean, these are poor people moving into the cities, so they're building the wrong sort of apartments.

And what's worse, to build all these massive cities, they've had to tear down what was there before, clearing rice fields and displacing by some counts tens of millions of villagers.

On the edge of Zhengzhou, Gillem and I came upon a strange sight.

Lesley Stahl: I'm just watching what they're doing, these—do you have any idea?

Gillem Tulloch: I think they're trying to recycle the bricks.

These villagers were salvaging what's left of their homes, bulldozed to make room for more empty condos, already encroaching in the distance.

Lesley Stahl: There are all these empty apartments over here. Can they conceivably move into those up-scale places?

Gillem Tulloch: Most people in China live on about less than $2 a day. And these apartments probably cost upwards of $50,000 or $60,000 U.S. So it's very unlikely.

Lesley Stahl: What will happen to them, do you think?

Gillem Tulloch: I mean, they'll be forced to relocate somewhere. I have no idea where they'll go.

These are the immediate casualties of the building boom. And there's another problem: analysts warn that all this building has created a bubble that could burst.

Lesley Stahl: So if the bubble bursts, who's left holding the bag?

Gillem Tulloch: There are multiple classes of people that are going to get wiped out by this. People who have invested three generations worth of savings—so grandparents, parents and children—into properties will see their savings evaporate. And then, of course, 50 million construction workers who are working on all these projects around China.

The prognosis of a bubble about to burst isn't only coming from financial gloom-and-doomers. We heard it from the most unlikely source.

Lesley Stahl: Are you the biggest home builder in the world?

Wang Shi: I think. Maybe.

Lesley Stahl: You may be?

Wang Shi: Yes. Only the quantity, not quality.

Wang Shi is modest, but his company, Vanke, is a multibillion-dollar real estate empire, building more homes than anyone in China. He was born on the frontlines of communism, and joined the Red Army. But he secretly read forbidden books about capitalism, so that when China liberalized its economy, he rushed to the frontlines of the

Chapter 5   China's Property Market

free market. Even he thinks today's situation is out of control.

Lesley Stahl: Are homes in China too expensive today?

Wang Shi: Yeah.

Lesley Stahl: Here's a number I saw. A typical apartment in Shanghai costs about 45 times the average resident's annual salary.

Wang Shi: Even higher, even higher.

Lesley Stahl: What does that mean for your economy if it's just too expensive for the vast majority of people to buy?

Wang Shi: I think that dangerous.

Lesley Stahl: Dangerous.

Wang Shi: That's the bubble. So I think that's the problem.

Lesley Stahl: Is there a bubble?

Wang Shi: Yes, of course.

Lesley Stahl: There is a bubble and the issue is whether it burst or not? That's the big issue—

Wang Shi: Yes, if that bubble—that's a disaster.

Lesley Stahl: If it burst?

Wang Shi: If it burst, that's a disaster.

To try and prevent the disaster the Chinese government decided to act. Heard of their one-child policy? Since 2011, China has had what amounts to one-apartment policy, where it's very hard to buy more than one apartment in major cities. Because of this, prices plunged. The bubble was being tamed. And yet, the taming was creating all kinds of unintended consequences.

Lesley Stahl: Are many developers in debt?

Wang Shi: Yes, yes.

Lesley Stahl: And are many of them stopping development in the middle of projects because they don't have the money to go forward?

Wang Shi: Yeah, that's problem. That's a huge problem.

Slowdown of construction led to a downturn in the overall economy. Unfinished projects dot China, and not just apartment buildings.

Lesley Stahl: Look at this. Can you believe it?

Analyst Anne Stevenson-Yang who has traveled across China showed us a giant project all but abandoned in the port city of Tianjin with concrete skeletons as far as the eye can see. The plan is to build a new financial district to rival Manhattan including a Lincoln Center and a World Trade Center, only taller. But it all seems frozen.

[Anne Stevenson-Yang: There's supposed to be a Rockefeller Center here.

Anne Stevenson-Yang: I hope they have a Christmas tree too. Skating rink.]

City officials told us everything stopped because developers want to build all the facades at once to match. But on the ground we heard a different explanation.

Lesley Stahl: Workers told us that many of these buildings haven't had any work done on them for weeks, months, as if the developers just don't have the money to go on.

Anne Stevenson-Yang: It's true. You see that happen first. The migrant workers will go home. That's often the first sign that the debt crisis is starting.

Lesley Stahl: The debt crisis?

Anne Stevenson-Yang: Well, when you stop paying your bills, then everything stops.

It could become a debt crisis because of the huge loans most of the developers took out. If developers can't repay them, the whole economy will seize up.

The government's great fear is that all this could lead to social unrest and that's not hypothetical.

When regulations caused property prices to drop, it infuriated all those homeowners who watched the value of their nest eggs plummet.

Lesley Stahl: And there's already been some demonstrations over real estate around the country.

Wang Shi: Yes.

Lesley Stahl: Have you had demonstrations against your showrooms anywhere? You're company?

Wang Shi: Often!

So often, Wang Shi shudders to think what would happen if the bubble actually burst.

Chapter 5 China's Property Market

Wang Shi: If that bubble breaks, who know what will happen? Maybe that—maybe—maybe the next Arabic Spring—

Lesley Stahl: Arabic Spring. You mean people coming out and demonstrating.

Wang Shi: Hmmm.

Lesley Stahl: A lot of economists say that it's too big for even this government to control.

Wang Shi: A ha. I believe that top leaders have enough wisdom to deal with that. I hope!

Lesley Stahl: You're doing this.

Wang Shi: But that's uncertain.

Meanwhile, people who can afford it are still buying as much real estate as they can. They're even finding ways around the one apartment restriction in big cities. Can't buy more in Beijing? Just cross the city line and the boom is in full swing. Flyers advertize new projects, potential buyers crowd buses to see new construction and new owners line up to register their new apts. Like us in our bubble, they just don't believe the good times will ever end.

Text 2

美媒称中国房地产泡沫即将破灭

北京时间 2013 年 3 月 6 日凌晨消息，哥伦比亚广播新闻（CBS News）周二发表评论称，由中国经济快速增长和中国新型中产阶级对房地产市场的庞大投资所创造的历史上最大的房地产泡沫可能即将破灭。中国房地产界大亨、SOHO 中国 CEO 张欣告诉哥伦比亚新闻记者莱斯利·斯塔尔，中国住宅物业市场的发展已经穷途末路。中国最大的地产商万科集团董事长王石对斯塔尔表示，由于去年数百万成屋的价格出现下跌，他已经看到了许多愤怒的投资者的抗议，担心一旦中国房地产泡沫破灭，会造成严重的后果。

张欣曾在华尔街当过分析师，她是全球第五大白手起家的亿万富翁。她和丈夫兼合伙人潘石屹共同建造了北京的一些最具标志性的新摩天大楼，这些摩天大楼标志着中国这几年火热的经济增长。张欣表示，她预计北京和上海的优质商业物业市场将继续增长，但是住宅物业市场则是另外一回事。她已经将企业的业务重心放在了优质商业物业上，并避开住宅物业项目。她表示："我的观点是中国住宅物业市场确实已经穷途末路。"这位现年仅47岁的SOHO中国CEO出身贫寒，她将自己的成功比喻成一种美国梦，并称中国是一个充满机遇的新土地。她告诉斯塔尔："中国这片土地比世界其他国家创造了更多白手起家的亿万富翁。"

这些亿万富翁的诞生是由中国经济的飞速发展所带来的。在过去仅仅三十年的时间里，中国一跃成为世界第二大经济体。然而，推动中国经济快速增长的一个主要力量是房地产市场投资。自1998年开始，中国政府允许公民拥有自己的住房，新兴的中产阶层开始抢购住房库存并创造了巨大的需求，因为在中国他们没有太多的选择进行投资和抵御通胀。当时，银行利率非常低，股市震荡并且政府禁止海外投资，投资者只好将资金投入房地产市场。这推动了房屋价格的一路飙升。斯塔尔报道称，在中国许多城市现在都能够看到数英里范围的住宅项目，这些住房已经售出，但是里面常常空无一人，因为它们仅仅是投资的工具。

中国政府已经意识到了这些问题。为了抑制房地产泡沫的增长，中国政府制定了许多限制投资者购买二套以上房产的政策措施，因而房屋价格出现了一定程度的下跌。但是这种在需求上的下跌导致许多开发商耗空了资金，并且不得不中途停止一些物业项目，这又进而导致了营建项目市场发展的放缓及中国经济增长的放缓。如果市场发展停滞，开发商将无法偿还银行贷款，债务危机就可能出现，这样，中国经济增长也将停滞。这与美国在房地产市场崩盘后出现的金融危机并没有什么不同。许多人担心这将导致中国的社会动荡。有一个人已经敲响了警钟，他就是中国最大的房地产商王石。

当他去年降低房价时，他的售楼大厅遭到了许多愤怒的购房投资者的打砸，民众的愤怒源于他们将毕生的积蓄投入了房市，但是这些投资随着房价的下跌出现了亏损。王石担心事情可能会变得更糟。他说："如果房地产泡沫破灭，谁也不知道会发生什么。"

Chapter 5 China's Property Market

Reading Tasks

❶ Reading Comprehension

Briefly answer the following questions about the two texts in English.

1) Why are Chinese people so crazy about property investment compared with other investment options in Text 1?
2) What are the reasons for many empty apartments in China in Text 1?
3) Do you agree with Wang Shi's observation that property prices in China are exorbitantly high in Text 1?
4) What is the stance of CBS on China's property market? Do you think it is biased or do you share the concern of bubbles being built across China in Text 1?
5) Who are the victims if the bubble in China's real estate market is burst in Text 1?
6) What do you know about Zhang Xin and her husband? What type of property do they develop in Text 2?
7) What are the differences between "商业地产" and "商品房" in Text 2?
8) Do you agree with Zhang Xin's observation of China's property market in Text 2?

❷ Language Exercises

Replace the expressions in bold in the following sentences/paragraphs without changing their meanings.

1) For three decades, China had been **nothing short of** a financial miracle: a state-controlled economy that managed to navigate its way **out of the tatters of** communism to become the world's second largest—deftly managed by government policies and decrees.
2) They're not allowed to invest abroad, banks offer **paltry** returns, and the stock market is a **rollercoaster**.
3) But 16 years ago, the government changed its policy and allowed people to buy their own homes and **the flood gates opened**.

4) Actually, property values have doubled and tripled and more—so people in the middle class have **sunk** every last penny into buying five, even 10 apartments, fueling a building **bonanza** unprecedented in human history.

5) And it's all **Potemkin**.

6) These villagers were **salvaging** what's left of their homes, bulldozed to make room for more empty condos, already **encroaching in the distance**.

7) There are multiple classes of people that are going to get wiped out by this. People who have invested three generations worth of savings—so grandparents, parents and children—into properties will see their savings **evaporate**.

8) The **prognosis** of a bubble about to burst isn't only coming from financial **gloom-and-doomers**.

9) He was born on **the frontlines of communism**, and joined the Red Army. But he secretly read forbidden books about capitalism, so that when China liberalized its economy, he rushed to **the frontlines of the free market**.

10) The bubble was being **tamed**. And yet, the taming was creating all kinds of **unintended consequences**.

11) Slowdown of construction led to a **downturn** in the overall economy. Unfinished projects **dot** China, and not just apartment buildings.

12) City officials told us everything stopped because developers want to build all the **facades** at once **to match**.

13) When regulations caused property prices to drop, it infuriated all those homeowners who watched the value of their **nest eggs** plummet.

14) Can't buy more in Beijing? Just cross **the city line** and the boom is **in full swing**.

Translation

1. **Provide the English equivalents to the following terms and expressions.**

   1) 空置房
   2) 烂尾楼
   3) 商品房
   4) 商业地产

5) 拆迁 6) 开发商
7) 限购 8) 售楼中心

2. **Translate the following paragraphs into English.**

推动中国经济快速增长的一个主要力量是房地产市场投资。自1998年开始，中国政府允许公民拥有自己的住房，新兴的中产阶层开始抢购住房库存并创造了巨大的需求，因为在中国他们没有太多的选择进行投资和抵御通胀。当时，银行利率非常低，股市震荡并且政府禁止海外投资，投资者只好将资金投入房地产市场。这推动了房屋价格的一路飙升。斯塔尔报道称，在中国许多城市现在都能够看到数英里范围内的住宅项目，这些住房已经售出，但是里面常常空无一人，因为它们仅仅是投资的工具。

中国政府已经意识到了这些问题。为了抑制房地产泡沫的增长，中国政府制定了许多限制投资者购买二套以上房产的政策措施，因而房屋价格出现了一定程度的下跌。但是这种在需求上的下跌导致许多开发商耗空了资金，并且不得不中途停止一些物业项目，这又进而导致了营建项目市场发展的放缓及中国经济增长的放缓。如果市场发展停滞，开发商将无法偿还银行贷款，债务危机就可能出现，这样，中国经济增长也将停滞。这与美国在房地产市场崩盘后出现的金融危机并没有什么不同。许多人担心这将导致中国的社会动荡。有一个人已经敲响了警钟，他就是中国最大的房地产商王石。

当他去年降低房价时，他的售楼大厅遭到了许多愤怒的购房投资者的打砸，民众的愤怒源于他们将毕生的积蓄投入了房市，但是这些投资随着房价的下跌出现了亏损。王石担心事情可能会变得更糟。他说："如果房地产泡沫破灭，谁也不知道会发生什么。"

IV Research and Discussion

Search the Internet for answers to the following questions and share your findings in class.

Besides the one apartment purchase restrictions, what other cooling measures have you heard of in China to tame the hot property market? Do you think it is an effective and equitable tool to tame the rising property prices?

Part 2 Beijing's Property Control Measures

Read the following four English texts, and carry out your reading tasks as directed.

Text 1

Housing Subsidies at Heart of Beijing's "New Deal"
Where Will Beijing Find 10 Million Housing Units?

The Chinese government aims to build or renovate 10m units of state-subsidized housing in 2011. There are four major categories that it will use to meet its target for the year.

1. Two million units of "economic use housing" and "double-limit housing". Both of these types of housing are sold at a discount to market prices although economic use housing is usually cheaper and harder to get.

2. Just over two million units of "public rental housing". These flats are rented out at low prices and can be bought by occupants over time but cannot be sold on the market.

3. More than 1.6 million units of "low-cost rental housing". These flats are rented out at even lower prices and are reserved for households on urban "minimum income insurance", subsistence living allowances paid by the state to the poorest eligible urban residents.

4. Four million new or renovated residential units in "shanty areas". This comprises a wide range of housing, in city suburbs, factory dormitories and accommodation at mines and on farms.

A huge portion of China's rapid growth in the past decade has been driven by investment in real estate and by the stimulus it gives related industries, ranging from steel and cement to makers of washing machines and cars. So by curbing rising prices and developers' profits, Beijing risks a wider economic slowdown, one reason why the

Chapter 5 China's Property Market

subsidized housing plan is so important.

In theory, the boom in subsidized housing will pick up the slack from slowing real estate investment while allowing rapid urbanization to continue by providing affordable homes for new migrants from rural areas.

Lessons from China's Housing Bubble
China's Nuanced Approach to Letting the Air out of Its Housing Bubble

Steve Weisman: Is China undergoing an asset and housing price bubble similar to the one that the United States went through that led to the current crisis? This is Steve Weisman at the Peterson Institute for International Economics with Nicholas Lardy, senior fellow at the Institute, who's been studying China and looking at this phenomenon recently. Thanks Nick.

Nicholas Lardy: Thank you, Steve.

Steve Weisman: Is China's asset price bubble something to worry about and are the Chinese worried about it?

Nicholas Lardy: Certainly, the Chinese are worried about it. Earlier this year, prices of real estate in China were rising at an all-time record level since they created a housing price index a number of years ago. So they have been concerned that a bubble is being created, if [it's] not already in existence.

Steve Weisman: What are they doing about it?

Nicholas Lardy: The authorities in China have taken a unique approach to dealing with the property bubble, rather than the kind of standard approach that you'd expect to see in a market economy, where you raise interest rates across the board in order to curtail the demand for housing. They have taken a very selective approach and made housing more expensive for investors, speculators, property flippers—who they believed constitute a significant portion of the kind of extra demand that is pushing prices up rapidly.

Steve Weisman: How did they accomplish that?

Nicholas Lardy: They basically discriminate against people [who] have more than one mortgage, [who] own more than one house. In the current environment, for example, if you want to take out a mortgage on a house that you are not going to live in, a nonowner-occupied house, you have to pay down 50 percent of the purchase price before you can get a mortgage—as compared to an ordinary buyer who, as a first-time buyer, would have to pay down only 20 percent. And the interest rate that the investors, if we want to call them that, would have to pay would be about 50 percent higher. In other words, if the standard mortgage was about 5 percent, the investor/buyer would have to pay 7.5 percent interest. And they also discriminate against these investors in terms of the tax treatment of property. They have to hold the property for five years in order to avoid a tax when they sell it. And for the owner occupier, they only have to hold the property for two years.

So, rather than pushing on the brakes [in a way] that affects the whole economy, all the interest-sensitive sectors of the economy, they go after only the housing market. They try to curtail demand by those people who they believe are speculators in the market and are responsible for a large part of the excess demand, particularly in the primary cities. There aren't maybe so many speculators in tertiary, secondary cities. But Beijing, Shanghai, some cities in South China, a popular resort-type city in Hainan Island way down in the South with a lot of beaches, they believe that speculators come in and buy up dozens of properties and then hold them off the market with the hope that they would be able to resell them in a substantial profit at some point in the future.

Steve Weisman: Do you suppose that China was listening to the debate in the United States in 2008–2009 about whether big steps like raising interest rates across the board can prick asset bubbles and they took a more carefully defined approach?

Nicholas Lardy: I think their approach is much more nuanced. It's very carefully targeted against a small subset of the buyers and does nothing to slow down demand for housing on the part of first-time buyers. China is undergoing rapid urbanization. There's a big demand for housing. They didn't want it to be unaffordable, and the way of doing that is to not to raise the interest rate or the down payment requirement for the first-time buyers but to raise it dramatically for the speculators, and that tends to hold down prices. They did this also starting in late 2007. Within a few months, property sales slowed down. A few months after that prices start to moderate. And within about eight months, China entered into a period where for six consecutive months housing prices actually fell. But they didn't fall dramatically; they were falling on a year over year basis by 2 or 3 percent per month. So they demonstrated in that previous case that there was a lot of air in the balloon, but they could let the air out gradually and have a modest price correction without popping the balloon and having a housing crash.

Text 3

China Embraces an Old Western Tradition: Property Taxes
Looking to Rein in China's Skyrocketing Home Prices, the Government Began a Pilot Program That Imposes Property Taxes on High-end Properties.

Two of China's fastest-growing cities, Shanghai and the western megalopolis of Chongqing, announced Thursday they would impose taxes on high-end properties, in pilot schemes that other Chinese cities are expected to follow.

The government is anxious to cool China's red-hot property market, fearing a bubble that could wreak havoc with the economy if it burst, and worrying about antagonizing young first-time buyers, many of whom are being priced out of the market.

Shanghai will levy an annual 0.6 percent tax on second houses, while Chongqing will charge between 0.5 percent and 1.2 percent on all residential properties, depending on its value.

Those rates are too low to deter speculative buyers of multiple houses, warns Ren Xianfang, a property analyst at HIS Global Insight, a macro-economic consulting firm in Beijing. "If they care they will pass those higher costs on to tenants," she predicts, "or they are leaving the properties empty which means they don't care whatever the tax is."

The new taxes do, however, point to a major shift in the way Chinese cities will raise tax revenue in the future, suggests Mr. Klibaner. Currently they make a large share of their income by selling land to developers, but "there is a finite amount of land use rights that can be sold," he says. "China needs to move to a more regular form of revenue generation", like annual property taxes. It will be a long time before China has the rules, regulations, land registries, and other infrastructure needed to impose U.S.-style taxes based on assessed property values, Klibaner says, "but this is the first step in the process."

Text 4

China Sends a Real Estate Mogul to Prison

To millions of Chinese, the enterprising banker from the gritty northern province of Shaanxi is known by the nickname House Sister, and it is not exactly a term of endearment.

On Sunday the woman, Gong Aiai, who was accused of amassing dozens of high-end properties by forging or illegally purchasing documents, was sentenced to three years in prison, according to the state-run Xinhua news service.

After her exposure earlier this year by online whistle-blowers, Ms. Gong and her voracious appetite for real estate became a lightning rod for the frustrations of poor and middle-class Chinese who have been priced out of the nation's booming property market. To many detractors, her case also provided further evidence of how government officials and executives at state-owned enterprises can use their positions to grow unimaginably rich.

Ms. Gong, a former vice president of the Shenmu Rural Commercial Bank, was accused of accumulating 41 apartments in Beijing and several others closer to home by presenting illicitly obtained national identity cards and hukou, the coveted residency permits required when buying residential property. Prosecutors say her real estate portfolio was worth $160 million.

The Beijing municipal government at the beginning of the year released a package of rules to restrict house purchases in the capital and rein in soaring property prices. Under

Chapter 5 China's Property Market

the rules, non-Beijing residents must have paid their monthly social security contribution or income tax for five consecutive years before they are eligible to buy their first apartment in the city. The rules also state that people with Beijing residence permits will be limited to two properties, and eligible non-locals will be allowed to buy only one. Beijing is worried that very high property prices, along with soaring food costs, could trigger social unrest as first-home buyers struggle to get a foot in the market.

Having multiple identity cards and hukou allows a person to skirt restrictions aimed at dampening real estate speculation and rules that bar out-of-towners from buying property in overheated markets like Beijing. During a brief trial last week, Ms. Gong denied the charges, according to the state news media.

Her downfall follows that of a number of other figures with grotesque spending habits. There was Brother Watch, a midlevel civil servant known for his large collection of luxury timepieces who was convicted of bribery last month, and Grandpa House, a former police chief in Guangdong Province who was accused of using fake identity cards to purchase 192 houses.

Although these and other cases were exposed by muckraking Internet sleuths or rivals of the accused, they have been viewed through the lens of the anti-graft campaign started by President Xi Jinping, who has promised to take down "tigers and flies" in his war on self-dealing, bribery and official extravagance. In September, Bo Xilai, once one of China's most powerful officials, was sentenced to life in prison for crimes that included bribe-taking and embezzlement of funds worth $4.4 million.

Ms. Gong's downfall, however, did little to mollify the public's anger. Writing on the nation's most popular microblog service, Sina Weibo, many people criticized the court for failing to address how Ms. Gong had accrued the money to buy so many properties.

❶ Summary Writing

Complete the following summary of the four English texts in Chinese by filling out the table.

中国房地产新政重拳频出			
从_____的角度	从_____的角度	从_____的角度	从_____的角度

❷ Reading Comprehension

Briefly answer the following questions about the texts in English.

1) Suppose Wang Gang wants to buy a second apartment in Xi'an for investment purposes. The apartment costs 1 million RMB and the standard mortgage rate of a commercial bank is 6%, how much would he have to pay as the down-payment and how much is the mortgage rate?

2) What is the role of the interest rate in the economy? Give examples to back up your points.

3) What is property tax and what's the difference between property tax and other types of tax associated with the property investment?

4) What are the benefits of property tax? Find evidence from the text and from the Internet resources to support your claim.

5) What are challenges of property tax collection? And what are the hurdles for the tax to be rolled out nationwide?

6) Describe your understanding of China's judicial system. How does China's judicial process work?

Chapter 5 China's Property Market

Ⅲ Language Exercises

1. **Search the texts and the Internet for expressions as requested.**

    1) Search Text 2 and the Internet for expressions associated with "楼市泡沫".
    2) Search Text 2 and the Internet for expressions associated with "房地产的投资行为".
    3) Search Text 2 and the Internet resources for expressions associated with "交通行业表达如何类比到经济表现".
    4) Search Text 2 for expressions associated with "房贷".
    5) Search the Internet for expressions associated with "利率".
    6) Search Text 3 and the Internet for expressions associated with "征税".
    7) Search Text 3 and the Internet for expressions associated with "试点".
    8) Search Text 4 and the Internet for expressions associated with "限购".

2. **Replace the expressions in bold in the following sentences/paragraphs without changing their meanings.**

    1) On Sunday the woman, Gong Aiai, who **was accused of** amassing dozens of high-end properties by forging or illegally purchasing documents, **was sentenced to three years in prison**, according to the state-run Xinhua news service.
    2) ...her **case** also provided **further evidence** of how government officials and executives at state-owned enterprises can use their positions to grow unimaginably rich.
    3) There was Brother Watch, a midlevel civil servant known for his large collection of luxury timepieces who **was convicted of** bribery last month.
    4) During a brief **trial** last week, Ms. Gong **denied the charges**, according to the state news media.
    5) **Prosecutors** say her real estate portfolio was worth $160 million.
    6) In September, Bo Xilai, once one of China's most powerful officials, **was sentenced to life in prison** for crimes that included **bribe-taking and embezzlement of funds** worth $4.4 million.

141

7) ...many people criticized the court for **failing to address** how Ms. Gong had accrued the money to buy so many properties.

IV Translation

1. **Provide the Chinese equivalents to the following terms and expressions.**

    1) economic use housing
    2) public rental housing
    3) low-cost rental housing
    4) shanty areas
    5) subsistence living allowances
    6) housing price index
    7) subsidized housing
    8) 2nd/3rd-tier cities
    9) the State Council/Cabinet
    10) residency permit
    11) anti-graft campaign
    12) online whistle-blowers
    13) self-dealing

2. **Translate the following sentences/paragraphs into Chinese.**

    1) A huge portion of China's rapid growth in the past decade has been driven by investment in real estate and by the stimulus it gives related industries, ranging from steel and cement to makers of washing machines and cars.

    2) So by curbing rising prices and developers' profits, Beijing risks a wider economic slowdown, one reason why the subsidized housing plan is so important.

    3) In theory, the boom in subsidized housing will pick up the slack from slowing real estate investment while allowing rapid urbanization to continue by providing affordable homes for new migrants from rural areas.

    4) The government is anxious to cool China's red-hot property market, fearing a bubble that could wreak havoc with the economy if it burst, and worrying about antagonizing young first-time buyers, many of whom are being priced out of the market.

    5) Currently they make a large share of their income by selling land to developers, but "there is a finite amount of land use rights that can be sold," he says. "China needs to move to a more regular form of revenue generation", like annual property taxes.

It will be a long time before China has the rules, regulations, land registries, and other infrastructure needed to impose U.S.-style taxes based on assessed property values, Klibaner says, "but this is the first step in the process."

6) Under the rules, non-Beijing residents must have paid their monthly social security contribution or income tax for five consecutive years before they are eligible to buy their first apartment in the city.

7) After her exposure earlier this year by online whistle-blowers, Ms. Gong and her voracious appetite for real estate became a lightning rod for the frustrations of poor and middle-class Chinese who have been priced out of the nation's booming property market.

8) Having multiple identity cards and hukou allows a person to skirt restrictions aimed at dampening real estate speculation and rules that bar out-of-towners from buying property in overheated markets like Beijing.

3. **Translate the following Chinese paragraph into English.**

中国的房地产市场在2008年金融危机时曾短暂停滞，但受到危机之后宽松的信贷政策及一系列优惠政策的刺激，从2009年第二季度开始迅速回升。进入2009年年底，深圳、北京、杭州等地的房价开始了爆发性增长，商品住宅均价相继突破了20000元/m²。同时，泡沫也不再局限于一线城市，而是显现了向二三线城市蔓延的趋势。政府因此快速出台了一系列房地产调控措施，遏制房价过快上涨。楼市新政旨在打击炒楼者和投机者，挤掉房地产市场的泡沫。抑制房价上涨的有效手段就是扩大供给，这包括保障性住房和商品房两方面。作为民生问题的住房问题，绝不是简单增加商品房供应或者打击投机就能轻易解决的。它需要政府调整自己的工作议程，把保障性住房建设放在一切调控的首位，把工作重心放在买不起商品房的国民身上。

Research and Discussion

The following is an excerpt from a Chinese news report on the unintended consequences of the housing control policies. Read and discuss the loopholes of the property cooling measures in class.

近日，上海爆出收紧房贷的传闻，楼市成交量随之暴涨，当地居民选择离婚买房的现象也进入"白热化"阶段。据报道，2017年8月29日，上海徐汇区民政局离婚登记处被前来办理离婚的市民挤爆，离婚的人群从早上7时多开始排队。下午4时30分离婚登记处不得不采取了临时"封闭"措施，并在门口贴出通知请需要办理离婚登记的当事人改日再来取号办理相关事务。

为了抑制房价，相关部门通过提高贷款首付、利率来严格收紧对二套的房贷，然而，"上有政策，下有对策"。自房产限购令政策实施后，在许多城市，为拆迁多得一套安置房而离婚早已不是新闻。有的地方出现一对夫妻离两次婚的情况，有些城市甚至离婚也预约到了半年以后，中国式"假离婚"并没有"犹抱琵琶半遮面"。

Part ③ Property Boom/Bust

Read the following English text and carry out your reading tasks as directed.

Effects of the Boom and Downturn of the Property Market on Different Players

When the Property Market Booms

For homeowners

When homeowners are seeing the value of their apartments fall as new homes in their neighborhoods are sold at a discount compared to what they paid earlier, they will feel pain and panic.

Chapter 5 China's Property Market

A group of around 400 homeowners in Shanghai demonstrated publicly and damaged a showroom operated by their property developer after the company said it cut prices. Home buyers had wanted to speak with the developer to refund or cancel their contracts but were unsuccessful, according to local media.

For real estate developers

If home prices continue to fall, home buyers could delay the purchase, leaving the developer with more unsold units and bigger debt.

In April, Fenghua's Zhejiang Xinrun Real Estate Co. defaulted on its loans and said ongoing projects had been halted.

There are signs that bigger developers are also starting to feel squeezed.

To entice homebuyers, major property developers are starting to take on construction costs themselves by delaying the down payment and mortgage payments for homebuyers until construction of the home is completed.

For banks

With real estate loans accounting for around 20% of all commercial bank loans, lenders face rising defaults, huge bad or nonperforming loans and losing significant money if the market takes a dive.

Some banks have disguised loans to property developers to skirt regulatory limits on lending, compounding the risks.

For governments

Local governments are heavily reliant on land sales for income, despite efforts in recent years to diversify their revenue sources.

A weakening housing market in China threatens to exacerbate an economic slowdown and also takes a bite out of local government coffers, which depend on land sales for revenue.

With many regional governments already taking on a huge pile of debt following the lending binge and construction boom induced by the global financial crisis, a sharp fall in housing prices could prove disastrous for both local economies.

For other industries

Most sold apartments are concrete empty boxes. So if the property sector slowed down, building materials, home appliances and furniture and home decor market would also suffer.

China's property market won't recover any time soon, say some analysts, who figure the downturn will shave the country's GDP growth by 1.4 percentage points in 2014 and 0.6 percentage points in 2015 if there are no drastic changes to policy.

When the Property Market Slows Down

For homeowners

Income growth is slowing as the economy matures, making homes steadily less affordable. People will swamp sales centers when new properties are put on the market.

In Shanghai, divorces have spiked as people take advantage of a loophole in regulations. Couples can get a preferential mortgage rate only on their first home. Divorced spouses can benefit by buying homes separately and then remarrying.

For real estate developers

Property developers will increase their borrowing and choose to be aggressive. They have driven up land prices at auctions. That is why Diwang (land king) emerge.

For governments

Governments in cities count on land sales as a source of revenue. Smaller cities have plenty of land for building but shrinking populations. Big cities, where people actually want to live and work, have limited lands to sell.

For other industries

There will be stronger demand for iron ore and copper and furniture and gizmos that fill new homes, in a way helping to stabilize the GDP.

Chapter 5　China's Property Market

Reading Tasks

I Summary Writing

Complete the following summary of the text in Chinese.

楼市低迷，谁会深受其害？

有房一族／业主：＿＿＿＿＿＿＿＿＿＿＿＿＿＿＿＿＿＿＿＿＿＿

开发商：＿＿＿＿＿＿＿＿＿＿＿＿＿＿＿＿＿＿＿＿＿＿＿＿＿＿

银行：＿＿＿＿＿＿＿＿＿＿＿＿＿＿＿＿＿＿＿＿＿＿＿＿＿＿＿

地方政府：＿＿＿＿＿＿＿＿＿＿＿＿＿＿＿＿＿＿＿＿＿＿＿＿

其他行业，如：＿＿＿＿＿＿＿＿＿＿＿＿＿＿＿＿＿＿＿＿＿＿

楼市繁荣会产生什么影响？

有房一族／业主：＿＿＿＿＿＿＿＿＿＿＿＿＿＿＿＿＿＿＿＿＿＿

开发商：＿＿＿＿＿＿＿＿＿＿＿＿＿＿＿＿＿＿＿＿＿＿＿＿＿＿

银行：＿＿＿＿＿＿＿＿＿＿＿＿＿＿＿＿＿＿＿＿＿＿＿＿＿＿＿

地方政府：＿＿＿＿＿＿＿＿＿＿＿＿＿＿＿＿＿＿＿＿＿＿＿＿

其他行业，如：＿＿＿＿＿＿＿＿＿＿＿＿＿＿＿＿＿＿＿＿＿＿

II Research and Discussion

What are the effects of the boom and downturn of the property market on different players? Work in groups of four by assuming a role of one player and share your viewpoints.

147

Part 4 China's Women and Property

Read the following English text and carry out your reading tasks as directed.

Watering the Gardens of Others

China's Women Are Being Shut out of the Land and Housing Market.

Mei Wu, a young lawyer in Shanghai, earns 1 million yuan ($160,000) a year. She recently left her abusive husband. Ms. Mei and her parents invested all their savings in her 5 million yuan home, which has tripled in value over five years. It was bought solely in her husband's name. She will now leave her marriage without her savings and without her home.

Hers is not an isolated case. Although the condition of women in China is better than in many developing countries, and has advanced dramatically in recent years in some respects, old customs and new laws have combined to short-change China's women in the property market.

One problem is a Chinese divorce law that went into force in 2011. The supreme court ruled that in the case of divorce, if the separating couple reaches no agreement on how to divide its assets, residential property can be granted in its entirety to the person in whose name it is registered. That is almost always men, due to the social norm that they are the "heads of house": They have claims on 87% of China's 109 trillion yuan property market, according to the National Bureau of Statistics. Yet women contribute to over 70% of mortgages and 90% of cash purchases of homes, a survey by Horizon Research found. Under the 2011 law, they forfeit that cash if their name is not on the deed. This is not a hypothetical scenario: The divorce rate in big cities like Beijing and Shanghai has soared towards 40%.

China's overheated housing market has made the problem worse. The average house price in China's "megacities" is 14 times average annual income—even London's property

Chapter 5 China's Property Market

market is twice as affordable. Yet young people hoping to marry have little choice but to buy: Families on both sides often believe a home is a prerequisite for marriage. As a result, a majority of the assets of Chinese households are invested in housing. To get onto the housing ladder and into the marriage market, homes are financed by a pooling of assets from partners, friends and family. "Assets pooled from different family members tend to flow toward men," says Ms. Hong Fincher. It used to be said in China that raising a daughter was like "watering someone else's garden". That is exactly what Chinese daughters are now doing.

In the countryside, the situation is especially dire. Large families are more common, but that is little solace for women. A 2010 government survey found that only one in four respondents agreed that sons and daughters had an equal right to inherit property. When villages distributed communal land to households in the 1980s, village committees made up of male household heads decided where it should go. Chen Junjie of the University of Illinois found that in many regions, boys were granted twice as much as girls. Only 17% of land leases contained women's names in 2011. The China Women's Federation, a government branch, found in 2004 that 70% of landless villagers were women. This is getting worse: The percentage of women who are landless more than doubled in the decade leading up to 2010. "We're seen as outsiders," one female farmer in Yunnan said, "village leaders put everything under men's names."

There is an even darker side to housing inequality. Surveys show that between 24%–40% of Chinese women have experienced domestic violence. Ms. Wu believes that owning her own home would have protected her from marital abuse. As domestic violence workers around the world know, husbands abuse most easily when the woman has nowhere to go. There are immense family pressures against divorce—and the loss of one's lifetime savings is a material obstacle. China's first bill on domestic violence will finally have its first reading in the legislature in August. For China's women, it cannot come a moment too soon.

Reading Tasks

I Research and Discussion

Search the Internet for answers to the following questions and share your findings in class.

1) How do you define domestic violence? What form of abuses do you think does violence take?

2) Do you think housing is a prerequisite for marriage? What do you think are the basic conditions for marriage?

3) If you want to purchase an apartment for you to get married, what do you think is the best way of financing it?

4) Are you willing to add your spouse's name or let your son add his fiancee's name to the deed?

5) Do you agree with the amendment of Supreme Court on the division of assets in case of a divorce?

6) Suppose you were a delegate to the NPC and participate in the reading of the Law. What should be included in this new anti-domestic violence law? List your suggestions.

7) Do you think the author presented a fair picture of Chinese women's status in the housing market?

II Translation

Complete the Chinese translation of the English text by filling in the blanks.

Watering the Gardens of Others China's Women Are Being Shut out of the Land and Housing Market	

Chapter 5 China's Property Market

Mei Wu, a young lawyer in Shanghai, earns 1m yuan ($160,000) a year. She recently left her abusive husband. Ms. Mei and her parents invested all their savings in her 5m yuan home, which has tripled in value over five years. It was bought solely in her husband's name. She will now leave her marriage without her savings and without her home.	吴梅（音）是一名上海的律师，年收入人民币一百万元（16万美元）。最近，她_____。吴女士和她的父母将所有存款都投资在了价值五百万元的房产上，现在5年过去了，房产价值翻了三倍，而因为_____，离婚后，吴女士将净身出户，没有存款，也得不到房子。
Hers is not an isolated case. Although the condition of women in China is better than in many developing countries, and has advanced dramatically in recent years in some respects, old customs and new laws have combined to short-change China's women in the property market.	这不是个例。尽管中国女性的地位比其他发展中国家要好得多，近年来在某些方面也取得了显著的进步，然而，由于_____。
One problem is a Chinese divorce law that went into force in 2011. The supreme court ruled that in the case of divorce, if the separating couple reaches no agreement on how to divide its assets, residential property can be granted in its entirety to the person in whose name it is registered. That is almost always men, due to the social norm that they are the "heads of house": They have claims on 87% of China's 109 trillion yuan property market, according to the National Bureau of Statistics. Yet women contribute to over 70% of mortgages and 90% of cash purchases of homes, a survey by Horizon Research found. Under the 2011 law, they forfeit that cash if their name is not on the deed. This is not a hypothetical scenario: The divorce rate in big cities like Beijing and Shanghai has soared towards 40%.	其中一个问题就是自2011年起开始生效的一部中国离婚法。最高人民法院规定，_____。而按照社会惯例，_____，据中国国家统计局的统计，在价值109万亿元的中国房地产市场中，男性拥有高达87%的产权。而事实上，零点研究咨询集团（Horizon Research）的调查显示，女性对房屋贷款和现金购房的贡献率分别为70%和90%。而_____。

151

China's overheated housing market has made the problem worse. The average house price in China's "megacities" is 14 times average annual income—even London's property market is twice as affordable. Yet young people hoping to marry have little choice but to buy: Families on both sides often believe a home is a prerequisite for marriage. As a result, a majority of the assets of Chinese households are invested in housing. To get onto the housing ladder and into the marriage market, homes are financed by a pooling of assets from partners, friends and family. "Assets pooled from different family members tend to flow toward men," says Ms. Hong Fincher. It used to be said in China that raising a daughter was like "watering someone else's garden". That is exactly what Chinese daughters are now doing.	中国的房地产市场过热也恶化了这一问题。中国一些"超大城市"的平均房价是平均年收入的14倍，就连伦敦房地产市场的价格也仅仅是人们所能承担价格的两倍。然而，想要结婚的年轻人却别无选择：双方家庭通常都认为房子是结婚的先决条件。因此，中国家庭绝大部分的资金都投资于房产。_____。社会学家洪理达女士（Ms. Hong Fincher）说："由多个家庭成员共同筹集的资产通常都流到了男性手中。"_____。
In the countryside, the situation is especially dire. Large families are more common, but that is little solace for women. A 2010 government survey found that only one in four respondents agreed that sons and daughters had an equal right to inherit property. When villages distributed communal land to households in the 1980s, village committees made up of male household heads decided where it should go. Chen Junjie of the University of Illinois found that in many regions, boys were granted twice as much as girls. Only 17% of land leases contained women's names in 2011. The China Women's Federation, a government branch, found in 2004 that 70% of landless villagers were women. This is getting worse: The percentage of women who are landless more than doubled in the decade leading up to 2010. "We're seen as outsiders," one female farmer in Yunnan said, "village leaders put everything under men's names."	在农村，形势尤为严峻。大家庭随处可见，但是这并没有缓解女性的状况。2010年一项政府的调查显示只有四分之一的受访者认为儿女均享有平等的继承权。_____。伊利诺伊大学的陈俊杰（Chen Junjie）发现，在很多地区，男孩得到的土地是女孩的两倍。2011年，只有17%的房契包含女性的名字。政府机构中国妇女联合会（China Women's Federation）在2004年发现70%没有土地的人为女性。情况日益恶化：截止到2010年的十年间没有土地的女性比例翻了一番。"我们被视为外人，"一位云南女农民说道，"村里的领导把什么都归到男性名下。"

Chapter 5 China's Property Market

There is an even darker side to housing inequality. Surveys show that between 24%–40% of Chinese women have experienced domestic violence. Ms. Wu believes that owning her own home would have protected her from marital abuse. As domestic violence workers around the world know, husbands abuse most easily happens when the woman has nowhere to go. There are immense family pressures against divorce—and the loss of one's lifetime savings is a material obstacle. China's first bill on domestic violence will finally have its first reading in the legislature in August. For China's women, it cannot come a moment too soon.

_____。调查显示，24%~40% 的中国女性都曾遭到家暴。吴女士认为，拥有自己的房子将会使她免受家暴。反家暴工作者都明白，如果女性无处可去，那么丈夫更易施暴。_____。中国首部反家庭暴力法最终将在 8 月进行第一轮审核。_____。

Business Application

1. This chapter explains the reasons why China residential property prices remain so high and gives you some basic idea on four types of policies used by government authorities to tame the market. Are there any new polices being implemented or in the works? Are they effective? Provide updates on government controlling measures.

2. Use any Internet resources you can find and summarize commonly used phrases expressing the following meanings and give examples in both Chinese and English.
    1) Verbal phrases indicating "increase".
    2) Verbal phrases indicating "decrease".
    3) Verbal phrases indicating "fluctuations".
    4) Adjective phrases indicating "the degree of change".
    5) Adjective phrases indicating "the pace of change".
    6) Verbal phrases indicating "ranking".
    7) Adverbial phrase indicating "同比" and "环比".

Chapter 6
China's High-Speed Rail

Overview

China is a country obsessed with rails. In the past, riding on a green train was the only means of transportation. Although we now have more travel options, trains are still an important part of our life and a topic of great concern. Indeed, China's railways have been through a lot of high-profile events, from the opening of high-speed links, to the accident in Wenzhou, from the overhauling of the Ministry of Railway, to Premiere Li Keqiang's "high-speed rail diplomacy". This chapter will take you through some of these events and help you see the trajectory of China's infrastructure construction in recent years.

Pre-reading Activities

1. What are some of the high-profile events you heard of regarding China's high-speed rail?

2. What are the reasons why it is imperative for China to develop a HSR network?

3. In addition to the high-speed rail, what other big infrastructure projects do you know that are under construction or in planning in China? What contribution does infrastructure build-out make to the overall economy?

4. Watch the video "The Incredible Chinese High-Speed Rail" by China CCTV.

5. Watch the video "China's Future Mega-Projects" from Youtube.

Part 1 Trajectory of China's HSR Development

Read the following two texts, one in English and one in Chinese, and carry out your reading tasks as directed.

Status Quo of Railway Transportation

High Economic Growth, a Large Population, and the Uneven Distribution of Resources Have Created Long-term Challenges to China's Logistics System.

Despite its rapid economic growth in the past few decades, China still faces bottlenecks in the distribution of its wealth, with a marked imbalance between the

Chapter 6 China's High-Speed Rail

geographic development of the coastal areas and that of inland and western China. China's galloping economic growth requires a highly efficient logistics system to provide fast, frequent, and inexpensive transportation services to move both people and cargo in large quantities.

Moreover, due to significant gaps in living standards and wage levels, there are more than 149 million "migrant workers" in China who travel to the coastal cities in the east and south in search of jobs. With scant financial resources, they travel mostly by trains or buses once or twice a year over hundreds of miles between their homes and workplaces. These massive migrations take place regularly every year: In February/March the migration moves east/south when Chinese New Year starts and west/north in January/February when the lunar calendar ends.

By 2010, China had about 91,000 kilometers of railways in operation, which provided transportation to 1,676 million passengers who had traveled 523 kilometers on average for the year. Relatively, rail passenger volumes accounted for about 31.5% of total passenger volumes in the country, versus 14.5% for air and 54% for highways. Yet the penetration ratio of rail traffic (the percentage of total rail passengers over total population) is only 125%, compared with 654% in India and 17,868% in Japan. The greater popularity of railway transportation in these countries stems from more frequent usage by people commuting between homes and workplaces (with average distances of 123 kilometers for India and 17 kilometers for Japan).

Another part of the equation is that the existing national railway network has been shared by cargo and passenger trains, which keeps operational efficiency low. From the perspective of capacity utilization, China's railways are probably the most burdened in the world. On average, there are 40,029 tons of freight and 360,304 passengers delivered on every kilometer of rail in China, versus 11,101 tons of freight in the U.S. and 13,835 tons in Russia, and 839,115 passengers in Japan and 122,136 in India.

In late-1990s China, the Ministry of Railways was eager to make room on its lines for an increasing number of freight cars, so it began phasing out sluggish passenger trains on short routes and hustling its long-distance trains—a campaign dubbed "Speed Up". The maximum locomotive speed was bumped from 30 to 100 miles per hour. The system's total capacity opened up, and the distance traveled by an average passenger more than doubled. The ministry laid a pilot set of high-speed tracks in northern China, began planning the Beijing-Shanghai link, and in 2004 awarded a series of contracts to companies from France, Germany, and Japan.

The Ministry of Railways purchased complete train sets from manufacturers like Alstom, Siemens, and Kawasaki—as well as the technology for brake systems, traction converters, and control networks, which the Chinese then assembled in their own factories. China's needle-nosed bullet trains can look quite distinctive with their white livery paint and "CRH"—China Railway High-Speed—in thick black block letters. But some are the Siemens Velaro model (a version of which set a 2006 world speed record at 250 mph); others are Alstom New Pendolinos (the favorite of Richard Branson's Virgin Trains in Britain); still others are the Zefiro 250 type, made by the Canadian company Bombardier and equipped with 480 beds. Nearly all high-speed train models that China uses today have been refitted with new domestic-made parts, reverse-engineered once the patented machinery was safely within the country.

This process, which the government euphemistically calls "digestion and re-innovation", demonstrates China's genius for improving foreign technology, a skill once dominated by the Japanese, and it set the course for a home-built industry that would soon be able to export its own train sets and parts. For a country that was still manufacturing and using coal-fired steam trains as recently as the late 1990s, the rapid absorption of high-speed rail marked noteworthy progress.

In 2008, the U.S. financial crisis soured the world economy, but the downturn was a great gift for Chinese rail. On Nov. 9, 2008—a hinge moment in railroad history—the central government announced a giant national stimulus package, and the following year it revealed that the largest chunk of money would go to improve public infrastructure. Investment in rail projects soared from $49 billion to $88 billion within the space of a year. And the original plan was to open 42 high-speed lines within the next three years.

Chapter 6 China's High-Speed Rail

China wants to put in place a comprehensive blueprint—the "Mid-to-Long-Term Railway Network Plan" to build a HSR network consisting of four vertical (north-south) lines and four horizontal (west-east) lines. From the first HSR project—the Qinhuangdao–Shenyang Passenger Dedicated Line, China has steadily expanded the overall construction plan of the HSR network. By January 2011, the network boasted an operational length of about 8,358 kilometers, the longest HSR network in the world. The three traffic hubs—Beijing, Shanghai and Guangzhou — are all linked up by HSR, with many more provincial capitals and metro regions being linked up soon.

Text 2

中国高铁的发展历史

进入21世纪后，我国经济继续高速发展，各项事业蒸蒸日上。但在铁路运输领域，我国铁路已经远远不能适应经济发展的需求。

铁路客货运的运能严重不足：就铁路发展的总体状况而言，总量偏少、运能紧张的问题仍然突出，突出表现为铁路网整体能力不足。全国每天货运装车的需求有14~16万车，铁路只能满足60%左右，有大量货物不能及时承运；全国铁路开行的客车每天提供的座席有242万个，而日均实际运量达到290多万人，客运高峰时每天达到420多万人，许多客车常年拥挤，很多人要站着乘车。遇到春节等重大节日时，由于增开大量的客车，必须停开货车确保客车开行，严重制约了铁路货运的健康发展。

铁路客货混运导致运输效率低下：目前我国铁路普遍采用的是客运与货运混线运输的方式。随着铁道部连续对列车进行的提速，目前我国的普通客运列车已经基本达到100~120 km/h的运行速度，部分特快列车可以达到140~160 km/h的运行速度。与之形成对比的是，由于货运列车载重较大，一般只能以80 km/h的速度运行，客货车之间运行速度差别较大，因此无法实现平图运行。货车只能在某些区间停车避让客车，严重干扰了运输秩序，降低了运输效率。因此，实现客货分线运输刻不容缓。

针对上述问题，2004年1月国务院通过了《中长期铁路网规划》，第一次明确提出发展高速铁路的计划。2003年10月12日，随着长春开往北京的T60次列车经由沈阳北站驶入秦沈客运专线，预示着中国建设的第一条高速客运铁路线——"秦沈客运专线"正式开通，也标志着我国从此迈入了高铁时代。根据《中国铁路中长期发展规划》，为满足快速增长的旅客运输需求，到2020年将建立省会城市及大中城市之间的快速客运通道，规划"四纵四横"铁路快速客运通道及三个城际快速客运系统，建设客运专线1.2万公里以上，客车速度目标值达到每小时200公里及以上。

"四纵"客运专线：北京—上海、北京—武汉—广州—深圳—香港、北京—沈阳—哈尔滨（大连）、杭州—宁波—福州—深圳。

"四横"客运专线：徐州—郑州—兰州、杭州—南昌—长沙—昆明、青岛—石家庄—太原、南京—武汉—重庆—成都。

三大城际客运系统：环渤海地区：北京—天津；长江三角洲地区：南京—上海—杭州；珠江三角洲地区：广州—深圳、广州—珠海、广州—佛山。

2016年印发的《中长期铁路网规划》更是首次明确提出要建设"八纵八横"高铁网，它是建立在2004年规划的"四纵四横"高铁网的基础之上的。原有的"四纵四横"高铁网中的纵线：北京到上海、北京到广州、哈尔滨到沈阳，以及东南沿海高铁；四条横线中的上海到昆明、上海到成都、徐州到兰州都已经通车。除正在建设的北京到沈阳，青岛到济南、石家庄外，我国"四纵四横"高铁网已经全部建成。

Reading Tasks

❶ Reading Comprehension

Briefly answer the following questions about the two texts in English.

1) Why does China want to develop a high-speed rail network?
2) How do you feel about riding on the train during the Chinese Lunar New Year travel rush?
3) Compare differences between a traditional train and a HSR train in terms of your user experience.

Chapter 6 China's High-Speed Rail

4) When was the first high-speed rail line completed?
5) What is the current high-speed rail network like?
6) How does the planned high-speed rail network look like?
7) What kind of technological shift has China's high-speed rail gone through?
8) Do you think China's high-speed rail is developing at a very fast rate?

II Translation

1. **Provide the English equivalents to the following terms and expressions.**

    1) 运输系统　　　　　　　　2) 客运专线
    3) 货运列车　　　　　　　　4) 内陆地区
    5) 高速铁路网　　　　　　　6) "四横四纵"
    7) 运输能力　　　　　　　　8) 运营效率
    9) 客流量　　　　　　　　　10) 运营里程
    11) 铁路提速　　　　　　　 12) 渗透率
    13) 最高时速　　　　　　　 14) 运输"瓶颈"
    15) 交通枢纽　　　　　　　 16) 分布不均
    17) 逐步淘汰

2. **Translate the following sentences/paragraphs into Chinese/English.**

    1) Another part of the equation is that the existing national railway network has been shared by cargo and passenger trains, which keeps operational efficiency low.

    2) China's needle-nosed bullet trains can look quite distinctive with their white livery paint and "CRH" —China Railway High-Speed—in thick black block letters.

    3) In 2008, the U.S. financial crisis soured the world economy, but the downturn was a great gift for Chinese rail. On Nov. 9, 2008—a hinge moment in railroad history—the central government announced a giant national stimulus package, and the following year it revealed that the largest chunk of money would go to improve public infrastructure.

    4) The three traffic hubs—Beijing, Shanghai and Guangzhou—are all linked up by HSR, with many more provincial capitals and metro regions being linked up soon.

5) 进入21世纪后,我国经济继续高速发展,各项事业蒸蒸日上。但在铁路运输领域,我国铁路已经远远不能适应经济发展的需求。

6) 客货车之间运行速度差别较大,因此无法实现平图运行。货车只能在某些区间停车避让客车,严重干扰了运输秩序,降低了运输效率。因此,实现客货分线运输刻不容缓。

Research and Discussion

Search the Internet for answers to the following questions and share your findings in class.

1) What sort of legacy do these events have on China's high-speed rail development?
2) How does the development of HSR correlate with China's "Belt and Road" Initiative?

Part 2 — News Reports on China's HSR

Read the following six English texts and carry out your reading tasks as directed.

Text 1

Severe Snowstorms Batter China

Severe snowstorms over broad swaths of eastern and central China have wreaked havoc on traffic throughout the country, creating gigantic passenger backups, spawning accidents and leaving at least 24 people dead, according to state news reports.

In Guangzhou, the booming southern industrial city, authorities said they expected as many as 600,000 train passengers would be stranded there by Monday, unable to board trains home. Green-uniformed anti-riot police were being deployed around the city's central railroad station as a precaution to keep order.

Chapter 6 China's High-Speed Rail

In order to cope with the rail travel crisis, authorities in Guangzhou have ordered a temporary halt to the sale of train tickets and urged migrants from other provinces to spend the Spring Festival in Guangdong Province. At its fastest, normal train service is not expected to resume before three to five days.

Text 2

China to Dismantle Railway Ministry

China will shake up its massive but troubled railway system and invite greater participation from private investors including foreigners, according to the head of the country's powerful Ministry of Railways.

Under a plan issued Sunday, the ministry will be dismantled and its administrative and commercial functions separated.

Currently, the ministry both regulates and operates China's rail system, which has made for a murky structure and impeded both competition and financing.

Under the new blueprint, the Ministry of Transport will absorb administrative duties including overseeing technology and safety standards and service and railway-project quality. A new entity, China Railway Corp., will focus on operational and commercial areas such as management of freight and passenger business as well as railway construction.

Details of the overhaul were outlined in a report delivered to the congress Sunday by State Councilor Ma Kai.

Shaking up the ministry will be a considerable task, but one that analysts say is necessary to keep China's economy and transportation sector humming.

Splitting it up into parts—which could eventually entail creating several regional rail companies—could intensify competition and improve fundraising. This could help reduce China's relatively high rail costs and fuel the system's continued development. It could also create additional business for international companies that supply parts and know-how for China's rail ambitions.

Text ③

High-Speed Rail Line Connecting Xinjiang and Gansu Set to Open

The first high-speed railway in the Xinjiang Uygur Autonomous Region will open in mid-November and cut journeys to nearby provinces from 12 hours to about eight hours.

The Lanzhou-Xinjiang High-Speed Railway, which began construction in 2009, will serve as a key link between the region and the provinces of Gansu and Qinghai. It will also help shorten travel time between Beijing and Urumqi, Xinjiang's capital, from 40 hours to less than 20.

The 1,776 km of track, which will be the longest high-speed railway line in the world, cost 143.5 billion yuan (HK$181 billion) including 31 stations. It will cross three major plateaus—Qinghai-Tibet, Loess and Pamirs—at speeds of up to 250 km/h.

Officials have given the project the ponderous name of the Lanxin Railway Second Double-Tracked Line. This is to distinguish it from a conventional line from Lanzhou to Xinjiang that was completed in 1962. Oddly, however, it does not follow the same route. Instead of heading north from Lanzhou along the old Silk Road through Gansu, it detours into adjacent Qinghai Province on the Tibetan Plateau and opts for a far tougher route through the snowy Qilian Mountains before re-entering Gansu 480 km later and picking up the old trail into Xinjiang.

There is little economic pull between Qinghai and Xinjiang. Just one flight a day takes off from Xining, the capital of Qinghai, to Urumqi. There are as many as eight a day from Lanzhou. In 2011 *China Daily*, an English-language newspaper in Beijing, quoted an unnamed researcher from the China Academy of Railway Sciences as saying it would be difficult to make any money from the line. "It's more of a political thing," he said. "It's more about national defence and ethnic unity."

One of the biggest challenges of the project was dealing with the geology of Qilian Mountain Tunnel No.1 in Qinghai, whose highest point is 4,211 meters above sea level.

The line is a key project for China's western development strategy, as well as an important transport corridor for the construction of the Silk Road Economic Belt.

Chapter 6 China's High-Speed Rail

Text 4

At Every Overseas Whistle Stop These Days, China's Leaders Peddle Their Nation's High-Speed Rail Construction as a Route to Modernization

On his tireless foreign travels, China's Prime Minister Li Keqiang, "the railway salesman" has already successfully pressed for contracts in Europe, Africa and South East Asia.

Undeniably, a sort of "high-speed rail diplomacy" has become an extra arm in the new Chinese government's foreign affairs.

The industry website Railyway.com calls rail China's "business card abroad" and the Communist Party's *Guangming Daily* newspaper claims China's high speed network is "the world's fastest and best".

Once famous as the world's factory for low-technology and labour intensive products, China is now adding bullet trains to the mix, a symbol of its ability to shift up the technology ladder.

Ambition doesn't stop there. Not content with a high-speed grid at home and lucrative railway contracts abroad, Beijing is considering both funding and building high-speed lines from west China through Central Asia to Europe and from south-west China through South East Asia to Singapore.

The challenges are immense: persuading Central Asian states to move to standard gauge tracks and tackling security to add to the enormous diplomatic, financial and technical hurdles.

But China has advantages in this game: enormous economies of scale, the absence of a political cycle to disrupt long-term planning.

Text 5

Chinese-led Consortium Wins Mexico High-Speed Rail Project

A Chinese-led consortium has won an uncontested contract for a multi-billion dollar high-speed passenger rail link between Mexico City and the central city of Queretaro.

The group led by China Railway Construction Corp., Ltd. was the only bidder for the 210-km (130-mile) line, despite earlier interest from rivals like German conglomerate Siemens and Canada's Bombardier.

Under the leadership of President Enrique Peña Nieto, Mexico has sought to forge closer business ties with China, while the world's No.2 economy has been looking to export more of its high-speed rail technology. The Export-Import Bank of China (EximBank) will finance 85 percent of the project's costs, the ministry said.

Mexico's government said on Monday the project would cost 50.82 billion pesos ($3.74 billion), including the build cost and five years of operation. That is less than the 58.95 billion pesos the consortium quoted for the deal.

Siemens' Mexico rail chief told *Reuters* last month that the company, along with Bombardier and France's Alstom PA, had asked for more time to prepare a bid, a request denied by the transport ministry.

Text 6

China Is "Surprised" as Mexico Revokes High-Speed Rail Deal

China has expressed surprise at Mexico's decision to revoke a £2.36 billion high-speed rail contract with a Chinese-led consortium.

The decision to scrap the deal, which was awarded on Monday, was made ahead of a state visit to APEC in Beijing by President Enrique Peña Nieto this week following

Chapter 6　China's High-Speed Rail

accusations from Mexican opposition politicians that the government was favouring the group led by China Railway Construction Corp.

The Chinese-led consortium became the sole bidder after 16 other groups pulled out and the proposal came with a 20-year, Chinese government-backed credit to cover most of the project's value, at interest rates below those available even to Mexico's government.

Mexico's Communications and Transport Ministry said it expects to re-run the tender in late November under the same terms, and would keep it open for six months to enable all interested parties to participate.

China Railway Construction could take part in the new tender and could be eligible for compensation, because Mexico's government withdrew the contract.

Reading Tasks

❶ Reading Comprehension

Briefly answer the following questions about the texts in English.

1) Describe in your own words in Chinese the reform carried out at the Ministry of Railways.
2) Why does Beijing want to break the Ministry of Railways into two separate organizations?
3) What is the significance of the Lanzhou-Xinjiang High-Speed Railway in relationship with "Belt and Road" Initiative? Do you agree with the stance taken by Text 3?
4) What do you know about the "Silk Road Economic Belt" and the "Maritime Silk Road" (now commonly referred to as the Belt and Road Initiative)?
5) What is "APEC"? What is its significance?
6) What is "投标" and "招标"? What are the differences between "bid" and "tender"?

Language Exercises

Search the texts and the Internet for expressions as requested.

1) Search both Text 1 and the Internet for expressions associated with "扰乱公共交通服务".
2) Search both Text 2 and the Internet for expressions associates with "整改" or "调整" of an organization.
3) Search both Text 3 and the Internet for expressions associated with "开通运营" of rail service.
4) Search both Text 5 and the Internet for expressions associated with "投标".

Translation

Proofread the following two Chinese translations of Text 4, the first one by news.sina.com and the second by the paper.cn. Discuss their differences in class.

版本一：

BBC：中国的高铁梦——到欧洲只要两天

在铁路行业网站Railway.com上，铁路被称为"中国的海外名片"。《光明日报》称，中国的高铁网络是"世界上最快、最好的"。

在不知疲倦的外访中，被称为"高铁推销员"的中国总理李克强，已经在欧洲、非洲和东南亚与多个国家签订了高铁合同。作为有名的低技术附加值和劳动密集型产业的世界工厂，中国现在开始生产高铁，这象征着中国有能力实现技术转型。

中国的雄心还不止于此。显然，国内的高速铁路和那些利润颇丰的海外铁路合同还不够。中国正考虑投资建设一条起于中国西部，穿越中亚，最后到达欧洲的高速铁路；一条起于中国西北，穿过东南亚，到达新加坡的铁路。

挑战是巨大的：需要说服中亚的国家采用相同标准的铁轨；通过多方外交来确保安全问题；资金和技术也面临难题。

但是在这个项目中，中国有着极大的优势：巨大的经济规模；长期、稳定的执政党确保了长期计划的实行；财力雄厚的国有铁路建设公司。

Chapter **6** China's High-Speed Rail

版本二：

看中国：中国的铁路梦——拥有巨量资金

铁路网站 Railway.com 称，铁路是中国的"海外商业名片"，《光明日报》称中国的高铁网络是"世界最快和最好的"。

"铁路推销员"李克强总理成功地在出访期间为中国高铁成功赢得了在欧洲、非洲和东南亚的铁路建设合同。一度以出口低技术和劳动力密集型产品的"世界工厂"而闻名的中国已将子弹头列车加入它的出口商品清单，这成为中国具备攀爬技术阶梯能力的象征。

但中国没有满足于国内的高铁网络和有利可图的海外铁路合同，还在考虑为建设从中国西部经中亚前往欧洲、从中国西南部经东南亚至新加坡的高铁，并为此提供资金。

这方面的挑战是巨大的：中国需要说服中亚国家采用标准铁轨、应对安全问题。此外还有巨大的外交、财政和技术障碍。

但中国也有自己的优势：规模经济庞大、政局稳定、拥有巨量资金的国营铁路建设商和媒体支持。

Part ③ Industry Implications of High-Speed Rail

Read the following English text and carry out your reading tasks as directed.

HSR Trains Transform China

The cavernous rail station here for China's new high-speed trains was nearly deserted when it opened less than four years ago.

Not anymore. Practically every train sold out, although they leave for cities all over the country every several minutes. Long lines snake back from ticket windows under the 50-foot ceiling of white, gently undulating steel that floats cloudlike over the departure hall. An ambitious construction program will soon nearly double the size of the 16-platform station.

Just five years after China's high-speed rail system opened, it is carrying nearly twice as many passengers each month as the country's domestic airline industry. With traffic growing 28 percent a year for the last several years, China's high-speed rail network will handle more passengers by early next year than the 54 million people a month who board domestic flights in the United States.

Business executives like Zhen Qinan, a founder of the stock market in coastal Shenzhen, ride bullet trains to meetings all over China to avoid airport delays. The trains hurtle along at 186 miles an hour and are smooth, well-lighted, comfortable and almost invariably punctual, if not early. "I did not think it would change so quickly. High-speed trains seemed like a strange thing, but now it's just part of our lives," Mr. Zhen said.

China's high-speed rail system has emerged as an unexpected success story. Economists and transportation experts cite it as one reason for China's continued economic growth when other emerging economies are faltering. But it has not been without costs—high debt, many people relocated and a deadly accident. The corruption trials of two former senior rail ministry officials this summer have cast an unfavorable light on the bidding process for the rail lines.

The high-speed rail lines have, without a doubt, transformed China, often in unexpected ways.

For example, Chinese workers are now more productive. A paper for the World Bank by three consultants this year found that Chinese cities connected to the high-speed rail network, as more than 100 are already, are likely to experience broad growth in worker productivity. The productivity gains occur when companies find themselves within a couple of hours' train ride of tens of millions of potential customers, employees and rivals.

Productivity gains to the economy appear to be of the same order as the combined economic gains from the usual arguments given for high-speed trains, including time savings for travelers, reduced noise, less air pollution and fuel savings, the World Bank consultants calculated.

Chapter 6 China's High-Speed Rail

Companies are opening research and development centers in more glamorous cities like Beijing and Shenzhen with abundant supplies of young, highly educated workers, and having them take frequent day trips to factories in cities with lower wages and land costs, like Tianjin and Changsha. Businesses are also customizing their products more through frequent meetings with clients in other cities, part of a broader move up the ladder toward higher value-added products.

Li Qingfu, the sales manager at the Changsha Don Lea Ramie Textile Technology Company, an exporter of women's dresses and blouses, said he used to travel twice a year to Guangzhou, the commercial hub of southeastern China. The journey, similar in distance to traveling from Boston to Washington, required nearly a full day in each direction of winding up and down mountains by train or by car.

He now goes almost every month on the punctual bullet trains, which slice straight through the forested mountains and narrow valleys of southern Hunan Province and northern Guangdong Province in a little over two hours, traversing long tunnels and elevated concrete viaducts in rapid succession.

"More frequent access to my client base has allowed me to more quickly pick up on fashion changes in color and style. My orders have increased by 50 percent," he said.

China relocated large numbers of families whose homes lay in the path of the tracks and quickly built new residential and commercial districts around high-speed train stations.

The new districts, typically located in inner suburbs, not downtown areas, have rapidly attracted large numbers of residents, partly because of China's rapid urbanization. Enough farm families become city dwellers each year to fill New York City, part of a trend visible during a series of visits to the Changsha High-Speed Rail Station over the last four years.

When the station opened at the end of 2009 in an inner suburb full of faded state-owned factories, the neighborhood was initially silent. But by 2011, nearly 200 tower cranes could be counted building high-rises during the half-hour drive from downtown

Changsha to the high-speed rail station. On a morning last month, only several dozen tower cranes were visible along nearly the same route. But a vibrant new area of apartment towers, commercial office buildings and hotels had opened near the train station.

China's success may not be easily reproduced in the West, and not just because few places can match China's pace of urbanization. China has four times the population of the United States, and the great bulk of its people live in the eastern third of the country, an area similar in size to the United States east of the Mississippi.

China's high-speed rail program has been married to the world's most ambitious subway construction program, as more than half the world's large tunneling machines chisel away underneath big Chinese cities. That has meant easy access to high-speed rail stations for huge numbers of people—although the subway line to Changsha High-Speed Rail Station has been delayed after a deadly tunnel accident, a possible side effect of China's haste.

New subway lines, rail lines and urban districts are part of China's heavy dependence on investment-led growth. Despite repeated calls by Chinese leaders for a shift to more consumer-led growth, it shows little sign of changing. China's new prime minister, Li Keqiang, publicly endorsed further expansion of the 5,900-mile high-speed rail network this summer. He said the country would invest $100 billion a year in its train system for years to come, mainly on high-speed rail.

The Chinese government is already struggling with nearly $500 billion in overall rail debt. Most of it was incurred for the high-speed rail system and financed with bank loans that must be rolled over as often as once a year. Using short-term loans made the financing look less risky on the balance sheets of the state-controlled banking system and held down borrowing costs. But the reliance on short-term credit has left the system vulnerable to any increase in interest rates.

"Even well-performing railways capable of covering their cash running costs and interest on their debt will almost certainly be unable to repay the principal without some long-term financing arrangements," said a World Bank report last year.

Another impact: air travel. Train ridership has soared partly because China has set

Chapter 6 China's High-Speed Rail

fares on high-speed rail lines at a little less than half of comparable airfares and then refrained from raising them. On routes that are four or five years old, prices have stayed the same as blue-collar wages have more than doubled. That has resulted in many workers, as well as business executives, switching to high-speed trains.

Airlines have largely halted service on routes of less than 300 miles when high-speed rail links open. They have reduced service on routes of 300 to 470 miles.

The double-digit annual wage increases give the Chinese enough disposable income that domestic airline traffic has still been growing 10 percent a year. That is the second-fastest growth among the world's 10 largest domestic aviation markets, after India, which now faces a slowdown as the fall of the rupee has made aviation fuel exorbitantly expensive for air carriers there.

High-speed trains are not only allowing business managers from deep inside China to reach bigger markets. They are also prompting foreign executives to look deeper in China for suppliers as wages surge along the coast.

"We always used to have go down south to Guangzhou to meet with European clients, but now they come up to Changsha more often," said Hwang Yin, a sales executive at the Changsha Qilu Import and Export Company.

The only drawback: "The high-speed trains are getting very crowded these days."

Reading Tasks

1 Summary Writing

Complete the following summary of the Text in Chinese.

高铁改变中国

变化一：_____ 变化二：_____

变化三：_____ 变化四：_____

173

Reading Comprehension

Briefly answer the following questions about the two texts in English.

1) How is the construction of HSR financed?
2) What does the sentence "Most of the debt was incurred for the high-speed rail system and financed with bank loans that must be rolled over as often as once a year" mean?
3) What does the sentence "Using short-term loans made the financing look less risky on the balance sheets of the state-controlled banking system and held down borrowing costs. But the reliance on short-term credit has left the system vulnerable to any increase in interest rates" mean?

Translation

1. Translate the following sentences/paragraphs into Chinese.

1) The cavernous rail station here for China's new high-speed trains was nearly deserted when it opened less than four years ago.
2) Practically every train sold out, although they leave for cities all over the country every several minutes. Long lines snake back from ticket windows under the 50-foot ceiling of white, gently undulating steel that floats cloudlike over the departure hall.
3) With traffic growing 28 percent a year for the last several years, China's high-speed rail network will handle more passengers by early next year than the 54 million people a month who board domestic flights in the United States.
4) The trains hurtle along at 186 miles an hour and are smooth, well-lighted, comfortable and almost invariably punctual, if not early. "I did not think it would change so quickly."
5) China's high-speed rail system has emerged as an unexpected success story. Economists and transportation experts cite it as one reason for China's continued economic growth when other emerging economies are faltering.
6) The corruption trials of two former senior rail ministry officials this summer have

Chapter 6 China's High-Speed Rail

cast an unfavorable light on the bidding process for the rail lines.

7) "Even well-performing railways capable of covering their cash running costs and interest on their debt will almost certainly be unable to repay the principal without some long-term financing arrangements,"...

8) Productivity gains to the economy appear to be of the same order as the combined economic gains from the usual arguments given for high-speed trains...

9) He now goes almost every month on the punctual bullet trains, which slice straight through the forested mountains and narrow valleys of southern Hunan Province and northern Guangdong Province in a little over two hours, traversing long tunnels and elevated concrete viaducts in rapid succession.

10) China's high-speed rail program has been married to the world's most ambitious subway construction program, as more than half the world's large tunneling machines chisel away underneath big Chinese cities.

11) That has meant easy access to high-speed rail stations for huge numbers of people—although the subway line to Changsha High-Speed Rail Station has been delayed after a deadly tunnel accident, a possible side effect of China's haste.

2. Translate the following paragraphs into English.

哪些行业将从高铁建设中获益或遭受冲击？

飞机：高铁给民航带来了直接的压力。例如，武广高铁在开通100多天后，自2010年3月28日起武汉飞广州的航班从每天最多13班减为最多10班。其中1 000公里、一个半小时以内航程的航线最易受到高速铁路的冲击。第一，这一航程加上到机场和办票的时间，乘坐飞机节省不了多少时间。第二，与飞机相比，高铁更准时，且不易受天气的制约。第三，高铁虽然速度快，但运行平稳，乘客在车厢内几乎感觉不到噪音。第四，乘客可以在列车中照常保持通信联络。

收费公路：高铁给收费公路带来的挑战相对要小一些，因为高铁缺少短途运输的灵活性。另外，尽管乘坐高铁可以节省旅途用时，但是高铁票价还是"吓退"了不少低收入乘客。预计2011~2013年，高铁将会分流1%~3%的收费公路的旅客。此外，由于高铁不承担货运，货运将会转移到普通的铁路运输上。据预测，到2015年，普通铁路将会分流 10%~12% 的收费公路的货物运输。

旅游业：乘高铁去临近城市所花费的时间将等同于驾车穿过一个大城市的时间。同一城市群中的城市将因高铁的连接而不再孤立，而是变得像大都市中彼此经济联系活跃的商业和生活区一样。高铁所应用的新科技将给中国人带来全新的休闲旅游体验。高铁可以缩短人们的旅途用时，为人们节省旅费，人们休闲旅游的频率也会增加。国内旅游市场目前仍集中于观光旅游，大部分游客只是参观自然景观与历史古迹。然而随着时间的推移，观光旅游在中国旅游业中所占的比重将不断下降。三小时交通圈城市群出现后，将会有越来越多的人利用周末到邻近城市的娱乐场所和度假村游玩，登山和运动型等旅游项目将会越来越受青睐。

经济型酒店：中国大规模的基础设施建设推动了经济的增长，也缩小了一线城市和二三线城市的差距，因此在未来十年间，二三线城市对经济型酒店的需求将会大幅上升。在认识到二三线城市的巨大潜力后，几乎所有的知名连锁经济型酒店都开始进军二三线城市，其中汉庭连锁酒店和 7 天连锁酒店遥遥领先：二者 45% 的连锁店都位于 2015 年将要建成的拥有最大交通量的 14 个超级交通枢纽城市。

物流业：当一部分客运列车走高铁线后，与高铁并行的既有线路货运能力得到释放，推动了中国铁路主要通道实现客货分线运输。例如，京沪高铁开通后，既有京沪线释放的运输能力每年可增运货物 5 000 万吨。和公路运输相比，铁路货运快且价格要便宜 1/2~1/3。据测算，在全社会货物运量中铁路货运比重每提高一个百分点，就可节约社会物流成本 212 亿元。高铁的开通运营有效增加了铁路货运能力，大大降低了全社会的物流成本和时间成本。

Ⅳ Research and Discussion

Search the Internet for answers to the following question and share your findings in class.

In additional to what is mentioned above, what may other industries stand to gain or become vulnerable due to the HSR build-out in China? Use evidence to support your claim.

Chapter ⑥ China's High-Speed Rail

Ⓥ Bilingual Debate

Take a stance on the following topic "The Benefits of China's High-Speed Rail Outweigh Its Harm" and state your reasons in both Chinese and English in class.

Part ④ High-Speed Rail in the U.S.

Read the following English text and carry out your reading tasks as directed.

An Unlikely Saviour
China Invests in America's High-Speed Rail

Xi jinping, China's president, visited America in September, 2015. He brought plenty of baggage: the controversy surrounding the manipulation of China's struggling economy, alleged cyberattacks on American government and businesses, and aggressive construction in contested parts of the South China Sea that has infuriated American allies. One Chinese observer told the *New York Times*, "Xi is obsessed with strategic rivalry with the United States."

But in one important area, that obsession seems to be working to America's benefit. Last week brought news of a big Chinese investment in what could become the first high-speed rail line in America. Construction on a 230-mile line between Los Angeles and Las Vegas will begin as early as next autumn, announced a Chinese Communist Party official. China Railway International U.S.A., a consortium led by China's national railroad, will provide an initial capital investment of $100 million for the line, which will first run from Las Vegas to the town of Victorville, about 80 miles from Los Angeles, and which officials hope will later connect to the city's downtown.

High-speed rail has many advocates in America. But the country that once thrived on its transcontinental railways has fallen hopelessly behind Europe and Asia following years of disinvestment and closures. The trouble is that the government has demonstrated a stubborn unwillingness to bring the network into the 21st or even mid-20th century. In his 2011 State of the Union address, President Obama proclaimed: "Within 25 years, our goal is to give 80% of Americans access to high-speed rail." But Republican governors of three states slated for big rail projects cancelled those plans and returned the money to the federal government. Jeff Denham, the chairman of the House of Representatives subcommittee in charge of railroads said last year: "High-speed rail can be a good idea; I just think it should be left up to the private sector." Even states that stand to benefit most from such investment seem ambivalent. Kevin McCarthy, the House Majority Leader, who represents perpetually congested California, told the *Wall Street Journal*: "I will do all that I can to ensure not one dollar of federal funding goes to boondoggles like California's high-speed rail."

Enter China. After XpressWest, the firm which had led the Los Angeles-Las Vegas rail project, couldn't secure a federal loan to build the line, China Railway International U.S.A. stepped in. The pair have now set up a joint venture. "It definitely speaks to the fact that our government is dragging their feet," says Andy Kunz, head of the U.S. High Speed Rail Association.

Mr. Kunz is happy to take the money where he can get it. And the American economy will benefit from improved transportation infrastructure, regardless of funding source. Commuters, too, will appreciate the convenience of an 80-minute train ride from Victorville to Las Vegas, considering the drive can take up to four hours. Still, American industry is missing out. No one thinks the investment in the rail line will be a big money spinner for China Railway International U.S.A. "Transportation isn't supposed to make money," says Mr. Kunz. Instead, China is taking a strategic step to boost its own industry. After investing in more miles of new high-speed rail than any other country in the world, it has developed the engineering know-how to build tracks and trains—which it now hopes to export to overseas markets. The United States is one of more than 20 countries where China aims to build a market for its rail industry.

Right-wing critics in America have long charged that government funding of public transit is akin to socialism. They can't be much happier to see the funding for a big American rail line coming from—in name, at least—a communist government.

Chapter 6　China's High-Speed Rail

Reading Tasks

I Reading Comprehension

Briefly answer the following questions about the text in English.

1) The U.S. is known for its technological prowess. Then why does it allow China to build a high-speed rail link from Las Vegas to Los Angeles?

2) What are the differences in financing for public infrastructure construction in the U.S. and China?

II Translation

Translate the following sentences into Chinese.

1) He brought plenty of baggage.
2) Xi is obsessed with strategic rivalry with the United States.
3) But in one important area, that obsession seems to be working to America's benefit.
4) High-speed rail has many advocates in America.
5) Enter China.
6) It definitely speaks to the fact that our government is dragging their feet.
7) Still, American industry is missing out. No one thinks the investment in the rail line will be a big money spinner for China Railway International U.S.A.
8) Right-wing critics in America have long charged that government funding of public transit is akin to socialism. They can't be much happier to see the funding for a big American rail line coming from—in name, at least—a communist government.

III Research and Discussion

Search the Internet for answers to the following questions and share your findings in class.

What are major differences in stance on high-speed rail development between the

Republican Party and the Democratic Party in the U.S. according to the passage? Can you list their differences on other social issues? Give concrete examples to show your points.

Business Application

The following is a guide written by a native English speaker on how to ride a conventional train in China. Based on your own high speed train riding experience, write a new guide on "How to Travel by HSR Train" in China.

How to Travel by Train in China

Traveling and Touring by Train in China Is Probably Easier than You Think It Is! Chinese Trains Are Inexpensive, Punctual and a Great Way to See the Country.

The Trains

Domestic trains run by the China Railway are broken down into "classes" which vary by speed and service. A letter (C, D, G, Z, T & K) preceding the numbers indicate the type of train. The "G" trains are the fastest and normally only service two end-points with maybe a couple of intermediate stops. These are fast trains that run on the regular passenger tracks. "D" trains are next fastest while "T" trains are quite slow.

Unless you are into punishing yourself you will want to travel in a sleeping car, not by coach. Within the sleeping car category, there are three types of accommodations available: Hard Class, Soft Class and Deluxe Soft Class.

The Hard Class sleeper is where most Chinese travel. Each compartment has 6 bunks—three on each side. If you are unlucky enough to be assigned a top bunk let's hope you aren't claustrophobic as you will have only about 18 inches of vertical "space" to accommodate you (not to mention the effort and contortions required to get up there!). The compartments are not enclosed, but are open to the aisle way, so are noisy. Across the aisle from the compartment is a single seat that folds down out of the wall. You can sit here (if it is available) but have to contend with a constant

Chapter 6   China's High-Speed Rail

flow of passengers scraping by you.

The Soft Class sleeper is where you will want to be. Each compartment has 4 beds—a lower and an upper on each side. There is an expansive window with a small table under it. Within the room and extending over the outer aisle way is an area to place your luggage. There is also space under the two lower bunks which everyone shares. Lower berth space is more expensive than upper berth space but it is worth the extra cost. Spending hours and hours in a windowless upper bed is not a great way to enjoy your visit to China.

Deluxe Soft Sleepers are two-bed compartments. This is perfect for a traveling couple as you don't have to share with others and you have a level of privacy you don't get with the Soft Sleeper compartment. The Deluxe Soft Sleeper is usually more modern and may have an actual closet in which to hang things, a hotel-type safe and even in-room sink and toilet facilities. Not all trains include Deluxe Soft Sleepers. Many "Z" trains do have these, but most "K" and "T" trains do not.

The CRH system is independent from the normal trains. This is the new high-speed rail system being built in China. The railroad right-of-way is elevated whereas the regular trains are at ground level. The facilities for the CRH are first-rate—putting similar modern airports to shame. In some cases the CRH station is completely separate from the regular train stations (as in Guangzhou) and in other cases they are combining existing regular rail station with the CRH station. When this is done everything is modernized. With this, gone are the dark and dingy 1980's stations. Everything is new and modern.

While CRH "G" trains are technically capable of going 380 km/h, they are currently limited to 250 km/h and less for energy conservation and safety reasons. Sleeping car service is not provided. A normal "fast train" trip from Beijing to Shanghai used to take 12 hours.

Train Tickets

There are various ways to buy train tickets in China although it is not easy for a tourist.

Tickets usually go on sale 20 days prior to departures via the official centralized website: www.12306.cn. This website is only in Chinese and requires a Chinese bank-issued card to pay.

Tickets now have the name and ID card number on the ticket (passport number for foreigners). This was put in place to eliminate scalpers. If you have someone buy tickets for you, you will need to provide them with your exact name and passport number (as with plane tickets). They will also need a copy of your passport if you wish to have the tickets delivered to you. When tickets are bought on-line, you are given a confirmation number which you need to bring along with your passport at the train station to pick up the paper ticket. You can do so just before your departure.

If you wait until you arrive in China to buy your tickets, tickets go on sale at the station or with ticket sellers all over town 18 days prior to the travel date. In some cases it may be difficult to obtain the tickets you want (such as deluxe soft sleeper) and alternatives may be either coach seating or Hard Sleeper, if anything. At peak times it is very difficult to get tickets as they may sell out in the first hour after going on sale.

If you are worried about obtaining a ticket there are ticketing agents that can procure your tickets but you will be paying a premium price and it is more expensive than obtaining your own. Such premium can be quite high. Tickets are good only for the name and passport number printed on them.

The Train Stations

The train stations are nearly always located in the center of town. Many large cities (and even some small ones) have more than one station! Guangzhou in the south and Beijing in the north both have three widely separated stations. Be sure you know which station your train leaves from!

The larger train stations usually have a large "square" out front. Many Chinese arrive hours early for their trains and are not admitted into the station. So you will find these squares filled with people sitting on their luggage, waiting for their train time.

There may be a very large electronic reader board above the entrance or off to the side with lists all the upcoming trains so those waiting will be informed.

Large stations also may have the "cattle gates" where you snake back and forth before arriving at the station entrance. Once at the entrance you will find a security screening area. This is nothing like the TSA security. Place your bags and other

Chapter 6 China's High-Speed Rail

carry items on a moving conveyor belt (it is low and easy to use) and walk around the machine to get your items on the other side. Some stations also have police to "wand" you, but foreigners are rarely asked to stop for this.

Once inside the station, look for the large electronic train board. If there are many trains, the screen may change a couple of times until you see your train listed. Look first for your train number and then the departure time—this should match your tickets. Then look for a number. This will be your train "waiting area". In smaller city/stations all passengers wait together in the same room. Larger cities/stations will have a designated "Soft Sleeper Waiting Area". It will be relatively uncrowded, have soft, cushy seating and will be a pleasant place to wait for your train. If you have trouble finding the proper waiting area, show your ticket to a railway employee. They will motion the direction to you.

While waiting, watch the TV monitors which will show you many of the scams designed to separate passengers from their luggage and valuables.

Keep an eye on the electronic reader board that displays your train number. It may or may not be in English but the train number and departure time are easy to figure out.

Generally the trains are loaded 30 minutes in advance of departure in originating cities. In intermediary cities, you may have a little as 3 minutes. When your reader board changes (or tells you it is boarding time), and you see masses of people pop up and head for the gate, that is your indication it is time to board. Note the platform number so you get the correct train. You may have your ticket punched as you leave the waiting area.

Follow the crowd. Again, every station is different. You may have to go up a few flights of stairs to cross over the tracks to your platform or you may have to go down to a subway to cross under the tracks. If you are lucky, there will be an escalator. More often than not you will have to carry your luggage up or down stairs. Some stairs have a small ramp to the side for pulling your wheeled luggage up or sliding it down as you go. In any case, this is not the most pleasant part of your journey as you are wrestling your items up and down stairways with a mass of other people doing the same.

Once on the platform there may be a train on both sides. Look for an overhead electronic reader board that displays your train number, departure time and often the current time. Most long distance trains will also have a placard on the center of the car showing the origin and final destination of the train. The car number is usually also written on a column or on the floor. Position yourself near the proper car so as to save time on boarding, especially in an intermediate city.

Now you need to find your car. Notice on your ticket that following the date will be a two-digit number followed by another number. The two-digit number is your car and the other number is your berth number in that car.

Every second car will have a vestibule open and with an attendant at the bottom of the stairs. There will be a small tab hanging out perpendicular to the train with the car number on it. Find your orientation (to know if the car numbers go from left to right or vice-versa) and head toward your car. At your car you will need to show your ticket to the car attendant who will motion you into the car to the right or to the left. Now all you have to do is to find your compartment and berth.

How It Works on the Train

Once in your compartment, you will stash your larger luggage overhead, under the lower bunk or (if there is no other space) under the table that is under the window. The Chinese tend to use the trains as a way to transport large items and to avoid shipping these, so you may find that they have every available space stuffed with their boxes and oversized-bags.

The beds are generally comfortable. When you enter your compartment each bed will have a stack of bedding—a sheet-covered comforter and one or two pillows. At bedtime you unroll your comforter and make up your bed. If you are a light sleeper it is recommended that you bring along a pair of ear-plugs.

At the end of the hall will be a hot-water dispenser that the passengers use to make noodles and tea. Use this water at your own risk—it will likely make you sick as it is "local" water and not purified. Never drink the water in the washroom—or use it to clean your toothbrush—even if you see other passengers doing this.

Shortly after departure your car attendant will come to visit. She may or may not speak English but will speak enough to get by. She will want your passport and your ticket. The passport and visa number are recorded in a book (the domestic Chinese will present their identification card in lieu of a passport). She will put your ticket into a space in a folder and hand you a plastic credit-card sized berth identification. Keep this with you for the duration of the trip (Note that this procedure is now being phased out with the issue of the real name system). Prior to your arrival city the car attendant will return to exchange your ticket for the berth identification card.

Meal Service

You have a number of choices for your meals: You can bring your own and eat in your room. Every train station has multiple vendors who can sell you tubs of dehydrated noodle dinners, sandwiches, and all manner of packaged goods and beverages. Most Chinese who travel by train bring their own food onboard and eat in the compartment.

You can eat snacks or meals in your room. During the meal periods, an attendant will pass through the train about every 15 minutes with a cart that has pre-packaged meals from the dining car. She may also have packaged sandwiches, noodles, beverages, etc.

You can eat in the dining car. The dining car generally separates the Soft Class sleepers from the Hard Class sleeping cars. Your car attendant can point you in the right direction to find the dining car.

Toilet Facilities on the Train

Each sleeping car has two toilet rooms. These may both be at one end of the car or there may be one at each end. Most are the traditional hole-in-the-floor type of facility. (Be careful not to lose your cell phone or other items down the hole). If you are lucky you will have a car with a "western" toilet. Some cars have both types.

Toilets in the "K" and "T" trains (and all normal class trains) dump directly on the railroad right-of-way. As such, the restrooms are locked while in the stations, for 10 to 15 minutes before arrival and a similar time after departure. The "Z" trains have holding tanks so are always available.

Toilet paper (and toilet seat covers) is generally not provided! Be sure to bring your own. Most food vendors sell a small packet of paper napkins that will suffice.

There is a separate room for shaving and makeup. This is near the toilets and will have from 2 to 3 sinks. Nothing is provided except water. So, plan ahead and bring your own washcloth and towel (travel stores carry a type of high-absorbency/quick drying towel) and soap.

The washroom is also the normal place for the Chinese passengers to get rid of their food items. There is usually a hole in the floor where they dump their soups and tea and a garbage bin where they stash their food packaging. So, it can be a busy place.

HSR build-out is part of China's infrastructure boom. Watch the video "China's Future Mega-Projects" from Youtube and use the Internet to check their latest progress. Report your findings back to class.

Chapter 7
China's Demographic Economics

Overview

This chapter begins with a bird's eye view of China's demographic challenges. As the most populous country in the world, China has started to relax its decade-old family control policy in recent years. What are economic considerations behind policy changes? Then it moves on to the two ends of the population spectrum. For the growing number of pensioners, do they have more options to support themselves? For China's newborns, how much does it cost to raise them up? Why do some rich Chinese families now choose to give birth in the United States? Should surrogacy and egg-freezing be legalized in China? These are some questions that you can find answers in this chapter.

Pre-reading Activities

1. Rapid ageing of the population plus a low birth rate, that's the situation China is facing today. What impact will these trends have on society and on individuals?

2. Some media say that labor shortages will place a huge burden on China's economy and shrink the manufacturing industry. Labor costs are expected to jump because of a short supply in labor resources, which could eventually lead to inflation. What's your take on such comments?

3. How can the country cope with these problems in terms of government policy?

4. The gender ratio is 51% to 49%. But some people, especially in rural areas, still prefer to have a male child over a female child, partly due to ancient Chinese traditions. Do you think this will affect the gender balance in China?

Chapter 7 China's Demographic Economics

Part 1
China's Demographic Challenges

Read the following two texts, one in English and one in Chinese, and carry out your reading tasks as directed.

Text 1

Demography: China's Achilles Heel

A Comparison with America Reveals a Deep Flaw in China's Model of Growth

Like the hero of "The Iliad", China can seem invincible. In 2010 it overtook U.S. in terms of manufactured output, energy use and car sales. Its military spending has been growing in nominal terms by an average of 16% each year for the past 20 years. According to the IMF, China will overtake U.S. as the world's largest economy in 2017. But when Thetis, Achilles's mother, dipped her baby in the river Styx to give him the gift of invulnerability, she had to hold him somewhere. Alongside the other many problems it faces, China too has its deadly point of unseen weakness: demography.

Over the past 30 years, China's total fertility rate—the number of children a woman can expect to have during her lifetime—has fallen from 2.6, well above the rate needed to hold a population steady, to 1.56, well below that rate. Because very low fertility can become self-reinforcing, with children of one-child families wanting only one child themselves, China now probably faces a long period of ultra-low fertility, regardless of what happens to its one-child policy.

The government has made small adjustments to the policy (notably by allowing an only child who is married to another only child to have more than one child) and may adapt it further. But for now it is firmly in place, and very low fertility rates still prevail, especially in the richest parts of the country. Shanghai reported fertility of just 0.6 in 2010—probably the lowest level anywhere in the world. According to the UN's population division, the nationwide fertility rate will continue to decline, reaching 1.51 in 2015–2020. In contrast, America's fertility rate is 2.08 and rising.

The difference between 1.56 and 2.08 does not sound large. But over the long term it has a huge impact on society. Between now and 2050 China's population will fall slightly, from 1.34 billion in 2010 to just under 1.3 billion in 2050. This assumes that fertility starts to recover. If it stays low, the population will dip below 1 billion by 2060. In contrast, America's population is set to rise by 30% in the next 40 years. China will hit its peak population in 2026. No one knows when America will hit its population peak.

The differences between the two countries are even more striking if you look at their average ages. In 1980 China's median (the age at which half the population is younger, half older) was 22. That is characteristic of a young developing country. It is now 34.5, more like a rich country and not very different from U.S., which is 37. But China is ageing at an unprecedented pace. Because fewer children are being born as larger generations of adults are getting older, its median age will rise to 49 by 2050, nearly nine years more than America at that point. Some cities will be older still. The Shanghai Population and Family Planning Committee says that more than a third of the city's population will be over 60 by 2020.

This trend will have profound financial and social consequences. Most obviously, it means China will have a bulge of pensioners before it has developed the means of looking after them. Unlike the rest of the developed world, China will grow old before it gets rich. Currently, 8.2% of China's total population is over 65. The equivalent figure in America is 13%. By 2050, China's share will be 26%, higher than in America.

In the traditional Chinese family, children, especially sons, look after their parents (though this is now changing). But rapid ageing also means China faces what is called the "4-2-1 phenomenon": Each only child is responsible for two parents and four grandparents. Even with high savings rates, it seems unlikely that the younger generation will be able or willing to afford such a burden. So most elderly Chinese will be obliged to rely heavily on social-security pensions.

China set up a national pensions fund in 2000, but only about 365m people have a

Chapter 7 China's Demographic Economics

formal pension. And the system is in crisis. The country's unfunded pension liability is roughly 150% of GDP. Almost half the (separate) pension funds run by provinces are in the red, and local governments have sometimes reneged on payments.

But that is only part of a wider problem. Between 2010 and 2050 China's workforce will shrink as a share of the population by 11 percentage points, from 72% to 61%—a huge contraction, even allowing for the fact that the workforce share is exceptionally large now. That means China's old-age dependency ratio (which compares the number of people over 65 with those aged 15 to 64) will soar. At the moment the ratio is 11—roughly half U.S. level of 20. But by 2050, China's old-age ratio will have risen fourfold to 42, surpassing U.S.. Even more strikingly, by 2050, the number of people coming towards the end of their working lives (i.e., those in their 50s) will have risen by more than 10%. The number of those just setting out (those in their early 20s, who are usually the best educated and most productive members of society) will have halved.

The shift spells the end of China as the world's factory. The apparently endless stream of cheap labour is starting to run dry. Despite pools of underemployed country-dwellers, China already faces shortages of manual workers. As the workforce starts to shrink after 2013, these problems will worsen. Sarah Harper of the Oxford Institute of Population Ageing points out that China has mapped out the age structure of its jobs, and knows for each occupation when the skills shortage will hit. It is likely to try to offset the impact by looking for workers abroad. Manpower, a business-recruitment firm, says that by 2030 China will be importing workers from outside, rather than exporting them.

Large-scale immigration poses problems of its own. U.S. is one of the rare examples of a country that has managed to use mass immigration to build a skilled labor force. But U.S. is an open, multi-ethnic society with a long history of immigration and strong legal and political institutions. China has none of these features.

In the absence of predictable institutions, all areas of Chinese society have relied on guanxi, the web of connections that often has extended family relations at the center. But what happens when there are fewer extended families? One result could be a move towards a more predictable legal system and (possibly) a more open political culture. And, as shifts in China's economy lead to lower growth, Chinese leaders will have to make difficult spending choices; they will have to decide whether to buy "guns or walking sticks".

China is not unique in facing these problems. All rich countries have rising pension costs. And China has some advantages in dealing with them, notably low tax rates (giving room for future increases) and low public expectations of welfare. Still, China is also unusual in two respects. It is much poorer than other ageing countries, and its demographic transition has been much more abrupt. It seems highly unlikely that China will be able to grow its way economically out of its population problems. Instead, those problems will weigh down its growth rate—to say nothing of the immense social challenges they will bring. China's Achilles heel will not be fatal. But it will hobble the hero.

Text 2

人口问题：未来中国面对的最大噩梦？

一、2017 年，漂亮数据中的不漂亮。

前不久统计局发布了 2017 年的宏观数据，这绝对是一份漂亮的数据清单。2017 年全年 GDP 超过 80 万亿，达到 82.71 万亿元，实际增长了 6.9%，是连续 7 年 GDP 增速下滑来的首次上升。

数据是超出所有人的预期的。根据《2017 年政府工作报告》，预计 2017 年中国的增速是 6.5% 左右，而此前 IMF、联合国、世界银行等国际组织预期 2017 年中国的增速也是 6.5% 左右。

不过，统计局没有提的是，这个数据包里有一个数据是大大低于预期的，那就是新出生人口数据。

2016 年是全面二胎政策的第一年，2017 年是第二年，国家卫计委在政策实施之初曾预测 2018 年将出现新生人口高峰，预计 2017 年出生人口最少为 2 023.2 万。

而现实数据却是，2016 年出生了 1 786 万人，2017 年出生了 1 723 万，同比减少了 63 万人。这就是说，二胎政策的第一年，人口出生高峰就可能过去了。

要指出的是，这还不是全部真相。

2017年出生的人口当中，二胎占比达到了51.2%，增长率为11%左右，也即2016年二胎占比为46.13%。这就是说，2017年，一孩人数为841万，比2016年的一孩人数962万，足足减少了121万人。

这意味着年轻人的生育意愿在不断下降。

从下面的中国人口结构图我们可以看到，45到49岁的人口高峰对应到25到29岁的人口出生高峰。考虑到现在受教育等各种因素导致生育年龄往后推迟5年，那么25到29岁的人口高峰也应该要对应0到4岁的人口高峰，即第三波婴儿潮。

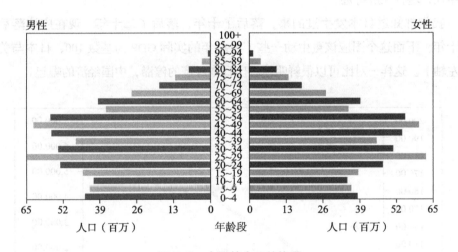

图7-1　中国的人口结构图

但事实上，我们看到，新的人口高峰并没有出现。0~4岁人口与5~9岁人口相比，仅仅是微增。

另外，从上面的人口结构图可以看到，之后的适龄生育父母人数进一步减少，20~24岁的人口比25~29岁少了一大截，后面跟着断崖。

这样的人口趋势下，再叠加生育意愿的下滑，后面的人口走势是什么样的，无须赘言。

二、AI 时代，人口真的不重要了？

这样的人口塌陷趋势，又会演化出什么呢？

不少人认为人口问题是危言耸听，他们的观点是技术在不断进步，尤其像 AI 这样的技术突破。但果真如此吗？

先看传统框架下，人口塌陷趋势会演化出什么？

有一个生动的案例，这就是我们的近邻日本。

看过日本的 GDP 增长，你就知道，谁没有年轻过呢？一个国家只要在自己年轻的时候干正事，GDP 都可以飞起，这跟人是一个道理。回首韩国的经济增长，在那个年代，堪称经济奇迹。

我们都知道日本发生过的事，落后了十年，落后了二十年，现在应该落后了三十年。下面这个图应该更生动一些（1990 年的实际 GDP 为基数 100，日本与美国看左轴）。这样一对比可以很鲜明地看出日本经济的停滞，中国经济的崛起。

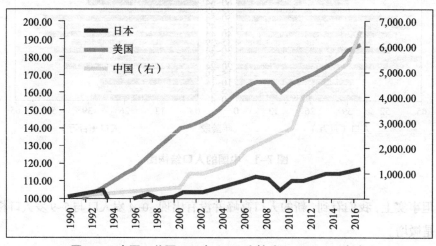

图 7-2　中国、美国、日本 GDP 比较（1990~2016 年）

一个国家的 GDP 波动是很正常的，一段时间增长，一段时间下跌，这就像一家公司一样，业绩有波动也是正常的。投资者不用过分关注一家公司一年的波动，上升到国家层面，也没必要过分强调一个国家一年的 GDP 波动。就如美国，涨涨跌跌，最终爬到了全球经济体第一的位置。

Chapter 7　China's Demographic Economics

但是像日本这种情况，近三十年的停滞，那就一定是决定经济大方向的因素出了问题。在日本这样一个稳定的国家里，导致大方向出问题的就只能是人口因素了。

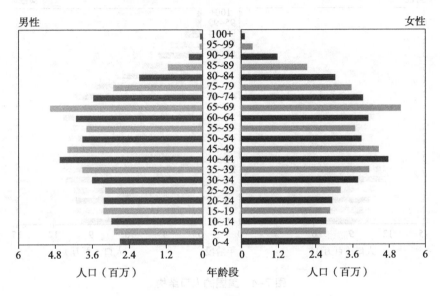

图 7-3　日本的人口结构

看过去五十年里日本与中国的劳动人口对比，你就能明白为什么中国会超过日本，为什么日本会落后了一个又一个十年。

从日本的人口结构基本可以断定，除非安倍能让日本的人口重新启动增长，否则日本的经济绝无可能再腾飞。

日本在过去三十年里，其技术相比 1990 年同样取得了令人瞩目的成就，但它并没有改变日本经济的萎靡状态。

与我们隔得比较远的欧洲，尤其是西欧，过去几年也过得不好，各种危机袭来。说到底，也是同一个原因，年轻的劳动人口在减少。难民的涌入或许会改变欧洲的人口结构，不过不同意识形态的人群涌入究竟会如何改造欧洲，还不得而知。

美国虽然说有不少问题，但经济实力一直是稳居世界第一的，金融危机之后的反弹力是很强的。看美国的人口结构，这几乎是经济发展不错的国家里（包括中国）

最漂亮的了。美国的中位数年龄是38.1岁,仅比中国稍大一点。而从人口结构来看,中国人口老龄化的程度超过美国只是时间的问题。

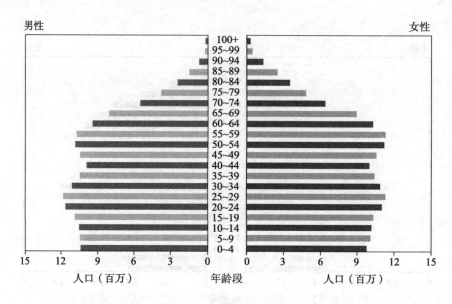

图 7-4 美国的人口结构

所以从传统的经验来看,人口是决定一个经济体大方向的关键因素。

未来会不会有变化呢?技术进步会不会让人口不再是决定一个经济体大方向的关键因素呢?

这个问题是很难说的,至少过去三十年的技术进步并没有让日本走出低迷。

再来看一个问题:技术可以进步背后的动机又是什么?技术会不断进步,说好听点,背后动机是人类追求更好的生活。接地气点,是两个动机,一是赚钱,二是兴趣。

兴趣就不用多说了,在今天这种越来越需要烧钱探索技术前沿的背景下,兴趣对技术的贡献比例很小,那就只有一个动机了,赚钱。技术进步能让企业赚钱,这又来自两个方面,一是改善消费者的需求,二是创造新的供给引领需求。

而这都离不开人口,它既需要天才的大脑,又需要大众的需求。美国为什么会

Chapter 7 China's Demographic Economics

引领全球技术的发展？一个原因是它太幸运了，天才的大脑都跑到它那儿了，另一个因素是其国内有庞大的需求。

也就是说，技术进步是很依赖人口的，它确实看人口的质量，但它也需要人口的数量。

从这点出发，即使在 AI 时代，人口因素仍然是很重要的。

三、AI 还没来临，人口老龄化问题步步紧逼。

更何况，AI 时代还没到来，它还需要很长的时间去实现大量的技术积累。

而中国人口问题上的一个缺陷是，比起日本和欧洲，它多了一个计划生育的变量。

因此到 2016 年，中国的人口结构即为图 7-1 所示。第三波婴儿潮没有如期而至，这还是在二胎政策全面放开的背景下。

这意味着什么呢？

人口老龄化，加速的人口老龄化，比日本和欧洲更快的人口老龄化。

而我们知道，财富是需要时间去创造和积累的，所以相比日本和欧洲，加速的人口老龄化背后一个尴尬的事实就是未富先老。

这个尴尬已经在中国一些省份出现了。

看前不久人社部发布的《2016 年中国社会保险发展报告》，不看不知道，一看吓一跳。

抚养比全国平均值是 2.8，也就是 2.8 个劳动力（缴养老保险）要养一位老人。这个数据在 2014 年是 2.97，2015 年是 2.87，2016 年降到了 2.8。很明显，数字一路下滑。

但这还不是全部。分地方看，广东的抚养比是 9.25，位居全国第一，超出全国平均水平的只有 8 个省，而数据最低的是黑龙江，仅 1.3，几乎相当于 1 个劳动力养一位老人。有虹吸效应的广东还好，而人口流出的省份先经历未富先老的尴尬。

抚养比让人直接联想到养老金，有多么恐怖的抚养比，就有多么恐怖的养老金：全国养老金余额平均还能支付 17.2 个月，广东和北京凭着抚养比和工资双高，不仅位居全国之首，而且可支付月数较 2015 年还是上升的。其他省份就没有这么幸运了，尤其是黑龙江，养老保险累计结余居然是 -232 亿元。

看 2016 年当期结余，有 7 个省份收不抵支。

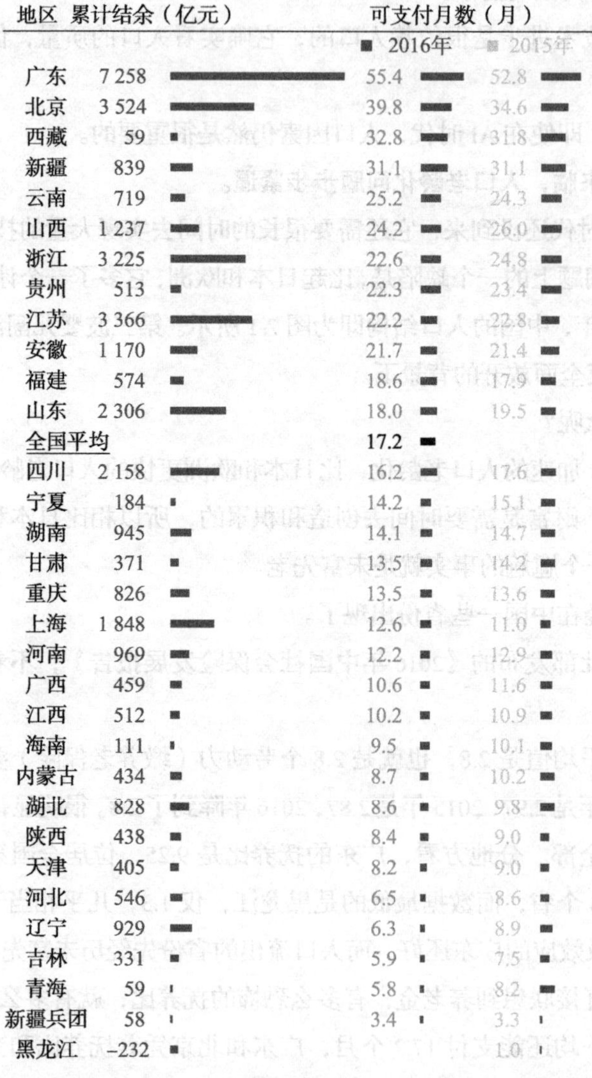

地区	累计结余（亿元）	可支付月数（月）	
		2016年	2015年
广东	7 258	55.4	52.8
北京	3 524	39.8	34.6
西藏	59	32.8	31.8
新疆	839	31.1	31.1
云南	719	25.2	24.3
山西	1 237	24.2	26.0
浙江	3 225	22.6	24.8
贵州	513	22.3	23.4
江苏	3 366	22.2	22.8
安徽	1 170	21.7	21.4
福建	574	18.6	17.9
山东	2 306	18.0	19.5
全国平均		17.2	
四川	2 158	16.2	17.6
宁夏	184	14.2	15.1
湖南	945	14.1	14.7
甘肃	371	13.5	14.2
重庆	826	13.5	13.6
上海	1 848	12.6	11.0
河南	969	12.2	12.9
广西	459	10.6	11.6
江西	512	10.2	10.9
海南	111	9.5	10.1
内蒙古	434	8.7	10.2
湖北	828	8.6	9.8
陕西	438	8.4	9.0
天津	405	8.2	9.0
河北	546	6.5	8.6
辽宁	929	6.3	8.9
吉林	331	5.9	7.5
青海	59	5.8	8.2
新疆兵团	58	3.4	3.3
黑龙江	−232		1.0

图 7-5 中国分地区企业养老保险基金可支付月数（2015~2016）

Chapter 7　China's Demographic Economics

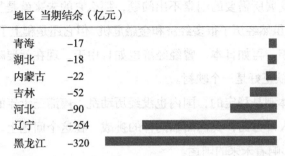

注：根据当期收入和支出计算得出

图 7-6　2016 年企业养老保险收不抵支地区情况

欧债危机的根源就是老去的人口再也支撑不起曾经的福利。很显然，对于东北三省等地方，如果没有其他途径，那么本质就与欧债危机一样，社保游戏玩不下去了。

目前还是国家维持着，2017 年 11 月 18 日，国务院对外公布了《划转部分国有资本充实社保基金实施方案》。这个划转显然是为了调节地方的不平衡，而这是一个由过去劳动力大迁徙带来的历史问题。像广东这些地方享受了大迁徙的红利，而锅却让东三省等劳动力输出省份背了。

但是，国有资本划转终究只能解决一时的地方不平衡的问题，它解决不了中国人口的日渐老去，以及伴随而来的抚养比下降问题。当人口老龄化加速到来时，社保游戏就不仅仅是东北三省这些地方玩不下去，还有更多的省份会玩不下去。

结语

欧债危机的解决途径之一是政府缩减支出，减少福利。但这个途径显然对中国是行不通的，因为中国相比欧洲，是未富先老，福利上面没有多少缩减的空间。如果支出无法削减，那就只能在开源上下功夫，即增加生育。

计划生育所造成的适合生育人口的减少是不可挽回的，现在能做的只能是提高生育意愿，而这需要很精细化的财政上的扶持，包括税收和奖励。

巴菲特曾说，不要关注一家企业一年的业绩情况，有波动是很正常的，应该要关注的是这家企业的"护城河"是不是越来越深。

这句话用到国家层面上也是如此。GDP 波动很正常，今年漂亮，明年难看，但是如果一个国家发展所需要的因素不出问题，那么它的未来就是呈上升趋势的。典型的例子是美国，虽然经历了很多经济和金融危机，但它还是爬上了世界第一的位置，并且保持了很多年。再如日本，曾经经济也如日中天，现在就要暗淡很多了。日经指数 20 多年的下跌正好是一个映衬。

日本的政治体制是稳定的，国内也没经历动乱，停滞三十年的经济增长只能归因于人口。而在人口方面，我们面临同样的挑战。在这个问题上，今天做出的任何一个选择，都将影响着未来的国运。

Summary writing

1. Complete the following summary of Text 1 in Chinese.

阿喀琉斯力大无比，但脚踝是其全身唯一一处"死穴"		
类比：中国飞速发展，但有制约发展的"软肋"：_____		
表现	1.（2015 年到 2020 年：中国：_____ VS. 美国：_____） 2.（2050 年：中国：_____ VS. 美国：_____）	
社会及经济影响	1._____ 3._____	2._____ 4._____
解决方法	好处：1._____ 坏处：1._____ 结论：_____	2._____ 2._____

Chapter 7 China's Demographic Economics

2. Complete the following summary of Text 2 in English.

China's Population Nightmare

What doesn't China's 2017 GDP figure tell us? _____
Is the population number relevant in the age of artificial intelligence?
_____
What are the demographic differences among Japan, China and U.S.?
_____
Japan: _____
China: _____
U.S.: _____
The driving force for development in the age of artificial age is: _____
Challenges brought by China's demographic shortfall: _____
Conclusion: _____

II Translation

1. **Provide the Chinese equivalents to the following terms and expressions.**

    1) 出生率   2) 死亡率
    3) 养老金   4) 老龄化
    5) 制造业产出   6) 军费开支
    7) 公共福利   8) 拖累（经济增长）
    9) 人口转型   10) 政治体系
    11) 拖欠支付   12) 名义值
    13) 就业不足   14) 入不敷出
    15) 劳动力短缺

2. **Translate the following sentences/paragraphs into Chinese.**

    1) Because very low fertility can become self-reinforcing, with children of one-child families wanting only one child themselves, China now probably faces a long period of ultra-low fertility, regardless of what happens to its one-child policy.

2) The shift spells the end of China as the world's factory. The apparently endless stream of cheap labor is starting to run dry. Despite pools of underemployed country-dwellers, China already faces shortages of manual workers.

3) The country's unfunded pension liability is roughly 150% of GDP. Almost half the (separate) pension funds run by provinces are in the red, and local governments have sometimes reneged on payments.

4) And, as shifts in China's economy lead to lower growth, Chinese leaders will have to make difficult spending choices; they will have to decide whether to buy "guns or walking sticks".

Research and Discussion

Search the Internet for answers to the following questions and share your findings in class.

1) Describe your understanding of the one-child policy that was implemented in China from around 1980 to 2003. What contributions does this policy make to China and what are its negative consequences?

2) In November, 2013, China allowed couples to have two kids if both of them are single child. In October, 2015, polices were further relaxed to allow all couples to have two kids. Do you think changes in law can reverse demographic challenges facing China? Do you think there will be a baby boom generation in China?

3) What is your attitude towards setting up a family? Do you want to stay single, be a DINK? Or do you want to have one kid or two kids? And what is the reason for your choice?

Chapter 7 China's Demographic Economics

Part 2
Challenges Facing the Old

Read the following four English texts and carry out your reading tasks as directed.

China's Pension System
China Has Made Great Strides in Expanding Pension Coverage for Its Population over the Last Fifteen Years.

Until the early 1980s (i.e., when China was still a planned economy), the state bore the entire cost of the urban pension plan system. As a result, there was no need for individual workers to contribute. However, following a series of reforms to the system, the cost is now shared by the state, companies, and workers. In addition to the existing urban workers' basic pension, public service workers' pension, and rural pension schemes, China's public pension system now also includes two pilot schemes, namely, the "urban social pension scheme" and the "new rural social pension scheme".

The urban workers' basic pension covers employees (of state-owned enterprises, collective enterprises, joint-stock companies, foreign-invested enterprises, private companies, and one-man businesses) and can be considered the cornerstone of China's pension system. Membership is mandatory. As of end of 2011, there were 284 million members, 216 million of whom were still working and 68. 26 million of whom were retired. The urban workers' basic pension is a two-tier pillar consisting of a (pay-as-you-go) social pooling element and (funded) individual accounts. Companies contribute 20% of their total wage bill to the social pool, while workers contribute 8% of their wages to their individual accounts. To receive a pension, members must have contributed for at least 15 years by the time they reach the age of retirement (60 for men, 55 for women in white-collar jobs, and 50 for women in blue-collar jobs). The income replacement rate is supposed to be 40%–50%.

Unlike the urban workers' basic pension, the public service workers' pension is still financed entirely by the state and has a high income replacement rate of 80%–90%. Because of regional differences in economic growth there is no nationwide rural pension fund. Instead, membership of the rural pension scheme, which is also open to rural enterprises, is voluntary and on a (funded) individual account basis. Reflecting the fact that economic growth in rural areas has lagged that of the country as a whole and that rural incomes are insufficient to be able to make pension contributions, the rural pension scheme has the lowest coverage among the public pension schemes and a very low income replacement rate.

With a view to establishing a universal pension scheme, the government introduced two new pilot schemes in designated regions: the "new rural social pension scheme" in 2009 and the "urban social pension scheme" in 2011. The latter extends pension eligibility in urban areas to those not covered by the urban workers' basic pension scheme. As of end of 2011, the two schemes had a total membership of 332 million, 240 million of whom were aged less than 60 and 91. 85 million of whom were pensioners.

Both schemes are voluntary and have many basic similarities. First of all, their two main sources of finance are individual contributions and government subsidies. Scheme members can choose within a given range how much to contribute to their individual accounts each month. The more they contribute, the more they will receive when they retire. Furthermore, those who have contributed for at least 15 years will receive a basic pension of at least RMB55 each month along with 1/139 of the balance of the principal and interest in their individual account when they reach the age of 60.

China Pension Reform Targets Civil Servant Privileges

China's 40 million public sector employees are to lose their exemption from paying into the state pension system, as the government looks to curb public outrage over excess benefits for civil servants.

Chapter 7 China's Demographic Economics

China's dual-track urban pension system—in which corporate employees must contribute 8 percent of their salary to the pension system but government employees contribute nothing—has been a source of populist outrage for years. The State Council, China's cabinet, announced a long-awaited plan that will move to equalize the two systems.

The plan applies to 8 million civil servants, who work directly for government agencies, as well as an additional 32 million employees of public institutions, including teachers, doctors and state researchers.

Employees will contribute 8 percent of their salary to the retirement insurance fund, while employers will contribute 20 percent. Before the reform there was no dedicated revenue source for public sector pensions, with the government simply paying retiree benefits out of general fiscal revenue.

While addressing concerns over fairness, the pension reform may do little to address the looming pension shortfall caused by China's ageing population.

The number of people aged 65 and over will rise from 132 million in 2015 to 331 million by 2050, while the number aged 15–64 will fall from 1 billion to 849 million, according to projections by the UN. That will cause the ratio of those aged 65 and over to those aged 15–64 to rise from 13 percent in 2015 to 39 percent by 2050.

Even with the current low dependency ratio, many provinces run annual shortfalls that have been filled by raiding current workers' personal retirement accounts—which were intended as a pre-funding mechanism to pay future benefits—to pay benefits owed to current retirees.

In theory, requiring China's 40 million public sector employees to pay into the system will reduce the shortfall. But in practice, experts say the government will face pressure to raise public salaries to compensate for the newly required employee pension contributions.

Despite low salaries, the civil service remains a popular career choice for young Chinese. Among graduates, 38 percent said they would prefer to work for the government, compared with 32 percent for private companies and 23 percent for a state-owned company, according to a survey last year by Hongwei Occupational Consulting. About 900,000 people sat for the civil service examination in 2014.

Text ❸

China: House-for-Pension Scheme vs. Tradition

China's government has come up with a novel idea to tackle the problem of an ageing population: It will try to persuade the elderly to pledge their homes for their pensions. Given currently high property prices, it sounds innovative and makes sense. But there's a big chance it won't be well received.

The State Council proposed running a pilot house-for-pension scheme, or reverse mortgage, in a recent document on pension service reform.

It noted that China was turning into an ageing society: The population of those aged 60 or more was 194 million at the end of 2012; it will reach 243 million in 2020 and 300 million in 2025.

Under the proposed scheme, elderly property-owners would pledge their homes to a bank or insurance company, and receive fixed monthly payments depending on the market value of the property and the applicant's life expectancy.

This type of product is not unknown in the west, where remortgaging properties is common. But it runs diametrically against the Chinese tradition of rearing children to help look after you in your old age, and then leaving the real estate to the children.

The proposal caused an outcry on the Internet. One unidentified netizen provided some number crunching:

You can receive around RMB3,700 ($605) monthly pension if you deed your flat with a value of RMB1 million for ten years; but you need to pay a mortgage of more than RMB10,000 for the same flat when you buy it in the first place.

But the argument is really about the willingness of China's parents to break the long tradition of relying on their children to help in their old age.

A survey published by the Shanghai team of the National Bureau of Statistics said 87.5 percent of respondents supported the tradition. The survey interviewed 2,248 residents aged 60 to 79 who have lived in Shanghai for more than a year. Surprisingly, 70 percent were open to the house-for-pension scheme; only 27 percent were firmly against the idea.

Chapter 7 China's Demographic Economics

Text 4

5 Things to Know About China's New Aged Care Law

Parents in China can now sue their grown children for both financial and emotional support.

The changes in the law in China reflect an increasingly urgent dilemma across the world: As populations age faster than ever before, families and governments are struggling to decide who will protect and provide for the old. Too often, the answer is nobody.

Here are five things to know about the situation in China, where filial piety, or respect for one's parents, was once a given:

Honor Thy Father and Mother—It's the Law

A handful of countries, such as China, India, France and Ukraine, require adult children to financially support their parents. Similar laws are in place in 29 U.S. states, Puerto Rico and most of Canada, but they are rarely enforced because government aid helps support the old. In Singapore, adult children who do not give their parents an allowance can face six months in jail.

Honey, so Nice That You Came

More than 1,000 parents in China have sued their children for financial support over the last 15 years. But the law now goes further to require that adult children regularly visit their parents. Employers are required to give workers time off to do so, although that provision may be hard to enforce.

Going Gray Before Getting Rich

China is not yet wealthy enough to keep up with its rapidly ageing population. It is projected to have 636 million people over age 50 by 2050, or nearly 49 percent of the population—up from 25 percent in 2010. Although a recent expansion of the medical system covers most Chinese, reimbursement rates remain low and out-of-pocket costs high. Many rural families cannot afford hospitals' huge up-front deposits.

The First Among 100 Virtues

A Chinese proverb calls filial piety, or respect for one's parents, "the first among 100 virtues". The ancient philosopher Confucius credited it as the bedrock of social harmony, and a popular song urges grown children to visit their parents often. Communities hold "best children" contests, and people compete for cash prizes. One county even made filial piety a condition for the promotion of local officials. And generations of Chinese have read the classic morality guide, "The Twenty-Four Filial Exemplars", where sons strangle tigers, let mosquitoes feast on their blood and proudly scrub bedpans for the sake of their parents.

At Home or away

Nursing homes are not an option for most Chinese. The few nursing homes in China supply only 22 beds for every 1,000 seniors, and most are too expensive for the average family. Even children who can afford nursing homes fear sending their parents away will mark them as unfilial.

Reading Tasks

❶ Summary writing

Complete the following summary of Text 1 in Chinese.

20 世纪 80 年代以前中国养老保险金体制

20 世纪 80 年代以前：＿＿＿＿＿＿＿＿＿＿＿＿＿＿
种类：＿＿＿＿＿＿＿＿＿＿＿＿＿＿＿＿＿＿＿＿＿
覆盖范围：＿＿＿＿＿＿＿＿＿＿＿＿＿＿＿＿＿＿＿
参与意愿：＿＿＿＿＿＿＿＿＿＿＿＿＿＿＿＿＿＿＿
缴纳标准：＿＿＿＿＿＿＿＿＿＿＿＿＿＿＿＿＿＿＿
资金来源：＿＿＿＿＿＿＿＿＿＿＿＿＿＿＿＿＿＿＿
获取养老金资格：＿＿＿＿＿＿＿＿＿＿＿＿＿＿＿＿
获取金额：＿＿＿＿＿＿＿＿＿＿＿＿＿＿＿＿＿＿＿

Chapter 7 China's Demographic Economics

II Reading Comprehension

Briefly answer the following questions about the two texts in English.

1) What is the difference between (pay-as-you-go) social pooling element and (funded) individual accounts in pension payment?
2) Will the amount of your pension influence your career choice? What do you believe are the most important factors in choosing a job? What are the most common terms for different types of employee compensation?
3) What is the reform of China's pension system? Use your own words to elaborate the point.
4) Do you support such reform on pension? And why?

III Research and Discussion

Search the Internet for answers to the following questions and share your findings in class.

1) Based on what you find from Internet resources and this passage, what are the benefits and drawbacks of "reverse mortgage"?
2) What are other ways proposed in China to help support the old in addition to pension reform and reverse mortgage? List your findings and their associated benefits and drawbacks in bilingual terms.

IV Language Exercises

Replace the expressions in bold in the following sentences/paragraphs without changing their meanings.

1) China's government has come up with a novel idea to tackle the problem of an ageing population: It will try to persuade the elderly to **pledge their homes for their pensions**.
2) The State Council proposed **running a pilot house-for-pension scheme**, or reverse mortgage, in a recent document on pension service reform.

3) **Under the proposed scheme**, elderly property-owners would pledge their homes to a bank or insurance company, and receive fixed monthly payments depending on the market value of the property and the applicant's **life expectancy**.

4) This type of product is not unknown in the west, where **remortgaging properties** is common. But it **runs diametrically against** the Chinese tradition of rearing children to help look after you in your old age, and then leaving the real estate to the children.

5) The proposal caused **an outcry** on the internet. One unidentified netizen provided some **number crunching**...

ⓥ Translation

1. Translate the following sentences/paragraphs into Chinese.

1) The urban workers' basic pension is a two-tier pillar consisting of a (pay-as-you-go) social pooling element and (funded) individual accounts. Companies contribute 20% of their total wage bill to the social pool, while workers contribute 8% of their wages to their individual accounts.

2) The income replacement rate is supposed to be 40%–50%.

3) China's 40 million public sector employees are to lose their exemption from paying into the state pension system, as the government looks to curb public outrage over excess benefits for civil servants.

4) The State Council, China's cabinet, announced a long-awaited plan that will move to equalize the two systems.

5) Before the reform there was no dedicated revenue source for public sector pensions, with the government simply paying retiree benefits out of general fiscal revenue.

6) Even with the current low dependency ratio, many provinces run annual shortfalls that have been filled by raiding current workers' personal retirement accounts—which were intended as a pre-funding mechanism to pay future benefits—to pay benefits owed to current retirees.

Chapter 7 China's Demographic Economics

7) In theory, requiring China's 40m public sector employees to pay into the system will reduce the shortfall. But in practice, experts say the government will face pressure to raise public salaries to compensate for the newly required employee pension contributions.

8) China: House-for-Pension Scheme vs Tradition.

9) You can receive around RMB3,700 ($605) monthly pension if you deed your flat with a value of RMB1 million for ten years; but you need to pay a mortgage of more than RMB10,000 for the same flat when you buy it in the first place.

10) Here are five things to know about the situation in China, where filial piety, or respect for one's parents, was once a given....

2. Translate the following paragraphs into English.

孝顺是中国社会最受珍视的传统美德。2013年7月1日，中国政府颁布了《中华人民共和国老年人权益保障法》，旨在强制成年子女看望年迈的父母。该法规定了子女的责任和关注"老年人精神需求"的义务。该法称，子女应该"经常"探视父母，并定期问候他们。用人单位应当给员工提供足够的探亲假，使他们有时间探望父母。

与其他工业化国家一样，时至今日，很多上了年纪的中国父母都抱怨见到子女的时间太少。子女们则表示，日常生活的压力，尤其是那些迅速扩张的城市带来的压力，使得他们根本抽不出探望父母的时间。

中国社会经济飞速发展，很多年轻人从农村搬出来到城市和城镇居住。这是城镇化的过程中的一个问题。老人的物质需求可以通过完善社会保障体系来解决，而精神需求就需要增加这条法律条文进行保障。

Ⅵ Survey

Conduct a survey on the following questions on campus and report your findings in class.

1) Talk to your parents about their plans for retired life.
2) Are you willing to financially support both your parents and in-laws when they are too old to do so themselves?

3) How do you plan to support yourself in old age? Do you want to live with your children or in a nursing home?

4) What role should China's government play to improve the wellbeing of old people? Is law-making a good step forward? Or should we push for more stringent punishment for those who don't honor their filial piety?

5) What safeguards should be taken to ensure the family leave won't be abused?

Part 3 Maternity Tourism

Read the following English text and carry out your reading tasks as directed.

Birth Tourists: Going for the 14th Amendment

Li lives in a boarding house in the affluent California city of Arcadia, about 13 miles northeast of downtown Los Angeles. She isn't alone. The other 29 units in her housing complex are either occupied or booked, all by Chinese women who are pregnant.

Like Li, who declined to disclose her real name, they are in the U.S. to get instant U.S. citizenship under the 14th Amendment to the U.S. Constitution for their newborns and to get around China's restrictive one-child policy, which doesn't bar having another child abroad.

Though there are no official statistics on how many women come to the U.S. to give birth, so-called maternity or birth tourism is legal as long as the woman has a valid tourist

Chapter 7 China's Demographic Economics

or business visa.

Birth tourism has been taking place for years in many major U.S. cities, and because of its proximity to Asia, it has become especially widespread in Southern California with the Los Angeles area as the epicenter. Last week, Los Angeles County inspectors cited 16 boarding-house owners for illegally operating them in residential zones and said they'll ultimately be shut down.

A two to three-month stay at one of the houses in the Los Angeles area can range from $12,000 to $50,000, which includes lodging, meals, transportation, prenatal and nursery care and assistance in documentation preparation after the child is born.

A deluxe package—with around-the-clock, one-on-one nursery services for the newborn, a personal beauty and fitness consultant, and seasonal dishes prepared by star chefs—can cost as much as $80,000.

"The word-of-mouth of my old clients brings me new customers, mainly from Beijing and Shanghai," said a Chinese woman who runs the boarding house where Li is staying until she gives birth in June, and who declined to give her name. "You know, people there are rich these days."

She said that this year only 30 percent of her clients are here for their first child. "The rest are for the second or even the third," she said, adding all her clients come from the Chinese mainland.

The increase in maternity tourism by Chinese stems in part from the U.S. government relaxing visa rules for the Chinese in June 2008, as well as Chinese being wealthy enough to pay the cost. By issuing more tourist visas, the U.S. was hopeful that deep-pocketed Chinese tourists could help revitalize the then sluggish economy.

"All of a sudden, some shrewd Chinese expectant parents figured out that they can benefit from this [U.S.] policy change," said Zhang Yong, an immigration attorney at a San Francisco-based law firm. "By manipulating contraception and pregnancy, and arranging travel plans accordingly, they can have their child born in the U.S. and take advantage of the automatic citizenship."

When Amy decided five years ago to travel to California from China on a tourist visa in her third trimester and give birth to her son Dylon, she believed the boy would later be grateful for her thoughtfulness.

"He will sooner or later recognize the value and weight of his U.S. birth certificate," said the 39-year-old manager for one of the nation's key players in the telecommunication industry.

Amy, who also declined to disclose her real name, said she paid approximately $30,000 for her child-bearing trip to the U.S., which she called the "best investment" she has ever made.

Amy remembered vividly being admitted to the labor and delivery unit at the Ronald Reagan UCLA Medical Center, on Dec 20, 2008. With Christmas a few days away, she said festive carols and decorations everywhere helped minimize her homesickness and loneliness and soothe the pain around her pelvic area.

Prior to the hospital, she lived in a single-family house that had been converted to a boarding home, sharing the two-story, 3,000-square-foot building with eight other pregnant women and three staff members for two months.

"I was all on my own," Amy said. "My husband wouldn't join me until my postpartum. Late pregnancy symptoms and the intense environment around (in the boarding home) were nothing but taxing. It all became worthy when I heard Dylon's first cry. I told myself from now on I am the mom of an American citizen."

Amy referred to provisions of the 14th Amendment, which ensures that "all persons born in the United States" are automatically granted citizenship and "full and equal benefit of all laws".

Foreign mothers giving birth on U.S. soil also generate a population of "anchor babies". As U.S. citizens, when the children become 21 they are eligible to sponsor their parents and relatives for legal immigration, functioning as the U.S. "anchor" for their extended immigrant family.

U.S. citizenship offers a wide range of government benefits and assistance programs, including social security, medicare, free public education and possible merit-based loans and grants for college and hassle-free tourism access to 186 countries.

In contrast, there is strong competition for a job and career development in the world's most populous nation. Although China is second to the U.S. in terms of economic strength, recent college graduates make a monthly salary of $450, according to a 2012 report by the

Chapter 7   China's Demographic Economics

China Data Center at Tsinghua University.

"I want my son to live an easy and happy life," said Amy, adding she doubts that would be possible in China. "I hope the U.S. citizenship can provide him another option."

It takes about eight to 10 years on average for a legal immigrant to obtain U.S. citizenship. "If something unpredictable happens, such as the gloomy economy or missing documentation, the waiting period could be longer," said Lu Ren, a New York-based immigration attorney, who said 70 percent of his clients are of Chinese origin. "So, the U.S.-born children are really on a fast track regarding the acquisition of their citizenships," he added.

In an online survey conducted in April by Tencent, China's largest Internet service provider, 69 percent of 101,529 respondents answered "Yes" to the question of "Will you choose to give birth in the U.S. if opportunity allows?"

Li and her husband, both senior engineers with a power company in Xi'an, Shaanxi province, said they have long dreamed of having another child to keep their 7-year-old daughter company. They intentionally dodge discussing having another child in public "just in case the rumors will backfire and be heard by our boss," said Li, 37.

Violation of the policy, no matter in public service or private sectors, can lead to demotion, job termination of the person involved, and a monetary penalty that can be two to six times a family's annual income.

"The fiscal penalty (of having the second child) is not a problem, what we can't afford is losing our job, retirement pension and health insurance, the sense of security when we are getting older," said Li.

In the fall of 2012, she said to her husband, "Why don't we try to have an American baby?", noting that the one-child restriction doesn't apply to those who give birth outside of China.

Li said she managed to get pregnant and continued to work throughout her first and second trimesters, and asked for a sabbatical leave of six months to cover her coming to the U.S., giving birth and completing the newborn's citizenship documentation and then returning to China and her company.

Li said she can't wait to start her motherhood again in June. "My daughter and husband will fly into LA to welcome our new family member, a boy we will name Arcadia," she said.

In Arcadia, six to eight boarding houses have been closed in the past several months, and an additional 12 are under investigation. Last year the city created a task force of police, fire and business-licensing departments to investigate boarding houses, according to Jason Kruckeberg, the city's development-services director.

"In Arcadia, boarding houses that are not state licensed are not permitted in a residential zone," he said. "We do not have a land use designation for these uses in commercial zones either."

Maternity houses have grown beyond the scope of just a zoning issue, said Los Angeles County Supervisor Don Knabe. He said conditions inside some boarding houses put the safety of the mothers and babies at risk. For example, she said, owners usually remove adjoining structural walls to create more divided rooms, making it unsafe for occupancy based on the standard for dwelling units. "We must do what we can to protect them and stop this illegal activity," said Knabe.

Zoning and building-code violations led authorities in the Los Angeles County city of San Gabriel to close three townhouses that had been converted to maternity-boarding centers early this year.

Mayor David Gutierrez said that while he understood why some foreigners would choose to have their children born in the U.S., the future welfare of the children of foreigners shouldn't affect "services and quality of life that we provided for U.S. residents".

Maternity tourism in Southern California made headlines in October 2011 with reports by U.S. media, including the Los Angeles Times, CBS News, CNN and NBC News about residents in a quiet neighborhood of Chino Hills, a suburb of Los Angles, demonstrating outside a maternity hotel with posters that read "No Chino Hills, no anywhere". Authorities closed it in December 2012.

Birth tourism also has reached the U.S. Congress. Some lawmakers have attempted to introduce bills to penalize maternity-hotel owners, as well as ask for a reinterpretation of the U.S. Constitution.

Chapter 7 China's Demographic Economics

Steve King, an Iowa Republican in the House of Representatives, sponsored a bill that would limit automatic citizenship to people with at least one parent being a U.S. citizen, a legal permanent resident or serving in the military.

U.S. Representative Judy Chu, a California Democrat, said she isn't convinced that birth tourism is a big-enough issue to warrant a reinterpretation of the Constitution.

"The 14th Amendment is fundamental to the U.S. and too important to change because of the practice of a few," said Chu, the first Chinese American woman elected to Congress. "It would be a severe disservice to our nation if millions of immigrants are painted with the same brush."

In TV footage broadcast by CBS News in January 2012, a Chino Hills resident, Rossana Mitchell, said, "When people think of the American dream, they are not thinking about birth tourism. They are thinking about people who come here, immigrate here, work hard, pay their taxes, become citizens and become Americans."

In response to Mitchell's comment, a man named Ottom wrote on the CBS News website comment section: "Their babies most likely grow up with their parents in China, not using U.S. resources. U.S. has millions of illegal immigrants who are gaining undeserved sympathy; they are the big problem compared with the minimal scale of the so called birth tourism. The notion that these parents are abusing the 14th Amendment is absurd. It will take at least 21 years for these Chinese parents to obtain U.S. green cards."

That's exactly Dylon's case. He went to China with his mother when he was 1-month old and makes trips to the U.S. every two years to renew his entry permit to China, which is issued by the Chinese Consulate General in Los Angeles. He also must come to the U.S. every five years to renew his passport.

"During each of our U.S. stays, we spent heavily in buying luxury suitcases, outfits and accessories on top of lodging and dining out," said Amy, adding that her son is contributing to the U.S. economic recovery at a very young age.

Echoing Ottom's points, another person named Nova left his comment on the CBS website: "Having some child who is likely to come back at 18 to attend college and stay for a job, contributes to the U.S. economy and pays income and social taxes. What's the problem here?"

I Research and Discussion

Search the Internet for answers to the following questions and share your findings in class.

1) What is a green card? What are the benefits of a green card? How to become a green card holder?
2) What are the paths to American citizenship? What are the responsibilities and benefits conferred by American citizenship? What are the differences in civil rights between a green card holder and a U.S. citizen?
3) What is the 14th amendment of the U.S. constitution? What is its bearing with U.S. citizenship?
4) What are some of the changes in U.S. visa polices for Chinese applicants in recent years?

II Reading Comprehension

Briefly answer the following questions about the text in English.

1) What are the benefits of giving birth in the U.S.?
2) What are the steps you need to take in order to give birth in the U.S.?
3) How much do you have to pay and can you break down the expenses?
4) What are the penalties if you violate China's one-child policy?
5) How do the authorities in the Great Los Angeles area respond to the rise of China's maternity tourism?
6) How do the American lawmakers respond to the rise of China's maternity tourism?
7) How do the average Americans respond to the rise of China's maternity tourism according to the CBS video?

Chapter 7 China's Demographic Economics

III Language Exercises

Search the texts and the Internet for expressions as requested.
1) Search the text and the Internet for expressions associated with pregnancy.
2) Search the text and the Internet for expressions associated with diplomatic rankings.

IV Translation

Translate the following sentences/paragraphs into Chinese.
1) Birth tourism has been taking place for years in many major U.S. cities, and because of its proximity to Asia, it has become especially widespread in Southern California with the Los Angeles area as the epicenter.
2) With Christmas a few days away, she said festive carols and decorations everywhere helped minimize her homesickness and loneliness and soothe the pain around her pelvic area. Late pregnancy symptoms and the intense environment around were nothing but taxing. It all became worthy when I heard Dylon's first cry.
3) It would be a severe disservice to our nation if millions of immigrants are painted with the same brush.

V Survey

The following is a survey conducted by MSN on Chinese people's attitudes towards U. S. maternity tourism. Conduct a similar survey based on the following questions on campus and report your findings in class.
1) If time could go backward 20 years and conditions permitted, would you want to be born in the U.S. and why?
2) Do you want to give birth to your own child in U.S. in the future or in any other country/region other than China?
3) What do you think are the most appealing incentives to have the child born in the U.S.?

如果条件允许你是否会选择赴美生子？		
选项	比例	票数
会	82%	2 966
不会	18%	634

你认为30万元生个美国宝宝靠谱吗？		
选项	比例	票数
会	54%	1 935
不靠谱	46%	1 664

你觉得赴美产子最吸引你的是以下哪点？		
选项	比例	票数
出生就是美国公民	47%	1 679
孩子生存压力小	32%	1 156
成年后可为父母申请依亲移民	9%	130
其他	13%	457

4) What do you think are the most effective disincentives to have the child born in the U.S.?

Part 4 Controversial Assistant Reproductive Methods

Read the following two English texts and carry out your reading tasks as directed.

Text 1

Childless Chinese Turn to American Surrogates

Chinese couples who are unable to have children are turning to a surprising place for help these days: the United States. By hiring American surrogates, Chinese couples get

Chapter 7 China's Demographic Economics

around a ban on surrogacy in China. They also get around the country's birth limits. And in doing so, they guarantee their children something many wealthy Chinese want these days. That's a U.S. passport. NPR's Frank Langfitt has more.

Frank Langfitt, Byline: Tony Jiang and his wife, Cherry, live in Shanghai and couldn't have children naturally. First, they turned to underground hospitals in China for surrogacy. It didn't go well. Tony says one of the surrogates ran away.

Tony Jiang: It was almost Chinese New Year's break. She became so homesick, so she flied back home. My wife was just two or three days away from embryo transfer. That was really ridiculous and disappointing.

Langfitt: So, Tony got online and found a fertility clinic in Orange County, California. Three years and $275,000 later, Tony and Cherry have a son and two girls, which, had they all been born in China, would've broken the law. The couple now works for the clinic, connecting it with Chinese clients, the vast majority of whom, Tony says, suffer from infertility. Others clients have included homosexuals and those barred from having a second child. Tony's first clients were a couple, both Communist Party members, who worked at a government-owned firm.

Jiang: They already become leaders in their companies. How could leaders, you know, violate this kind of regulations? You could be easily laid off if somebody knew you already have two kids.

Langfitt: The wife had nearly died giving birth to their first son. The couple did have a second child through surrogacy, who, because he was born overseas, didn't violate Chinese law. Still, they're very cautious about appearances.

Jiang: Only their closest friends, relatives, know they have two boys. All their colleagues, leaders or their boss don't know.

Unidentified Woman: Passport.

Langfitt: Chinese women routinely fly to the U.S. to give birth, so their children can get an American passport and enjoy the benefits that come with it, including clean air and a U.S. education. Birth tourism is so common, and it provided the plot for a popular movie last year called "Finding Mr. Right".

(Soundbite of movie, "Finding Mr. Right")

Jason Benson: (As immigration officer) Why did you come to the U.S.?

Tang Wei: (As Jia Jia) Oh, to travel.

Amy Kaplan: My name is Amy Kaplan, and I'm the director of West Coast Surrogacy and West Coast Egg Donation.

Langfitt: Kaplan says Chinese surrogacy took off in recent years through word of mouth. Her clinic, which helped and now employs Tony Jiang, saw their first Chinese client in 2009.

Kaplan: And as I look at it now, those incoming clients are waiting for a surrogate. We currently have 47 percent from mainland China.

Langfitt: There are no hard numbers on Chinese surrogacies. But Kaplan figures, in California alone, there are perhaps several hundred right now. She says her firm only works with clients who can show a medical need for surrogacy, not those who just want a passport for their kid. Kaplan says perfectly healthy couples have forged medical records to try to meet the requirements.

Kaplan: The surrogates are putting their own health at risk for another person. And for immigration reasons, to me, that's just not—that's not ethical.

Mark: I know what is my dream, to have a baby. For my status, to have a baby is not easy.

Langfitt: This is a Shanghai businessman who gave his English name as Mark. His status is gay, which is still pretty taboo in China. So he went to U.S. to quietly start a family. Last year, he had a daughter, Yifan.

Mark: When I hold her, look at her, my heart was expanding. She looks exactly like my mirror image.

(Laughter)

Langfitt: Mark, who is 34, chose the U.S. because it gave Yifan a clear, legal identity, including a U.S. passport, which she can use to attend school there in the future. Like many Chinese at his age, Mark is disappointed with China's education system.

Mark: For Chinese school, you are not allowed to have a free talk. So you just sit there

Chapter 7 China's Demographic Economics

quietly, just passively receiving knowledge. But in U.S., it's different, be more innovative, creative and have a free spirit.

Langfitt: When Yifan reaches high school, Mark plans to move to U.S. and educate her there. Chinese parents often have specific concerns and novel demands of their American surrogates. At first, Tony Jiang did.

Jiang: I remember very clear about, you know, how panicked I was in the first 12 weeks.

Langfitt: When his surrogate, a woman in northern California named Amanda Krywokulsky, was carrying his first daughter, Tony was worried about radiation. Amanda remembers.

Amanda Krywokulsky: Once the pregnancy was confirmed, they had asked about me wearing a, like a lead apron kind of when I used the microwave, which I thought was kind of weird.

(Laughter)

Langfitt: Tony says some couples apply the principles of traditional Chinese medicine to pregnancy and childbirth, which clash with American behavior.

Jiang: I saw my surrogate when delivering. She was chewing ice, so that's quite weird. Most of my clients actually don't understand or don't suggest their surrogates to drink icy water during pregnancy because they believe these cold things could arouse miscarriage.

Langfitt: Some of Tony's clients even tried to have lifestyle provisions written into the surrogacy contracts.

Jiang: Don't eat seafood, don't drink ice water, limit activities in the first four weeks at least. And they say, I will pay you four months' salary last if you can bed to four weeks. People raise these kinds of ridiculous provisions. But finally, they understand the situation and they let it go.

Jennifer Garcia: My name is Jennifer Garcia. I'm a surrogacy case coordinator at Extraordinary Conceptions in Carlsbad, California.

Langfitt: Garcia says some Chinese clients don't just want American surrogates. They also want American eggs.

Garcia: They all say the same thing: tall, blond, blue-eyed and pretty.

Langfitt: She says they see an egg from a tall woman as a way to genetically trade up for stature.

Garcia: Because I know in the Asian culture, people are a little bit shorter. They just want really tall children and strong boys. And they're thinking that the Caucasian girl is stronger and taller, therefore, they'll have stronger, taller children.

Langfitt: Garcia and other clinicians expect Chinese demand for American surrogates to continue to grow even with the recent relaxation of China's population policy. There was a rush to conceive children earlier this year, the Year of the Horse, which according to the Chinese zodiac, is especially auspicious for boys.

Text 2

China Debates Egg-Freezing Ban for Single Women

Modern science has done a lot to help adults who were once unable to produce children. But a fertility research group notes that many countries have passed laws to limit use of that technology.

The group, the International Federation of Fertility Societies, has ties to the World Health Organization. It reported that in 2013, most Southeast Asian nations and many Islamic countries bar unmarried women from using the new technology to have children.

The People's Republic of China is among those governments that have banned single women from freezing their eggs for future use. This ban has led to a public debate in China. Those objecting the loudest are women who want reproductive rights. They want the right to decide on their own methods of family planning.

National Debate over Freezing Eggs

This debate heated up when a Chinese actress, Xu Jinglei, reported that she had gone to the United States two years ago to have nine of her eggs frozen.

Xu Jinglei, Chinese actress, froze her eggs in the United States because China bars that practice.

Chapter 7 China's Demographic Economics

Xu Jinglei is 41 years old. She said her eggs were frozen so that she could possibly have her own children in the future—in her words, to save herself "an option".

After news of her U.S. visit spread, China's state media reported comments of Chinese health and family planning officials. They said that freezing ones eggs is considered an assisted reproductive treatment. They noted that it and other reproductive treatments are illegal for single women in China.

The health commission's rule took effect in 2003. It denies this treatment to "single women and couples and who are not in line with the nation's population and family planning regulation".

Some Chinese have come out against the ban. The writer and race car driver Han Han expressed his protest on Weibo, a popular social media site. He asked why a woman can't have a baby without being married. "Can't she use her own eggs?" he asked.

His reaction was widely shared by others on social media. Some people said the ban is a sign of "gender inequality since men in China are allowed to donate sperm".

Sperm and Eggs Not Treated Equally

Already, the ban has created problems for a Los Angeles reproductive clinic. The center had planned to advertize its egg-freezing treatment on Alibaba's group-buying website, Juhuasuan.

Last month, the same website successfully connected seven sperm banks in China to more than 22,000 men who offered to serve as sperm donors. However, the site is taking a more careful policy toward women's egg-freezing programs.

Melanie Lee of Alibaba Group says, "A Los Angeles clinic approached us, and, yeah, we had initial discussions, but nothing came out of those discussions." She adds, "I think we have to look at the regulations that are currently in place to see what the regulations will allow."

Freezing Eggs Is a Practical Insurance Policy

A 26-year-old woman, who gave her name as C.C. Chen, is from Shaanxi Province. Ms. Chen says she would freeze her eggs if she had enough money for the treatment. She says it is a realistic and practical thing to do.

"Women these days face increased pressures from the society and work. They may suffer a greater chance of infertility when they get old. So, if we can freeze our eggs at a younger age, it will be very practical and a precautionary measure," she says.

Yaya Chen is a sociologist with the Shanghai Academy of Social Sciences. She agrees that freezing eggs is like a reproductive insurance policy, for both single and married women. She adds that China should use the reproductive treatment and others to help deal with a falling birth rate and ageing population.

She says, "I think restrictions should be fully relaxed to give single women rights to give birth either via assisted reproduction or by natural birth. Governments can provide some guidance but each woman should have absolute reproductive rights."

In late 2013, the Chinese government began to ease its "one-child policy". Now, Chinese couples are legally permitted to have two children when at least one parent is an only child.

But that has so far failed to increase the birth rate. At the same time, other people wishing to have babies will face punishment and their children will be barred of Chinese citizenship.

There are other reasons why Chinese health officials argue against the egg-freezing procedure. One reason is the survival rate of the eggs. Some officials say that less than 50 percent of the eggs survive the process. Also, the cost of freezing eggs can be high.

The health commission told VOA that "the egg-freezing procedure falls in the category of the assisted reproductive treatment and is currently under a clinical study phase, whose development the commission will closely follow to ensure its safety and effectiveness".

In other parts of the world doctors are less concerned about the survival rate of frozen eggs. Hsin-fu Chen is a gynecologist with National Taiwan University Hospital in Taipei. He has this to say about the survival rate.

"The [egg-freezing] technique is very mature, so, the survival rate after thawing could be as high as 90 to 95 percent."

Chapter 7 China's Demographic Economics

Reading Tasks

I Summary Writing

Complete the following summary of Text 2 in Chinese.

姓名	身份	观点
Han Han		
Melanie Lee		
C.C. Chen		
Hsin-fu Chen		

II Reading Comprehension

Briefly answer the following questions about the two texts in English.

1) How do the West and the East clash culturally in case of a surrogacy?
2) What are the health risks associated with surrogacy? What are the moral hazards associated with surrogacy?
3) What is the trigger of the debate on egg freezing ban in China?
4) Do you think it is a discrimination in China that sperm donation is allowed, yet egg freezing is banned?
5) What does the sentence "Freezing eggs is a practical insurance policy" mean?
6) What are the health risks associated with egg freezing? What are the moral hazards associated with egg freezing?
7) What are the reasons for Chinese health officials to argue against egg-freezing?

III Research and Discussion

Search the Internet for answers to the following questions and share your findings in class.

1) What are the major types of surrogacy?

2) Which countries in the world allow surrogacy? Which countries ban surrogacy and which countries ban only commercial surrogacy?

3) What stance do you take on surrogacy?

4) Should surrogacy be legalized in China? Take a stance and defend your position in class.

5) What stance do you take on egg-freezing?

6) Should egg-freezing be legalized in China? Take a stance and defend your position in class.

7) In addition to surrogacy and egg-freezing, what other assistant reproduction methods have you heard of? Are they all legalized in China?

Business Application

The following English text calculates how much it costs to raise a baby in Beijing several years ago. First have a read and calculate the expenses associated with your growing up. Then conduct a survey on how much it costs to raise a baby today.

The Cost of Raising a Child in Beijing

Now everybody says there is no happiness. Everyone is anxious, saying the pressure is high. In fact, the pressure is nothing more than two things, one is that the house is too expensive, the other is the child's education costs are too high. So how much money will it take to raise a child in China? Some estimate that raising a child until he graduated from college takes at least 500,000–1,300,000 yuan. If he studies abroad, at least 2 million yuan. At first-tier cities like Beijing, Shanghai and Guangzhou, people have to spend more money. So how much money will a family spend to raise a child in Beijing? let's calculate this in details.

1. **Pregnancy: 10, 500 yuan**

   Pregnancy examination, drugs, etc., cost about 1 500 yuan.

Chapter 7 China's Demographic Economics

Chicken, fruits and other nutritional supplements, etc., cost about 4,000 yuan.

Radiation-proof clothes and maternity dress cost about 2,000 yuan.

Beijing ordinary maternity hospital natural labour fee cost about 3,000 yuan. For caesarean birth, the cost ranges from 8,000 to 10,000 yuan.

2. 0–3 years: around 41,000 yuan

If the 0-to-1-year-old baby is not sick, milk and clothing cost about 1,500 yuan a month. If the baby does not drink milk, then cost about 1,000 yuan a month, and 12,000 yuan in the first year.

For the 1-to-3-year-old baby, a variety of early childhood materials and toys cost about 5,000 yuan. Life and clothing cost about 1,000 yuan a month. So together, about 29,000 yuan.

3. Kindergarten (pre-school) 3–6 years old: around 95,600 yuan

For better nursery, the sponsorship fee ranges from 20,000 to 60,000 or even more.

A normal nursery in Beijing costs at least 1,500 yuan a month, about 500 yuan for meal, and other incidental expenses of 100 yuan. In total at least 2,100 yuan a month, and 75,600 yuan for three years.

4. Primary school: 122,000 yuan

Although there is no tuition fee compulsory education, school-selecting fee and training fee together cost at least 50,000 yuan.

Then books, mobile phone and other things cost about 2,000 yuan a year, and 12,000 yuan for six years. Clothing and living expenses cost at least 1,000 yuan a month on average and 72,000 yuan for six years.

5. Junior school: 40,000 yuan

Like elementary school, middle school is also part of compulsory education, so free of tuition. Miscellaneous fees are also not high: public school fees cost about 500 yuan a semester and 3,000 yuan for three years. School's missed-lessons-making-up cost, Interest classes fees, meals are also not high, about 1,000 yuan a term, and 6,000 yuan for three years. However, the school tolls may cost much. Electronic dictionary,

MP3, computers, etc., will cost the family several thousand yuan for three years. So in total 15,000 in junior middle school.

But the same thing that cannot be ignored is that many people will choose better middle school, so this will also lead to a sponsorship fee of 50,000 to 100,000 yuan.

Food, clothing and travel costs are about 20,000 to 30,000 yuan for three years.

On the whole, for three years of junior high school, if there is no school-selecting fee, the total cost is 40,000 yuan; if you want to select school, about 80,000 to 150,000 yuan.

6. High school: 50,000 yuan

If the child is good at the test and admitted to a key school, then the general tuition fee each semester is only 1,200–1,500 yuan; if he chooses boarding, 2,000 yuan a semester. Miscellaneous fees are 5,000–6,000 yuan for three years.

If the child is not good at the test, and then study at a general public high school, tuition is 900 yuan each semester. However, if he is transferred to a better school, the tuition is about 3,000–4,500 yuan per semester, and a one-time school-selecting fee is about 10,000–20,000 yuan. Miscellaneous fees are about 30,000 yuan for three years.

If he chooses private high school, the tuition and other fees can come up to 150,000 yuan.

Meanwhile, the high school learning is more competitive, so students have to participate in various classes out of school, which costs several thousand or even more than 10,000 yuan.

High school students are interested in computers and other electronic products, and their demand is higher than junior high school students'. Even the family with the worst conditions also spends 5,000 or 6,000 yuan on computers and other items a year, and about 50,000 to 200,000 yuan for three years.

Chapter 7 China's Demographic Economics

7. University: 70,000 yuan

After graduating from high school, some people are admitted to the university.

Generally four-year tuition is about 20,000 yuan; miscellaneous fees and living expenses are 800–1,000 yuan a month. Plus school-home traffic fees and travel cost, all of these cost about 40,000 yuan and 60,000–70,000 yuan for four years.

Some parents' budget is relatively high, and the total cost can come up to 150,000 to 200,000 yuan.

The cost of postgraduate education and studying abroad depends on individual's situation. If the child wants to continue postgraduate studies, parents have to prepare 100,000 to 800, 000 yuan for the child.

Compare the two sets of figures and account for the reasons for such differences in English.

The Cost of Raising You Up 20 Years Ago	
Phase	Cost (Currency: yuan)
Pregnancy	
0–3 Years Old	
3–6 Years Old	
Primary School	
Junior School	
High School	
University	
Total	

The Cost of Raising a Child Up Today	
Phase	Cost (Currency: yuan)
Pregnancy	
0–3 Years Old	
3–6 Years Old	
Primary School	
Junior School	
High School	
University	
Total	

In my opinion, the gaps between the two sets of figures are caused by:

- _____
- _____
- _____

Chapter 8
RMB Exchange Rate

Overview

The RMB exchange rate has been a topic of mutual concern in Sino-U.S. relations. The U.S. has always put much pressure on China to raise its currency, and RMB indeed has risen a lot since the exchange rate reform was launched in 1994. Starting in 2014, RMB, however, gradually embarked on a downward trend and despite the fall in value, it still joined the IMF's currency basket in 2016. One can't help wondering: How is exchange rate determined? Will the newly elected U.S. President still make a fuss on the currency issue? What are the pros and cons of being a global currency? This chapter tracks the trends of RMB in recent years and hopefully provides some clues to the questions.

Pre-reading Activities

1. What are the pros and cons of a strong RMB?

2. What are the pros and cons of a weak RMB?

3. Watch the "Commercial *Currency Fight*" by CMS Forex and think about why a stable exchange rate is very important for a country.

4. What is exchange rate? What are the factors that can affect the exchange rate?

5. What is balance of payment? What are its two components? Specifically, how is exchange rate linked to the balance of payment?

6. Watch the Q&A session on RMB exchange rate during Chinese Premier Wen Jiabao's press meeting at the end of the closing meeting of the Third Session of the 11th National People's Congress.

Chapter 8 RMB Exchange Rate

Part 1 — U.S.' and China's Stance on RMB Valuation

Read the following two English texts and carry out your reading tasks as directed.

Text 1

U.S.' Stance on RMB Valuation

The following is the text of a letter by members of the U.S. Congress, urging action against China's currency policy, as posted on the Web-site of Rep. Mike Michaud (D-Maine).

Dear Secretary Geithner and Secretary Locke:

We write to express our serious concerns about China's continued manipulation of its currency. By pegging the renminbi (RMB) to the U.S. dollar at a fixed exchange rate, China unfairly subsidizes its exports and disadvantages foreign imports. As we work to promote a robust U.S. economic recovery, it is imperative that we address this paramount trade issue with all available resources. We urge your agencies to respond to China's currency manipulation with the actions outlined in this letter. Doing so will allow American companies and workers to compete fairly against their Chinese counterparts and will boost U.S. economic recovery and growth.

The impact of China's currency manipulation on the U.S. economy cannot be overstated. Maintaining its currency at a devalued exchange rate provides a subsidy to Chinese companies and unfairly disadvantages foreign competitors. U.S. exports to the country cannot compete with the low-priced Chinese equivalents, and domestic American producers are similarly disadvantaged in the face of subsidized Chinese imports. The devaluation of the RMB also exacerbates the already severe U.S-China trade deficit. Statistics show that between January 2000 and May 2009, China's share of the U.S. trade deficit for non-oil goods grew from 26% to 83%—an untenable pattern for American manufacturers. And finally, China's exchange-rate misalignment threatens the stability of the global financial system by contributing to rampant Chinese inflation and accumulation of foreign reserves. For these compelling reasons, we ask your agencies to pursue the course of action below.

First, we urge the Department of Commerce to apply the U.S. countervailing duty law in defense of American companies who have suffered as a result of the currency manipulation. The U.S. is permitted to respond to subsidized imports where the elements of a subsidy are met under the countervailing duty law. The countervailing duty law outlines a three-part test to identify the presence of a countervailable subsidy: 1) that it involves a financial contribution from the government; 2) that it confers a benefit; and 3) that is specific to an industry or a group of industries. China's exchange rate misalignment meets all three parts of this test and therefore merits the WTO-permitted application of countervailing duties.

Second, we ask the Department of Treasury to include China in its bi-annual agency report on currency manipulation. Since 1994 Treasury has not identified China as a country that manipulates its currency under the terms of the Omnibus Trade and Competitiveness Act of 1988 ("Trade Act of 1988"), but Secretary's Geithner testimony to the Senate acknowledging that fact surely justifies the inclusion of China in the report. After labeling the country as a currency manipulator, Treasury should enter into negotiations with China regarding its foreign exchange regime. These combined actions will signal the government's willingness to take decisive action against China's currency manipulation, including the potential filing of a formal complaint with the World Trade Organization.

The recommendations identified above must be done in concert with intense diplomatic efforts, not only with China but also with the IMF and multi-laterally with other countries. Through a combined strategy of legal action and international pressure, it is possible that China will revisit its undervaluation of the RMB. If these efforts are not successful, we ask the Administration to consider all the tools at its disposal, including the application of a tariff on Chinese imports, to respond to China's currency manipulation.

Chapter ❽ RMB Exchange Rate

The economic impact of the RMB undervaluation on American businesses and workers is too great for the Administration not to pursue a comprehensive effort.

This economic downturn has underscored the pressing need to promote policies that protect U.S. jobs and U.S. businesses. Addressing China's manipulation of its currency must be a critical part of our strategy to rebuild our economy and establish safeguards against future financial crises. The Administration has the legal ability and resources to protect American businesses in the face of China's RMB devaluation, and we urge you to exercise this authority expeditiously.

Thank you for your consideration of this letter. We look forward to your response.

March 15, 2010

Text ❷

China's Stance on RMB Valuation

Chinese Premier Wen Jiabao met the press at the end of the closing meeting of the Third Session of the 11th National People's Congress (NPC), China's top legislature, in Beijing on Sunday morning of 2009.

The following is an excerpt of the transcript of the press meeting's Q&A session on RMB exchange rate.

Good morning, Premier Wen, I'm Jeff Dial from the *Financial Times*. I'd like to ask a question about Chinese currency policy. The economy is now growing very strongly in China, you recover very quickly, and inflation is now arising almost close to the 3% target you set for the year. So regardless of pressure and comments from other countries, isn't it now in China's interest to begin appreciating your currency? Thank you.

温家宝：第一，我认为人民币的币值没有低估。让我们看一组数据，去年我们统计了 37 个国家对中国的出口情况，其中有 16 个国家对中国的出口是增长的。就是先生所在的欧盟地区，出口总体下降 20.3%，但是对中国的出口只下降 15.3%。如果我举一个德国的例子，那就是去年德国对中国的出口多达 760 亿欧元，创历史最高。美国去年出口下降 17%，但是对中国的出口仅下降 2.2%。中国已经成为周边国家包括日本、韩国的出口市场，也成为欧美的出口市场。

第二，在国际金融危机爆发和蔓延期间，人民币汇率保持基本稳定对世界经济复苏作出了重要贡献。人民币汇率机制改革是从2005年7月开始的，到现在人民币的币值对美元升值21%，实际有效汇率升值16%。我这里特别强调指出，2008年7月到2009年2月，也就是世界经济极为困难的时期，人民币并没有贬值，而实际有效汇率升值14.5%。在这期间，2009年，我们的外贸出口下降了16%，但是进口只降低了11%，顺差减少了1020亿美元。人民币汇率在国际金融危机蔓延中基本稳定，对世界经济复苏起了促进作用。

第三，一国的汇率是由一国的经济决定的，汇率的变动也是由经济的综合情况来决定的。我们主张自由贸易，因为自由贸易不仅使经济像活水一样流动，而且给人们带来和谐与和平。

我们反对各国之间相互指责，甚至用强制的办法来迫使一国的汇率升值，因为这样做反而不利于人民币汇率的改革。

在贸易问题上，我们主张协商，通过平等协商总会找到互赢或者多赢的渠道。

第四，人民币将继续坚持以市场供求为目的（基础）、有管理的浮动汇率制度。我们将进一步推进人民币汇率形成机制的改革，保持人民币汇率在合理均衡水平上的基本稳定。

谢谢你。

Reading Tasks

❶ Reading Comprehension

Briefly answer the following questions about the two texts in English.

1) How is currency manipulation defined according to the letter in Text 1?
2) What are the impacts of the undervalued yuan in Text 1?
3) What are the recommended actions outlined in the letter in Text 1?
4) What are the three elements of a countervailable subsidy in Text 1?

Chapter **8** RMB Exchange Rate

5) What is the consequence by identifying China as a currency manipulator in Text 1?
6) What will be the final resort of the U.S. to China as suggested by the congressmen in Text 1?
7) What is line of logic of Premiere Wen regarding the RMB exchange rate change in Text 2?
8) Explain the meaning of "real" and "effective" in the term "real effective exchange rate" in Text 2.

II Research and Discussion

Search the Internet for answers to the following questions and share your findings in class.

1) What are common types of trade barriers in international trade?
2) What are the mandates of WTO and IMF? What are the differences between these two important organizations?
3) It is widely regarded that the WTO, IMF and World Bank are the trinity of the global financial institutions. What is the World Bank? What are its responsibilities?

III Translation

1. Provide the English equivalents to the following terms and expressions.

1) 人民币
2) 美元
3) 汇率政策
4) 汇率机制
5) 低估
6) 升值
7) 贬值
8) 中间价报
9) 突破关口
10) 汇率区间
11) 收支平衡
12) 经常账户（贸易）盈余
13) 外汇储备
14) 汇率失调
15) 操纵汇率
16) 反补贴关税

17) 保护主义　　　　　　　　18) 盯住美元
19) 不再盯住美元　　　　　　20) 名义汇率
21) 实际汇率　　　　　　　　22) 汇率缺乏弹性
23) 一次性升值　　　　　　　24) 渐进升值
25) "一篮子"货币　　　　　　26) 加权/剔除通货膨胀率
27) 向WTO申诉　　　　　　　28) 贸易争端
29) 有管理的、市场决定的浮动汇率

2. **The following is the verbatim translation provided by the interpreter Zhang Lu at the press conference. Read it and comment on her delivery based on criteria of accuracy, fluency and adequacy.**

　　英国《金融时报》记者：您好。我想问一个有关中国货币政策的问题。现在中国经济发展速度很快，中国经济迅速实现企稳回升，中国的通货膨胀也在上涨，几乎已经达到了您在《政府工作报告》中定下的今年通胀保持在3%左右的水平目标。不管外界给中国什么样的压力或者对中国的货币政策做出什么评论，我想问，让人民币升值难道不是符合中国自身利益的一件事吗？

　　First, I don't think the RMB has depreciated. Let's take a look at a set of figures here. We did a survey of exports of 37 countries in the world towards China last year, and 16 out of the 37 countries export more goods to China. Talking about Europe where this journalist comes from, on the whole, exports of European countries have decreased by 20.3%, yet its exports to China only fell by 15.3%. Last year, Germany's exports to China reached 76 billion euros, reaching a historical high. And last year, exports of the United States dropped by 17%, but its exports to China only declined by 2.2%. From this we can see that China has become an important export market for its neighboring countries, including Japan and ROK. It is also a major export market for European countries and the United States.

　　Second, since the outbreak of the international financial crisis, we have made strong efforts to keep RMB exchange rate at a stable level. This has played an important role in facilitating the recovery in the global economy. We have started to reform the RMB exchange rate regime from July 2005 and since then RMB has appreciated by 21% against the U.S. dollar. The real effective exchange rate of RMB rose by 16%. Here I would like

Chapter 8 RMB Exchange Rate

to point out that between July 2008 and February 2009, in the midst of raging international economic crisis, the RMB did not devalue, and actually the real effective exchange rate of RMB rose by 14.5%. In 2009, our exports dropped by 16%, but our imports only declined by 11%. And China's trade surplus declined by 102 billion U.S. dollars. The stable RMB exchange rate level in the midst of the international financial crisis has played an important role in promoting a recovery in the global economy.

Third, the exchange rate policy of a country is decided by this country's economic conditions. Any change in the exchange rate policy is responsive to the overall situation of the economy of that country. We call for a free trade because we are of the view that free trade will help keep the economy going and will also bring peace and harmony to the people.

We are opposed to the practice of engaging in mutual finger pointing among countries, or taking strong measures to force other countries to appreciate their currencies, because this kind of practice is not in the interest of the reform of RMB exchange rate regime.

On trade issues, we have always maintained that trade disputes should be resolved through consultations, and we believe that equal consultations will always lead to win-win or all-win solution.

Fourth, we will continue to implement a managed market-based and floating RMB exchange rate regime; we will continue to reform the RMB exchange regime and keep RMB exchange rate basically stable at an appropriate and balanced level.

Thank you!

Ⅳ Language Exercises

Replace the expressions in bold in the following sentences/paragraphs without changing their meanings.

1) The impact of China's currency manipulation on the U.S. economy **cannot be overstated**.

2) ...China's exchange-rate misalignment threatens the stability of the global financial system by contributing to **rampant Chinese inflation** and **accumulation of foreign reserves**.

3) For these **compelling reasons**, we ask your agencies to pursue **the course of action** below.

4) The U.S. is permitted to respond to subsidized imports **where the elements of a subsidy are met** under the countervailing duty law.

5) China's exchange rate misalignment meets all three parts of this test and therefore **merits** the WTO-permitted application of countervailing duties.

6) The recommendations identified above must be done **in concert with** intense diplomatic efforts, not only with China but also with the IMF and multi-laterally with other countries.

7) If these efforts are not successful, we ask the Administration to consider all the tools **at its disposal**, including the application of a tariff on Chinese imports, to respond to China's currency manipulation.

8) This economic downturn has **underscored the pressing need** to promote policies that protect U.S. jobs and U.S. businesses.

9) Here I would like to point out that between July 2008 and February 2009, **in the midst of raging international economic crisis**, the RMB did not devalue, actually the real effective exchange rate of RMB rose by 14.5%.

10) We are opposed to the practice of engaging in **mutual finger pointing** among countries, or taking strong measures to force other countries to appreciate their currencies, because this kind of practice is **not in the interest of** the reform of RMB exchange rate regime.

Chapter 8 RMB Exchange Rate

Part 2
The Fall of RMB's Value

Read the following two English texts and carry out your reading tasks as directed.

Text 1

U.S. Calls on China to Do More to Overhaul Exchange Rate Policy

Jack Lew, U.S. Treasury secretary, has called on Beijing to renew a pledge to overhaul its exchange rate policy in his first visit to the Chinese capital since the renminbi began to reverse its climb against the dollar in 2014.

The renminbi has weakened about 4 percent against the dollar since January, ending four years during which the currency appreciated almost 12 percent. The renminbi trades at RMB6.24 to the dollar, after flirting with the RMB6 level.

"It is important that China demonstrate a renewed commitment to move to a more market-determined exchange rate, which will help provide for more balanced domestic growth and global trade, while also moving to a more transparent exchange rate policy," Mr. Lew said on Tuesday in Beijing, where he met Li Keqiang, the Premier, and Zhou Xiaochuan, China's central bank governor.

The renminbi has appreciated about 30 percent since 2005, in an ascent that was carefully managed by the People's Bank of China. At the height of the global financial crisis, the central bank in effect re-pegged the Chinese currency at RMB6.8 to the dollar to relieve pressure on China's export sector, before allowing it to resume its climb in the middle of 2010.

While the PBOC widened the renminbi's daily "trading band" in March, increasing the amount the currency was allowed to rise or fall each day, Chinese authorities grew concerned that companies and traders saw it as a one-way bet that encouraged inflows of "hot money".

China's official reserves increased by $129 billion in the first quarter of this year, reaching a high of $3.95 trillion. Many analysts attributed the build-up in part to Beijing's purchase of dollars in an effort to curb the renminbi's rise, which Washington wants to continue as it seeks to reduce its chronic trade deficit with the world's second-largest economy.

In its semi-annual currency report released in April, the U.S. Treasury expressed "serious concerns" about the Chinese government's attempts to rein in the renminbi's appreciation although it stopped short of designating Beijing a "currency manipulator".

The renminbi's recent depreciation led Mr. Lew's agenda in his meetings with Chinese leaders. Mr. Lew had raised concerns over Beijing's intervention in its currency markets in a way that made clear the U.S. regarded recent movements as a policy of the Chinese government and not the result of market forces.

Mr. Lew previously visited Beijing in November. That trip coincided with a Communist party plenum in which the new leadership promised to let market forces play a "decisive role" in the economy.

"As China's economy continues to grow, it is important that China do so in a way that is fair, balanced and consistent with international trade rules," Mr. Lew said on Tuesday. "Market access and the exchange rate are top priorities for us. The challenge for China is going to be the follow-through."

Text ②

The Chinese Devaluation of the Yuan

Just over one week ago the People's Bank of China (PBOC) surprised markets with three consecutive devaluations of the yuan, knocking over 3% off its value. Since 2005, China's currency has appreciated 33% against the U.S. dollar and the first devaluation on August 11 marked the largest single drop in 20 years. While the move was unexpected and believed by many to be a desperate attempt by China to boost exports in support of an economy that is growing at its slowest rate in a quarter century, the PBOC claims that the devaluation is all part of its reforms to move towards a more market-oriented economy. The relative size of the devaluation appears to be in line with market fundamentals and thus, at least for now, the PBOC's claims can be believed.

Devaluation: Just the Result of Free-Market Reform Policies

China's president Xi Jinping has pledged the government's commitment to reforming China's economy in a more market-oriented direction ever since he first took office over two years ago. That and the fact that China is determined to be included in the IMF's special drawing rights (SDR) basket of reserve currencies make the POBC's claim that the devaluation was the result of measures taken to allow the market to have a more instrumental role in determining the yuan's value more believable.

The IMF re-evaluates the currency composition of its SDR basket every five years, the last time being in 2010. At that time the yuan was rejected on the basis that it was not "freely usable", but the devaluation, supported by the claim that it was done in the name of market-oriented reforms, is being welcomed by the IMF as it gets set to consider the yuan's inclusion. But despite this welcomed response, the IMF has stressed that China will still have to do more and be willing to progress towards a "freely floating exchange rate".

Devaluation Consistent with Market Fundamentals

While the drop in the value of the yuan was the largest in 20 years, the yuan is still stronger than it was only a year ago in trade-weighted terms. Over the past 20 years, the yuan has been appreciating relative to nearly every other major currency. This includes appreciation against the U.S. dollar. Essentially, China's policy has allowed the market to determine the direction of the yuan's movement while restricting the rate at which it appreciates. But, as China's economy has slowed significantly in the last number of years while the U.S. economy has done relatively better, a continued rise in the yuan's value no longer aligns with market fundamentals.

Understanding the market fundamentals allows one to see the small devaluation by the PBOC as a necessary adjustment rather than a beggar-thy-neighbor manipulation of the exchange-rate. While many American politicians may grumble, China is actually doing what the U.S. has prodded it to do for years—allow the market to determine the yuan's value. So long as there are no major declines in the yuan's value going forward it appears that the PBOC can be taken at its word.

The Bottom Line

Despite surprising markets and being critiqued for exchange-rate manipulation, China has a good reason for the recent devaluation of the yuan. With slower growth in China and a strengthening U.S. dollar, allowing the yuan to depreciate is in line with market fundamentals. Regardless of the fact that China's exports may get a boost from the depreciating yuan, the move is consistent with the Chinese government's commitment to letting the market play a greater role in determining economic outcomes.

Reading Comprehension

Briefly answer the following questions about the two texts in English.

1) According to Text 1, what is the agenda of Jack Lew, U.S. Treasury secretary during his visit to Beijing? Why is he still not satisfied with RMB's fall in value?

2) Describe in your own words the line of reasoning behind the sentence "If RMB kept on rising, companies and traders saw it as a one-way bet that encouraged inflows of 'hot money'" in Text 1.

3) Both texts mentioned changes of RMB at some important time-points. List them in the chronological order in Chinese.

4) According to Text 1, Mr. Lew's visit coincided with a Communist party plenum. Which communist party plenum does the text refer to? What is a communist party plenum and how often is it held?

Chapter 8 RMB Exchange Rate

5) What is the viewpoint presented in Text 2 about RMB's fall in value? Why does the text believe the fall is in line with market fundamentals?

Research and Discussion

Search the Internet for answers to the following questions and share your findings in class.

1) Who is Zhou Xiaochuan? What sort of track record does he have and what contribution does he make to China's financial liberalization?
2) How does a central bank control the monetary supply within a country?
3) How does a central bank influence its currency exchange rate in the international market?

Translation

Translate the following sentences/paragraphs in Chinese.

1) While the PBOC widened the Renminbi's daily "trading band" in March, increasing the amount the currency was allowed to rise or fall each day, Chinese authorities grew concerned that companies and traders saw it as a one-way bet that encouraged inflows of "hot money".
2) China's official reserves increased by $129 billion in the first quarter of this year, reaching a high of $3.95 trillion. Many analysts attributed the build-up in part to Beijing's purchase of dollars in an effort to curb the renminbi's rise, which Washington wants to continue as it seeks to reduce its chronic trade deficit with the world's second-largest economy.
3) The relative size of the devaluation appears to be in line with market fundamentals and thus, at least for now, the PBOC's claims can be believed.
4) Understanding the market fundamentals allows one to see the small devaluation by the PBOC as a necessary adjustment rather than a beggar-thy-neighbor manipulation of the exchange-rate.

Part 3 RMB's Addition to the IMF's Currency Basket

Read the following English text and carry out your reading tasks as directed.

IMF to Add China's Yuan to Its Official Basket of World Currencies

Steve Inskeep, Host: Currency in China does not look any different today, but it means something different than in the past. That's because the International Monetary Fund accepted China's renminbi as an official currency. It's alongside the British pound, the Japanese yen, the euro and the U.S. dollar. Let's bring in David Wessel. He is director of the Hutchins Center at the Brookings Institution and a contributor to *The Wall Street Journal*. David, good morning.

David Wessel: Good morning, Steve.

Inskeep: So what precisely did the IMF do?

Wessel: Well, the IMF keeps its books in an artificial currency called special drawing rights, which, as you said, has had four currencies for the last quarter century or more. And now there's a fifth—the Chinese renminbi. It doesn't have a lot of practical significance, but it has huge symbolic importance, a sign that China is really joining the big powers of the world economy. Let's listen to how Christine Lagarde, the Managing Director of the IMF, described the decision yesterday.

(Soundbite of archived recording)

Christine Lagarde: The addition is a recognition of the significant reforms which have been conducted, of the significant opening up of the Chinese economy, of the financial, more market-driven principles that are being used by the Chinese authorities going forward.

Inskeep: Wow, that sounds impressive, but I can imagine someone arguing with every single point that Lagarde makes there, David Wessel, saying that China's economy is more open, more transparent, that we know what China's doing with its currency. Is all of that

Chapter 8 RMB Exchange Rate

true?

Wessel: Well, I'm sure it was controversial. The rules say that a currency has to be issued by a country that plays a big role in world trade. There's no question China qualifies on that count. But the rules also say that the currency has to be freely usable. And, as my Brookings colleague Eswar Prasad put it, the IMF didn't break the rules, but it certainly bent them. And you know, China's so important now that they got the approval of at least the required 70 percent of the IMF voting shares for this change and had the blessing of the U.S. government, which is the IMF's largest shareholder, even though China's critics in Congress called on the IMF not to do this.

Inskeep: David, you mentioned that this change is symbolic, that the IMF gave its stamp of approval to this currency. But there's something that's a lot more practical that I want to ask about here, and that's currency that's actually used for global transactions. Right now it's the most common the dollar. If you're buying and selling oil, for example, you're going to do it in dollars no matter what country you're in. Is there a possibility that China's currency could gradually replace the dollar in many transactions around the world?

Wessel: Well, there's a possibility, a slim one I think. So as you know, once upon a time, the British pound was dominant. And then the U.S. dollar replaced it. And for the longer run, we may look back on this step—this symbolic step—as a big one towards elevating the Chinese renminbi. I think it's more likely it'll supplant the pound or the yen or the euro as the primary alternative to the U.S. dollar rather than replace the U.S. dollar. But that really depends on two things—one, whether China wants that and two, whether it's willing to take the steps necessary to accomplish that goal. Being a reserve currency is a mixed blessing. Your currency is a little stronger on the exchange markets. And you also have to be willing to have a much more open—China would have to continue to have a lot more financial liberalization, a lot more market forces in its economy if people were really going to feel confident to put lots of their money into the Chinese currency.

Inskeep: OK, David, thanks very much, as always.

Wessel: You're welcome.

Inskeep: Always a pleasure talking with you. David Wessel is director of the Hutchins Center on Fiscal and Monetary Policy at the Brookings Institution and is also a contributing correspondent to *The Wall Street Journal* and a regular guest right here on Morning Edition from NPR News.

Reading Tasks

❶ Research and Discussion

Search the Internet for answers to the following questions and share your findings in class.

1) What is special drawing right?
2) What is the role of the SDR?
3) How is SDR valued?
4) What are the criteria for a currency to be included in SDR?
5) What are the implications for RMB's inclusion in SDR?

❷ Language Exercises

Replace the expressions in bold in the following sentences/paragraphs without changing their meanings.

1) There's no question China qualifies **on that count**. But the rules also say that the currency has to be freely usable. And, as my Brookings colleague Eswar Prasad put it, the IMF didn't **break the rules**, but it certainly **bent them**.

2) David, you mentioned that this change is symbolic, that the IMF **gave its stamp of approval** to this currency.

3) China's so important now that they got the approval of at least the required 70 percent of the IMF voting shares for this change and **had the blessing of** the U.S. government, which is the IMF's largest shareholder, even though China's critics in Congress called on the IMF not to do this.

4) I think it's more likely it'll **supplant** the pound or the yen or the euro as the primary alternative to the U.S. dollar rather than replace the U.S. dollar.

5) Being a reserve currency is **a mixed blessing**. Your currency is a little stronger on the exchange markets.

Translation

Translate the following dialogue into English.

A: 今天一早打的来学校，刚好就听到广播里头在说"人民币入篮"之类的，你听说了吗？那是什么呀？

B: 哦，你说的是 IMF 于当地时间 11 月 30 日在美国把人民币纳入 SDR 货币篮子的事儿吧。

A: 什么是 SDR？麻烦帮忙解释一下。

B: IMF 是国际货币基金组织，里头有个特别提款权就叫作 SDR，也被称为货币篮子。

A: 似懂非懂啊，我还有好多问题迫不及待地想了解，这篮子里原来都有些什么？这 SDR 又是怎么来的？

B: 那我就来科普一下吧，SDR 货币篮子里原来有美元、欧元、英镑、日元这四种货币。它是在"二战"后的布雷顿森林体系出现危机后应运而生的新的货币体系。

A: 究竟 SDR 要做些什么？人民币纳入 SDR 就马上生效了吗？

B: 并不是，新的货币篮子正式生效得到 2016 年 10 月 1 日。届时人民币的权重将为 10.92%。SDR 是 IMF 成员国对可自由使用货币配额的潜在债权。通俗地说就是当 IMF 成员国没有钱的时候，可以用自己分到的份额先抵债。

A: 哦，意思是如果某人缺钱花了，可以先临时从家里借点儿垫着，救个急。那么国际货币基金组织宣布人民币纳入 SDR 意味着什么呢？

B: 首先当然意味着人民币成为一种新的储备货币了，中国将在未来世界经济活动中争取到更大的话语权。这是对中国一系列具有重大意义经济改革的认可，更是对中国政府未来遵守市场化规则的认可，具有很大的象征意义。

A: 难道人民币加入 SDR 仅仅只有象征意义吗？

B: 当然不是，从中国国内的情况来看，人民币加入 SDR 将推动国内金融改革，中国的资产价格将逐步跟国际接轨，资产泡沫问题将逐步得到解决。

A: 我最关心的是人民币加入 SDR 对普通中国老百姓的生活有什么影响，会带来什么好处。

B: 问得好，人民币加入 SDR，最大的好处当然是，以后中国人去国外旅游就可以直接使用人民币结算了。当然只是原则上如此，实际在其他主权国的货币使用情况，还是得由当地政策决定。

A: 哦，听起来不错，至少刷卡没问题，不用再购买外币还款了，出国旅行好像变得更省心，"说走就走"的旅行好像不再是梦想了。

B: 算是这样吧。其次，个人跨境投资会更便捷，到国外置业、去境外炒股都可以直接使用人民币。最后，企业进出口商品、跨境交易投资可采用人民币计价，降低了汇率风险和汇兑成本，为美元波动"牵肠挂肚"的日子将成为历史。

A: 这么说，难道完全没有弊端吗？人民币会因此贬值吗？

B: 也不能说是弊端，但确实有了更多的挑战。人民币成为国际储备货币之后，需要承担国际资本流动的责任，承担责任就意味着承担风险。贬值和升值都只是一时的波动。

A: 所谓能力越大，责任越大。看来政府当务之急就是要做好经济转型工作，实施好"一路一带"的战略。练好内功是以不变应万变的根本对策。

Part 4 President Trump's Stance on RMB

Read the following English text and carry out your reading tasks as directed.

Trump's China Stance Spurs Trade War Worries

At a Florida campaign stop in August, presidential candidate Donald Trump made

Chapter 8 RMB Exchange Rate

a promise for his first day in office: "I'm going to instruct my treasury secretary to label China a currency manipulator! The greatest in the world!"

Trump told supporters that China keeps its currency artificially low to flood the U.S. with cheap imports, putting Americans out of work.

But is it true?

"What is very important to note," says China-based economist Christopher Balding, "is that they're manipulating it the opposite of how President-elect Trump thinks they're manipulating it."

Trump's understanding of this issue, says Balding, is outdated. Years ago, China did, in fact, keep its currency artificially weak so that its exports remained cheap. But in the past couple of years, China's economy has suffered and wealthy Chinese are sending their money out of the country. Worried about inflation, China is now manipulating its currency to keep it artificially high.

If China allows its currency to float, as Trump wants, it wouldn't rise, says Moody's Analytics Chief Economist Mark Zandi. "It's likely to fall. In fact, right now it's falling—the market forces are pushing it down. So you may not get what you want."

And that would make Chinese exports even cheaper, which is what Trump was mad about in the first place.

One reason to label China a currency manipulator is that it'll provide legal and moral grounds to impose high tariffs on Chinese imports, another Trump campaign promise. Zandi and his colleagues at Moody's ran an economic model on what would happen if the U.S. imposed such tariffs on China.

"The Chinese economy would weaken," says Zandi. "And then, of course, the entire global economy would suffer because the U.S. economy is the largest on the planet, and China is the second largest. It's the kind of path we took back in the 1930s."

A year after the stock market crashed in 1929, President Herbert Hoover signed the Smoot-Hawley Act, which raised tariffs on thousands of imported goods. President Hoover's protectionist justification was similar to Trump's today.

In the end, the Smoot-Hawley Act was disastrous. Other nations retaliated with their own trade barriers, contributing to the severity of the Great Depression.

Zandi's economic modeling predicts that similar tariffs imposed on China's almost half-a-trillion dollars' worth of imports to the United States would spur a recession by 2018 that would last at least two years.

But not every economist agrees with this.

"The U.S. is in a very, very different position today—the opposite position than it was in 1930," says Michael Pettis, an economist at Peking University.

Pettis says that in 1930, the U.S. ran a large trade surplus with the rest of the world, much like China does today. But today, the U.S. runs a trade deficit with much of the world. Pettis says trade wars tend to hurt surplus countries like China much more severely than deficit countries like the U.S.

"If you intervene in trade, that's probably good for the U.S., certainly bad for China," Pettis says. Tariffs "reduce the ability of the surplus country to acquire foreign demand, and they also allow deficit countries to get more of their domestic demand".

Pettis says it would only likely be good for the U.S. economy in the short run, though, as inflation would be a likely result. What's clear, he says, is that a trade war would be disastrous for China because it would lead to either higher debt or tens of millions of lost jobs.

Pettis says the better path for sustained mutual growth is not tariffs, but something else Trump has already proposed: a gigantic investment in U.S. infrastructure. "If you build infrastructure, that's great for the U.S. and good for China," says Pettis.

It's good for the U.S. because it creates jobs, and good for China because it would continue to export goods to America without trade barriers. And if there's anything most economists agree on, it's that the world's two largest economies have become so co-dependent, that what's good for one is good for the other.

Chapter 8 RMB Exchange Rate

Reading Tasks

❶ Summary Writing

Complete the following summary of the text in Chinese.

> **If President-elect Donald Trump Labels China a Currency Manipulator and Imposes High Tariffs on Chinese Goods, What Will Happen?**
>
> Mark Zandi: _____
> Michael Pettis: _____
> Differences of the two experts: _____
> Common ground of the two experts: _____

❷ Reading Comprehension

Briefly answer the following questions about the text in English.

1) Trump accuses China of manipulating its currency to gain trade advantages. Does this NPR news report support or oppose his line of reasoning?
2) Why does President Trump target China's RMB on his campaign stops?
3) Is a trade war the best path for China and the U.S. to solve trade disputes?
4) Why is infrastructure the best path for sustained mutual growth for China and the U.S.?

❸ Language Exercises

1. **Replace the expressions in bold in the following sentences/paragraphs without changing their meanings.**

    1) Trump told supporters that China keeps its currency artificially low to **flood** the U.S. with cheap imports, putting Americans out of work.
    2) One reason to label China a currency manipulator is that it'll provide **legal**

255

and moral **grounds** to impose high tariffs on Chinese imports, another Trump campaign promise.

3) Other nations **retaliated with** their own trade barriers, contributing to the severity of the Great Depression.

4) ...the U.S. **ran a large trade surplus** with the rest of the world, much like China does today. But today, the U.S. **runs a trade deficit** with much of the world.

2. Search the Internet for videos on Trump lashing out on China and summarize as many relevant expressions as possible and share your findings in class.

Business Application

After you read the texts in this chapter, you probably have some basic idea of the influence of RMB exchange on international trade and how RMB has changed in value in the past decade. The following is an editorial. Provide an English translation using expressions you have learned in this Chapter.

　　自 2001 年加入世贸组织以来，中国承接了来自其他国家和地区的大量产业转移，迅速成为全球第一大出口国以及仅次于美国的第二大工业制造国。

　　但在西方国家，2007 年的次债风暴触发了世界金融危机，美国等西方工业国家因此而受到重创，大量金融机构因卷入金融衍生品交易而倒闭。一夜之间，流动性过剩变为流动性短缺，实体经济和消费等经济活动因"缺血"而陷入萧条，大量商人破产、工人失业。2009 年 10 月，失业率达到 10.2% 的高位，已经接近美国人所能容忍的底线。

　　美国的救市方法，一是向金融机构注入大量救命资金以恢复流动性；二是重振制造业，创造更多的出口和更多的就业机会以实现美国宏观经济的再平衡。前总统奥巴马曾誓言，要在五年内把美国的出口额翻一番。很

Chapter 8　RMB Exchange Rate

显然，要实现这一目标，剑锋必指外汇储备最多的中国。因为美国人认为人民币被人为操控压低价格，致使中国产品获得了对美国的不正当竞争优势，造成了美国的巨额贸易逆差和中国巨大的贸易盈余。因此，人民币必须大幅升值，这样才有利于美国减小逆差、降低失业率，从而摆脱当前的金融危机，最终达到实现经济再平衡的目标。此种声音经过美国主流媒体的热炒，大有泰山压顶之势。

人民币汇率问题显然已经成了中国一个两难抉择的问题。如果不升值就有可能被贴上"汇率操纵国"的标签，所有输美产品会被征收高额关税或者遭遇大量贸易壁垒，引发两国的贸易大战；如果大幅升值，所有出口企业都将因此而处于困境之中。

而实际上，中美两国的产品具有很大的互补性，至少在目前阶段还不是那种具备竞争性的"零和"游戏，因为中国的产品大多是中低端产品，美国现在已经不生产了，而美国的高科技产品却因诸多的限制无法进入中国。因此，人民币升值不会大幅减少美国的贸易逆差和失业率。但美国为什么要炒作人民币汇率问题呢？我想，这里面水很深，绝不仅仅是一个经济问题，应该还有更多深远的战略意图。

由于美国居高不下的失业率和中期选举的临近，美国政客炒作人民币话题无非是想找个替罪羊转移民众视线，赢得民心。但中美贸易战一旦开打，就绝不仅仅是一场商战，局限在经济领域；而是一场经济战争，涵盖了政治、经济、军事、文化等各个领域。假设中国的人民币升值了，美国不向中国进口，也会向印度、越南、孟加拉、巴西等国进口，单纯靠人民币升值来解决对华的贸易逆差是不可能的。美国当前的问题是要处理好自己的"双赤字"，加快结构调整，促进经济复苏和就业。另外，中国持有巨额美国国债，也可以算作美国利益的最大拥有者，打开贸易战引起中国抛售美元资产对谁都没有好处。当前中美贸易的主流一定是双方共赢的，中美贸易更多的是共同利益，谁也离不开谁。

Chapter 9
European Debt Crisis and Brexit
Overview

This chapter focuses on the European debt crisis and the Brexit. Starting around 2012, the European sovereign debt crisis, much like the black death in the 14th century, has quickly spread from Greece to other periphery countries in Europe and has showed no signs of abating ever since. Why were some Europe Union member countries afflicted with such a severe problem? How to contain the crisis? Fast forward to 2016, the U.K. voted to pull out of the European Union through a referendum. Why did Britons want a break from the E.U.? Is the debt crisis a factor? Hopefully you can find answers to these questions after you learn this chapter.

Pre-reading Activities

1. What is the European Union? How has the organization evolved? How many members are there in the European Union? What are the criteria of becoming an European Union member? How does the accession process work? What are the advantages and drawbacks of being an E.U. member?

2. What is the Schengen Agreement? How does it affect Chinese people? In what way is the current Syrian refugee crisis related with the Schengen agreement?

3. What is the eurozone? What are the differences between a Schengen area, eurozone and an E.U. member?

4. What are the major political institutions in the European Union? What are their respective mandates? And what are their differences?

5. What do the following terms refer to? And what are their differences? Provide their Chinese equivalents.

U.K.	Britain	British Isles
England	Scotland	Ireland
Northern Ireland	Republic of Ireland	
Common Wealth	British Overseas Territories	

6. How is the U.K.'s political system structured? What are major political parties in the U.K.? What are the differences in their attitude towards the E.U.?

7. Watch "A Brief Summary of the History of the E.U." by the *Economist*.

8. Watch "Why Brexit Happened—and What to Do Next?" delivered by Alexander Betts on TED.

Chapter **9** European Debt Crisis and Brexit

Part 1
European Debt Crisis Explained

Read the following two texts, one in English and one in Chinese, and carry out your reading tasks as directed.

Text 1

Greece's Debt Crisis
Possible Causes of Greece's Crisis

Greece's current economic problems have been caused by a mix of domestic and international factors. Domestically, high government spending, structural rigidities, tax evasion, and corruption have all contributed to Greece's accumulation of debt over the past decade. Internationally, the adoption of the euro and lax enforcement of E.U. rules aimed at limiting the accumulation of debt are also believed to have contributed to Greece's current crisis.

Domestic Factors

 High government spending and weak government revenues

Between 2001 and 2007, Greece's GDP grew at an average annual rate of 4.3%, compared to the eurozone average of 3.1%. High economic growth rates were driven primarily by increases in private consumption (largely fueled by easier access to credit) and public investment financed by the E.U. and the central government. Over the past six years, however, while central government expenditures increased by 87%, revenues grew by only 31%, leading to budget deficits well above the E.U.'s agreed-upon threshold of 3%. Observers also identify a large and inefficient public administration, costly pension and healthcare systems, tax evasion, and a general "absence of the will to maintain fiscal discipline" as major factors behind Greece's deficit.

According to the OECD, as of 2004, spending on public administration as a percentage of total public expenditure in Greece was higher than in any other OECD member, "with no evidence that the quantity or quality of the services are superior". This trend has continued. Greek government expenditures in 2009 accounted for 50% of GDP, with 75% of (non-interest) public spending going to wages and social benefits. Successive Greek governments have taken steps to modernize and consolidate the public administration. However, observers continue to cite overstaffing and poor productivity in the public sector as an impediment to improved economic performance. An ageing Greek population—the percentage of Greeks aged over 64 is expected to rise from 19% in 2007 to 32% in 2060—could place additional burdens on public spending and what is widely considered one of Europe's most generous pension systems. According to the OECD, Greece's "replacement rate of 70%–80% of wages (plus any benefits from supplementary schemes) is high, and entitlement to a full pension requires only 35 years of contributions, compared to 40 in many other countries". Absent reform, total Greek public pension payments are expected to increase from 11.5% of GDP in 2005 to 24% of GDP in 2050.

Weak revenue collection has also contributed to Greece's budget deficits. Many economists identify tax evasion and Greece's unrecorded economy as key factors behind the deficits. They argue that Greece must address these problems if it is to raise the revenues necessary to improve its fiscal position. Some studies have valued the informal economy in Greece at between 25%–30% of GDP.

Structural policies and declining international competitiveness

Greek industry is suffering from declining international competitiveness. Economists cite high relative wages and low productivity as a primary factor. According to one study, wages in Greece have increased at a 5% annual rate since the country adopted the euro, about double the average rate in the eurozone as a whole. Over the same period, Greek exports to its major trading partners grew at 3.8% per year, only half the rate of those countries' imports from other trading partners.

Some observers argue that for Greece to boost the competitiveness of its industries and reduce its current account deficit, it needs to increase its productivity, significantly cut

Chapter 9 European Debt Crisis and Brexit

wages, and increase savings. As discussed below, the Papandreou government has begun to curb public sector wages and hopes to increase Greek exports through investment in areas where the country has a comparative advantage. In the past, tourism and the shipping industry have been the Greek economy's strongest sectors.

International Factors

Increased access to capital at low interest rates

Greece's adoption of the euro as its national currency in 2001 is seen by some as a contributing factor in Greece's buildup of debt. With the currency bloc anchored by economic heavyweights Germany and France, and a common monetary policy conservatively managed by the ECB, investors have tended to view the reliability of euro member countries with a heightened degree of confidence. The perceptions of stability conferred by euro membership allowed Greece, as well as other eurozone members, to borrow at a more favorable interest rate than would likely have been the case outside the E.U., making it easier to finance the state budget and service existing debt. This benefit, however, may also have contributed to Greece's current debt problems: Observers argue that access to artificially cheap credit allowed Greece to accumulate high levels of debt. Critics assert that if the market had discouraged excess borrowing by making debt financing more expensive, Greece would have been forced to come to terms earlier with the need for austerity and reform.

Issues with E.U. rules enforcement

The lack of enforcement of the Stability and Growth Pact is also seen as a contributing factor to Greece's high level of debt. In 1997, E.U. members adopted the Stability and Growth Pact, an agreement to enhance the surveillance and enforcement of the public finance rules set out in the 1992 Maastricht Treaty's "convergence criteria" for EMU. The rules call for government budget deficits not to exceed 3% of GDP. The 1997 Stability and Growth Pact clarified and sped up the excessive deficit procedure to be applied to member states that surpassed the deficit limit.

The European Commission initiated an excessive deficit procedure against Greece in

2004 when Greece reported an upward revision of its 2003 budget deficit figure to 3.2% of GDP. Subsequent statistical revisions between 2004 and 2007 revealed that Greece had violated the 3% limit in every year since 2000, with its deficit topping out at 7.9% of GDP in 2004. The Commission also noted that Greece's debt had been above 100% of GDP before Greece joined the euro, and that the statistical revisions had pushed the debt number up as well. This points to a broader problem of a monetary union without a fiscal union.

Text 2

为何会爆发欧债危机

欧债危机是一个复杂的系统问题，涉及欧元、欧元区相互矛盾的货币政策与财政政策问题，以及欧盟内部各国发展不平衡等多种因素。

1999年欧元的正式启动对全球经济和欧元区内部均产生了巨大的影响，欧元成为仅次于美元的第二大结算货币和储备货币，削弱了美元在全球贸易结算体系和金融体制中的垄断力量。在某种意义上，欧元与美元是一种竞争关系，欧元区国家因此获得了与美国类似的廉价发行货币、发行债务的能力，这也为欧债危机的发生埋下了伏笔。

欧元的汇率一直呈现剧烈波动的态势。欧元汇率的高企大大削弱了欧洲（除德国外）制造业在全球的竞争力，但是欧元的长期升势却增强了欧元区对区外资金的吸引力，推动欧洲国家以金融服务业为代表的其他产业的蓬勃发展，掩盖了制造业整体衰落的趋势。与此同时，欧元的强购买力满足了欧元区国家高福利政策的需要，为这些国家提供了资金支持。但是，全球金融危机发生后，欧洲金融服务业进入了整体衰退周期，发生了冰岛国家破产等极端事件，打击了人们对欧洲非实体经济的信心，继而以希腊、葡萄牙、爱尔兰、西班牙等靠借债维持高福利的国家直接出现了主权债务危机，并引起了波及全球经济的欧债危机。

欧元区成员国发行和使用统一的货币——欧元，实施相对统一的货币政策、汇率和利率。但是，欧元区缺乏统一的财政政策，各国实施相对独立的税收政策，拥有独立的发债权力。对于任何一个经济体而言，货币政策和财政政策是调控经济的两个互补工具，而欧元区内的货币政策与财政政策的不协调，必将导致各国

Chapter 9　European Debt Crisis and Brexit

内部和整个欧元区的政策层面及整个经济实体的矛盾发展，这也是欧债危机爆发的重要原因之一。

欧盟内部各国之间发展的不平衡自始至终都存在。德国作为欧盟的核心国家，其制造业的竞争优势变得更加明显，形成了少数国家实体经济快速发展，而其他国家必须依靠以金融服务业为代表的虚拟经济的繁荣才能生存的局面，即德国输出商品、希腊等国输出债务的循环发展局面。当希腊发生主权债务危机之后，这些国家高负债经营的状态难以继续，欧元区国家也到了重构彼此关系的阶段，这种关系的重构过程将是一个痛苦而漫长的过程，这也解释了欧债危机到目前为止一直持续不断，甚至愈演愈烈的原因。

那么，欧债危机到底会产生哪些影响呢？

欧盟是全球第一大经济体，欧元区 17 个国家是欧盟内部最发达的部分，是欧盟的主要构成部分，所以欧债危机的发展趋势将直接影响到全球经济的走势。目前，全球经济正处于危机之后的恢复期，中国、巴西、印度等新兴国家是危机后表现最优异的国家，但也面临内外政策难以抉择的难题。欧债危机的解决需要全球各主要经济体的协同努力，否则欧债将会在更长的时间内困扰全球经济。

欧洲是全球最重要的进口市场之一，而欧债危机的爆发和欧元的贬值，大大削弱了欧元区国家乃至欧盟的购买能力，并会抑制日本、中国、美国等欧洲主要贸易伙伴的出口增长，其中，中国 2011 年的出口额已经低于去年同期对欧洲的出口额，东南沿海地区的出口型经济遭受了严重的冲击。欧洲进口市场的萎缩必将对全球经济的复苏带来负面影响。

任何事物均具有两面性，欧债危机虽然极大地打击了欧元区经济的近期走势，但伴随着欧元的贬值，对于欧元区的制造业而言，却是一个有利的因素。如果欧元长期贬值，这将增强欧元区国家出口产品的竞争力，有利于欧元区国家产业结构的调整、就业市场的恢复，以及欧元区国家的经济复苏。

目前，欧盟国家及国际货币基金组织正在采取措施救助以希腊为代表的欧债"重灾区"国家。例如，欧洲两大央行——欧洲央行与英国央行决定推出总规模约 1700 亿美元的新一轮宽松措施。同时，两大央行分别决定维持 1.5% 和 0.5% 的利率水平不变。欧洲各国官员还计划将欧洲金融稳定基金从 4400 亿欧元提高至 2 万亿欧元，以救助希腊、爱尔兰、葡萄牙、西班牙和意大利等危机国家。随着上述措施的实行,欧债危机的恶化态势将得到缓解。虽然上述国家面临削减赤字的短期阵痛,但是紧缩方案对于上述国家经济的长期健康发展是有利的。

总而言之,欧债危机将延缓全球经济的复苏,但伴随着救助方案的实施,相关政策的积极效应将在今后一段时间内逐渐显现,预计不会出现与2008年类似的第二次金融海啸。只是全球经济的复苏将经历一个相对漫长的过程,需要用耐心和痛苦的调整来赢得全球经济的真正回暖。当然,尽管已经达成共识,但如果欧盟及相关国家或组织的救助措施不够及时或有效,仍然不排除出现一次更严重的衰退的可能性。

❶ Reading Comprehension

Briefly answer the following questions about the two texts in English.

1) What do you know about Greece? What are the strong drivers of Greek economy? Why does the text believe Greece is marked by "structural rigidities"?

2) Based on the above two texts, explain in the most simple bilingual terms why Greece is suffering from a sovereign debt crisis.

3) What are the "convergence criteria" in the Maastricht Treaty? Are these criteria seriously implemented when new members were admitted into the E.U.?

❷ Translation

1. Provide the English/Chinese equivalents to the following terms and expressions.

1) 削减赤字
2) 紧缩方案
3) 欧元区
4) 救助基金
5) 主权债务危机
6) OECD
7) social benefits
8) structural rigidities
9) tax evasion
10) lax enforcement of E.U. rules
11) current account deficit
12) economic heavyweights

Chapter ⑨ European Debt Crisis and Brexit

13) shipping industry
14) monetary union
15) fiscal union
16) Maastricht Treaty
17) excess borrowing
18) budget deficits
19) service existing debt
20) excess borrowing

2. **Translate the following sentences/paragraphs into Chinese.**

1) Many economists identify tax evasion and Greece's unrecorded economy as key factors behind the deficits. They argue that Greece must address these problems if it is to raise the revenues necessary to improve its fiscal position.

2) With the currency bloc anchored by economic heavyweights Germany and France, and a common monetary policy conservatively managed by the ECB, investors have tended to view the reliability of euro member countries with a heightened degree of confidence.

3) The perceptions of stability conferred by euro membership allowed Greece, as well as other eurozone members, to borrow at a more favorable interest rate than would likely have been the case outside the E.U., making it easier to finance the state budget and service existing debt.

4) Over the same period, Greek exports to its major trading partners grew at 3.8% per year, only half the rate of those countries' imports from other trading partners.

Part ②
Debt Crisis in Greece

Read the following English text and carry out your reading tasks as directed.

Greek Debt Crisis and the PIIGS: Europe's Financial Swine Flu

With last year's swine flu scare already a distant memory, the risk of a new epidemic is spreading across Europe. This time the fears have to do not with the H1N1 virus, but with the debt contagion facing Europe's PIIGS: Portugal, Ireland, Italy, Greece and Spain. With each of these countries carrying high debt-to-GDP ratios, financial markets are growing increasingly skeptical that Greece's debt crisis will be successfully quarantined within its borders.

The last two weeks have seen downgrades in Greek, Portuguese, and Spanish bonds, tumbling stock markets, and flight from the euro to the safe haven of the dollar. All of this has occurred despite last Sunday's joint commitment by the IMF and E.U. to a $145 billion bailout package for Greece.

So why hasn't the bailout helped mollify market skittishness? And what will it take for Europe to convince financial markets that it has the situation under control?

The simple answer is that addressing Greece's problems does nothing to ease fears that other countries might also be carrying unsustainable debt loads. And so long as there are fears about these economies, markets will not be satisfied. But there's more to the story than just this. Europe could have signaled strength to financial markets when putting together the Greek rescue package. Instead, it gave them more reason to worry when it comes to the other PIIGS. Specifically, markets are looking for three things in a bailout, and on each criterion, the Greek package has not scored so well.

First, markets want to know that the financial resources provided in a rescue package are actually sufficient to truly solve the problem. On this count, there are already concerns that the amount of financial assistance for Athens is not enough, despite the IMF's insistence to the contrary. If markets feel that Greece will still be carrying an unsustainable debt load upon the expiration of the bailout, they have little reason to feel confident today. In short, markets view a half-hearted bailout as merely delaying the inevitable. Given the trouble the other PIIGS are in, investors wonder whether future rescues might face a similar shortfall, or even whether there will be enough resources to go around if more economies catch the bug.

Second, markets want to see resolve on the part of lending states and institutions. Here again, the Greek bailout does not earn high marks. It took months of contentious public debate among eurozone countries over whether the more fiscally sound members should

Chapter 9 European Debt Crisis and Brexit

toss Greece a life raft or teach it a lesson by letting it drown. From the beginning, the idea of bailing out another eurozone member for fiscal irresponsibility has been incredibly unpopular across Europe, but especially in Germany, the continent's largest economy and financial leader.

Of course, European finance ministers ultimately caved in last weekend, when they agreed on the terms of the rescue, but not before suggesting to financial markets that they have neither the resolve nor the political will to address multiple casualties. Markets clearly viewed the lengthy and messy process by which European leaders arrived at a coordinated response as a sign of weakness when it comes to other PIIGS.

Third, markets need to believe that the debtor state is committed to implementing the fiscal reforms necessary to get its financial house back in order. Greece has promised to slash its budget deficit, mainly through cutting public sector wages and pensions, but the past several days have seen increasingly riotous protests from the sectors directly hurt by these measures. The more volatile Greece's domestic situation becomes and the longer the process drags out, the more markets will suspect that Athens will not be able to follow through on its promises. If Greece backs out, the fundamental problems facing the economy will be left unsolved, and what little market confidence in its future health that currently exists will unravel. Even worse, the flow of rescue funds might be cut off if Germany and other lenders feel that Athens is reneging on the deal.

Given that the same kinds of conditions will be attached to any future PIIGS bailout, the scene playing out in Greece is suggestive of what may happen elsewhere. Indeed, recent protests in Spain and Portugal over budget cuts foreshadow more of the same.

What should Europe do now? First, eurozone lenders need to reassure markets that they will live up to the commitments they have already made to Greece. German Chancellor Angela Merkel has already taken the first step in this direction. Next, they need to unequivocally state that, should Athens live up to its end of the deal, the current package is by no means the final offer. They might even consider announcing that they are beginning private negotiations with Greece to determine the next wave of assistance. Hopefully, by showing a more united and firm commitment to markets on the Greek problem, Europe will signal that it is serious about solving this problem no matter where it spreads. Finally, they need to encourage other PIIGS to continue taking measures to rein in deficits, despite their unpopularity.

Unlike H1N1, there's no vaccine for Europe's financial swine flu. Markets are fickle things, and small concerns can mutate into major catastrophes. In the end, it largely comes down to communication. If Europe can effectively communicate that it has the requisite resources and resolve to address the PIIGS debt crisis, markets should respond positively. If not, the pandemic will spread.

Research and Discussion

Search the Internet for answers to the following questions and share your findings in class.

1) If left on its own, what will eventually happen to Greece and the euro?
2) What are the possible recourses for the Greek government to solve the debt crisis?
3) Will the money lent to Greece come with no strings attached? If the answer is no, then what could the conditions possibly be?
4) How will Greeks respond to these conditions?

Summary Writing

Complete the following summary of the text in Chinese.

作者认为希腊救助方案不理想，因为：
1. _____
2. _____
3. _____

Chapter 9 European Debt Crisis and Brexit

> 按照作者的观点，要彻底解决危机，欧盟应该：
> 1. _____
> 2. _____
> 3. _____

Language Exercises

1. **Replace the expressions in bold in the following sentences/paragraphs without changing their meanings.**

   1) The last two weeks have seen downgrades in Greek, Portuguese, and Spanish bonds, **tumbling** stock markets, and **flight** from the euro to **the safe haven** of the dollar.

   2) It took months of **contentious public debate** among eurozone countries over whether the more fiscally sound members should **toss Greece a life raft** or teach it a lesson by **letting it drown**.

   3) Third, markets need to believe that the debtor state is committed to implementing the fiscal reforms necessary to **get its financial house back in order**.

   4) If Greece **backs out**, the fundamental problems facing the economy will be left unsolved, and **what little** market confidence in its future health that currently exists will **unravel**.

   5) Indeed, recent protests in Spain and Portugal over budget cuts **foreshadow more of the same**.

2. **The author compares the debt crisis to a flu crisis. Observe the following analogies and make up new sentences using the same rhetorical device.**

   1) With last year's swine flu scare already a distant memory, the risk of a new epidemic is spreading across Europe.

   2) With each of these countries carrying high debt-to-GDP ratios, financial markets are growing increasingly skeptical that Greece's debt crisis will be successfully

271

quarantined within its borders.

3) Unlike H1N1, there's no vaccine for Europe's financial swine flu. Markets are fickle things, and small concerns can mutate into major catastrophes.

4) If not, the pandemic will spread.

Ⅳ Translation

1. Provide the Chinese equivalents to the following terms and expressions.

1) mollify market skittishness
2) rescue package
3) on each criterion
4) to the contrary
5) half-hearted bailout
6) delaying the inevitable
7) cave in
8) slash budget deficit
9) drag out
10) follow through on its promises
11) live up to its end of the deal

2. Translate the following text into Chinese.

One reason why the crisis has hit the eurozone before other regions is that its countries have renounced the money-printing and devaluation options by adopting a common currency.

When debt gets too high, a number of problems arise. First, a spiral is set off in which lower credit ratings for a country lead to higher borrowing costs, in turn increasing the deficit. Markets already seem unwilling to fund some countries at sustainable rates: By the time Greece turned to the IMF and its E.U. partners for help, its short-term bond yields were nearly 20%. RaminToloui of PIMCO, a fund-management group, explains the process this way: "When government debt reaches extreme levels, concerns about government creditworthiness become so severe that additional government spending produces increases in long-term interest rates that exacerbate, rather than ameliorate, the economic contraction."

Second, once a country is stuck in this debt trap, it has to bring in austerity programmes to reduce the deficit; but such austerity holds back economic growth because

Chapter 9 European Debt Crisis and Brexit

higher taxes and lower spending reduce demand. Like the Red Queen in Lewis Carroll's "Through the Looking-Glass", the country has to run as fast as it can just to stand still. Ireland has been the good boy of the sovereign-debt markets, taking quick action to reduce its deficit through measures such as cutting public-sector pay. But other countries may not be in a rush to emulate it: its nominal GDP has fallen by over 16%.

Third, larger government deficits imply greater government interference in the economy and thus a less efficient use of resources. One study found that each percentage-point increase in the share of GDP devoted to government spending reduced growth by 0.12%–0.13% a year.

An even bigger problem may be the unfunded liabilities that government faces from ageing populations. This is a double burden: Benefits for growing numbers of pensioners will have to be paid for by a shrinking band of workers.

For Greece, dodgy accounting disguised the size of its government debt. Its businesses remained uncompetitive, causing a large trade deficit. The economy is riddled with inefficiencies and restrictive practices. For example, cruise ships are not allowed to take on new passengers at Greek ports, and the number of lorry licences is still the same as in 1990 even though GDP has doubled. Such restrictive practices are keeping transport costs too high. According to Yannis Stournaras of IOBE, a think-tank, it is cheaper to transport goods to Athens from Italy than from Thebes, just 32 miles away.

Greece is an exemplar of the flaws in the European welfare model. The state gets remorselessly bigger because political parties of the right and left have bought votes by providing supporters with jobs or subsidies. Public-sector workers were mollycoddled with pay for 13 or 14 months per year and arcane allowances for things like firewood or carrying files between office floors.

Tax evasion is widespread. A report by the London School of Economics estimates that it reduced Greece's potential tax yield by 26%. It is normal to do deals under the table. On the birth of his baby daughter one parent was asked to hand over €2,500 in cash to the doctor, in exchange for a receipt for €1,500. The Greeks are attempting to tackle this issue. The austerity packages introduced over the past 12 months require higher earners to provide receipts for expenditure before they can qualify for their tax-free allowance.

Therefore, spiraling debt costs also forced the government to turn to the IMF as well as to its E.U. partners. But it remains to be seen whether the population will tolerate the austerity needed to bring the debt burden down to a reasonable level. The most recent package of cuts provoked a wave of strikes and riots in which three bank employees died.

3. **Translate the following dialogue into English.**

A: 奇怪，人家要借钱给他还不要，希腊人脑子烧坏了吗？

B: 你这人看新闻只看标题啊？借钱是有附带条件的，要减少政府开支，还要加重税赋。

A: 可是这要求合理啊，不就是因为政府假造财政数字、掩饰负债，才造成现在的情况吗？负债的人要还债，本来就应该撙节开支。

B: 看来你不是只看标题哦，你说的不错，但是你叫已经失业、生活贫穷、账户里取不出钱来的人民接受加税，可能吗？

A: 确实是有种雪上加霜的感觉，但是这才是面对债务的态度。

B: 说是这样说，难道是人民叫政府去举债乱花钱吗？你叫人民加税，那你有办法给他工作吗？

A: 只看眼前的话，当然会觉得这是个很冷血的条件，希腊政府大概也不愿意接受，所以才叫人民公投吧。

B: 现在看起来，要骂希腊，甚至骂其他被新闻媒体称为"欧猪五国"的国家好像很容易，但到底是什么让这些国家陷入这样的困境呢？

A: 不就是政府财政不透明、人民好吃懒做吗？

B: 我觉得事情没有这么黑白分明的。当然，希腊的财政体制不好，再加上政府隐匿公债数字、假造数据，使得金融海啸之后整个情况一发不可收拾。

A: 这都是事实啊。

B: 但是从另一方面想，要是没有信用评等单位，一下子把它的信用评等降那么多，要是它不在欧元区，可以自行调整币值，像冰岛那样，情况会有何不同呢？

A: 冰岛是另外一回事，冰岛倒闭的是银行，希腊是国家欠了太多的债。

B: 我要说的是，问题不会只是希腊单方面的，还有许多因素值得我们去发掘。

Chapter 9 European Debt Crisis and Brexit

Part 3
Brexit Explained

Read the following English text and carry out your reading tasks as directed.

Brexit Explained: What It Means and Why It Matters

What Is Brexit?

As a portmanteau of the words "Britain" and "exit", Brexit is the nickname for a British exit of the European Union after the June 23 referendum asking voters: "Should the United Kingdom remain a member of the European Union or leave the European Union?"

Who Can Vote?

British or Irish citizens who live in the U.K.

Commonwealth citizens who are residents of the U.K.

British citizens who live overseas but have been registered to vote in the U.K. in the last 15 years.

Irish citizens living overseas who were born in Northern Ireland and who have been registered to vote in Northern Ireland in the last 15 years.

Why Are Britons So Wary of Europe?

Spend enough time in the United Kingdom, and you will hear people refer to "the Continent". Travel agency windows advertize flights and package tours "to Europe", as if it were someplace else.

As Mr. Peterson of Stanford put it, "Britain has always kept Europe at a distance, even when they were favorable to the E.U."

Britain initially refused to join the European Economic Community when it was founded in 1957. It became a member in 1973, only to have a crisis of confidence that led to a similar exit referendum two years later. (The pro-Europe campaign won that round with 67 percent of the vote.)

275

A strain of populist opposition to Europe remained in the decades that followed. Britain has never joined other countries in using the euro as currency, for example, or participated in the union's Schengen Area open-borders agreement.

Why Do Some People Want to Leave the E.U.?

Since the economic meltdown of 2008, and the financial catastrophe in Greece, some Brits have become more skeptical about the benefits of remaining in the E.U., especially as the British economy has remained relatively strong.

Conservative MP Boris Johnson, a former mayor of London, has been the public face of the "leave" campaign.

Johnson says he rejects E.U. control over British policy, and believes that severing ties completely, as opposed to reform, is the only way to go.

"There is only one way to get the change we need, and that is to vote to go, because all E.U. history shows that they only really listen to a population when it says no. The fundamental problem remains that they have an ideal that we do not share. They want to create a truly federal union, a pluribus, when most british people do not," He wrote in the telegraph.

How Has Immigration Been a Factor in the Debate?

While some simply don't like the idea of giving the E.U. control over trade deals and foreign policy, others are scared that Britain's stronger economy makes it a magnet for low-wage European immigrants from hard-hit countries like Poland and Greece.

Some argue this strains not only the U.K. job market, but also its social services as well, like the National Health Service.

This is where the Brexit debate has turned ugly.

Nigel Farage, the leader of the right-wing U.K. Independence Party, released a poster in favour of leaving the E.U. that showed masses of dark-skinned men, presumably refugees, that read: "Breaking Point: The E.U. has failed us all. We must break free of the E.U. and take control of our borders."

Treasury secretary Harriett Baldwin called the poster "vile xenophobia," but its

Chapter 9 European Debt Crisis and Brexit

message enjoys some resonance. UKIP got 12. 6 percent of the vote in last year's election, and concerns about immigration factor heavily into pro-Brexit rhetoric.

Why Do Some People Want to Stay?

Those in favour of remaining think the benefits far outweigh the negatives. The E.U. is the world's largest economic free-trade zone, and British businesses save on import/export costs.

Prime Minister David Cameron, a noted opponent of Brexit, has warned that leaving would throw the economy into short-term turmoil and could undo the country's gains since the economic recession.

"After six years of sacrifice, when risks to our economy are still high, wouldn't the gravest risk be walking out of the biggest single market in the world?" He wrote in an editorial for *The Sun*.

Why Is the Referendum Being Held Now?

While Cameron is opposed to the leaving the E.U., he promised to redraft the terms of Britain's involvement and hold a referendum on the issue during his 2015 election campaign. At the time, this was seen as a way to appease voters who might have been swayed by far-right parties like UKIP.

In May, a new agreement between the E.U. and the U.K. was ratified. If Britain votes to remain in the E.U., it will go into force, and gives Britain more autonomy.

It also restricts some of the social welfare that E.U. immigrants can receive in Britain, and includes guarantees that Britain won't have to bail out other European countries, like Germany did with Greece.

What Will Happen to Britain If It Leaves?

Projections differ significantly over the precise economic effect, but there is a consensus that leaving would hurt Britain financially, at least in the short term.

Without access to the union's open markets, Britain would probably lose trade and investment. And while the influx of migrant workers has created anxiety over British culture and identity, losing that labor force could lead to lower productivity, slower economic growth and decreased job opportunities, a study by Britain's National Institute of Economic and Social Research found.

A Brexit could also quickly spawn or err a "Scexit". Nicola Sturgeon, the first minister of Scotland, has said that if Britain votes to leave the European Union, she will hold a new referendum in which Scots could vote to exit Britain—and then rejoin the union as an independent nation.

Scotland's voters rejected such a measure by nearly 10 points in 2014, but analysts say a Brexit could change that because the Scots overwhelmingly support European Union membership.

If Scotland were to leave, that could dramatically alter Britain's political character, as Scotland's members of Parliament lean to the left.

What Are the Wider Ramifications?

Britain makes up about a sixth of the European Union's economy. A Brexit, Mr. Klaas said, "would be akin to California and Florida being lopped off the U.S. economy".

That destabilization could affect the United States' economy: Last week, the Federal Reserve in Washington cited the possibility of a Brexit as a reason to not raise interest rates.

There could be political consequences, as well. If Britain leaves the union, that could give momentum to the nationalistic, anti-migrant message and policies of populist, far-right parties that are already rising across Europe.

The implications for the European project itself are unclear, but that uncertainty may be the greatest threat to the union, which has helped bring Europe 70 years of peace and is already under growing strain.

It also undermines trust between member states, whose commitments seem less reliable every time one of them toys with leaving.

"Members of the eurozone will realize that things can come unstuck," Mr. Grant said. "Entropy can happen."

In his view, Germany already has too much power in the bloc, and a British exit

Chapter 9 European Debt Crisis and Brexit

would make that imbalance more pronounced. It would undermine the European Union's legitimacy and make it more difficult to respond to internal crises, like the Greek economy or the migrant influx, and to outside security threats, he said.

Mr. Klaas said, "A more unified Europe is a powerful counterbalance to people like Vladimir Putin."

"Putin has stayed silent on this," he said of the Russian leader. "But he's probably silently cheering the pro-Brexit side."

Reading Tasks

❶ Reading Comprehension

Briefly answer the following questions about the text in English.
1) Who can vote in the referendum on the U.K. leaving the Europe Union?
2) What is the time-line in the U.K.'s efforts to break away from the European Union according to the text?
3) Do you think the European debt crisis is also a factor in the Brexit debate? Use the text and your background knowledge to support your points.
4) How will Russia respond to the results of the referendum?

❷ Summary Writing

Complete the following summary of the text in Chinese.

英国脱欧

参与公投的对象：_____   为何要举行公投：_____
英国与欧洲大陆的关系：_____   公投的核心问题：_____
退欧派主张：_____   留欧派主张：_____
脱欧短期影响：_____   脱欧长期影响：_____

279

Language Exercises

Replace the expressions in bold in the following sentences/paragraphs without changing their meanings.

1) Conservative MP Boris Johnson, a former mayor of London, has been **the public face** of the "leave" **campaign**.

2) Johnson says he rejects E.U. control over British policy, and believes that **severing ties** completely, as opposed to reform, is **the only way to go**.

3) ...others are scared that Britain's stronger economy makes it **a magnet for** low-wage European immigrants from hard-hit countries like Poland and Greece.

4) This is where the Brexit debate has **turned ugly**.

5) Some argue this **strains** not only the UK job market, but also its social services as well, such as the National Health Service

6) UKIP got 12.6 percent of the vote in last year's election, and concerns about immigration **factor** heavily into **pro-Brexit rhetoric**.

7) Prime Minister David Cameron, a noted opponent of Brexit, has warned that leaving would throw the economy into short-term **turmoil** and could **undo the country's gains** since the economic recession.

8) At the time, this was seen as a way to **appease** voters who might have been **swayed** by far-right parties such as UKIP.

9) A Brexit could also quickly **spawn** or err a "Scexit". Nicola Sturgeon, the first minister of Scotland, has said that if Britain votes to leave the European Union,...

10) It also **undermines trust** between member states, whose commitments seem less reliable every time one of them **toys with** leaving.

11) Britain makes up about a sixth of the European Union's economy. A Brexit, Mr. Klaas said, "would be akin to California and Florida being **lopped off** the U.S. economy".

12) "Members of the eurozone will realize that things can **come unstuck**," Mr. Grant said. "**Entropy** can happen."

Chapter 9 European Debt Crisis and Brexit

13) ...a British exit would make that imbalance more **pronounced**. It would undermine the European Union's **legitimacy** and make it more difficult to respond to internal crises, like the Greek economy or the migrant influx, and to outside security threats, he said.

Part 4
Aftermath of Brexit Referendum

Read the following English text and carry out your reading tasks as directed.

All You Need to Know after the U.K. Decides to Leave the E.U.
Why Is the Result of the Referendum?

A referendum—a vote in which everyone (or nearly everyone) of voting age can take part—was held on Thursday 23 June, 2016, to decide whether the U.K. should leave or remain in the European Union. Leave won by 51.9% to 48.1%. The referendum turnout was 71.8%, with more than 30 million people voting.

What Changed in Government after the Referendum?

Britain got a new Prime Minister—Theresa May. The former home secretary took over from David Cameron, who announced he was resigning on the day he lost the referendum. Like Mr. Cameron, Mrs. May was against Britain leaving the E.U. but she played only a very low-key role in the campaign and was never seen as much of an enthusiast for the E.U. She became PM without facing a full Conservative leadership contest after her key rivals from what had been the Leave side pulled out.

Where Does She Stand on Brexit?

Theresa May had been against Brexit during the referendum campaign but is now in favour of it because she says it is what the British people want. Her key message has been that "Brexit means Brexit" and she triggered the two year process of leaving the E.U. on 29

March. She set out her negotiating goals in a letter to the E.U. council president Donald Tusk.

Why Did She Call a General Election?

Theresa May became prime minister after David Cameron resigned, so had not won her own election. She ruled out calling a snap election when she moved into Downing Street, saying the country needed a period of stability after the upheaval of the Brexit vote. She said she was happy to wait until the next scheduled election in 2020.

But she surprised everyone after the Easter Bank Holiday by announcing that she had changed her mind with an election being called for Thursday, 8 June 2017.

The reason she gave was that she needed to strengthen her hand in Brexit negotiations with European leaders. She feared Labour, the SNP and other opposition parties—and members of the House of Lords—would try to block and frustrate her strategy, making the country look divided to other E.U. leaders and making her government look weak.

What Happened in the Election?

Mrs. May's gamble backfired and she lost her overall majority and ended up with fewer MPs than before the campaign, meaning she no longer has enough Conservative MPs to guarantee winning votes in the House of Commons.

Because of that she has done a deal with Northern Irish party the Democratic Unionists, which has 10 MPs, to enable her to form a minority government.

The DUP, which has long been an Eurosceptic party, broadly shares Mrs. May's Brexit strategy and has committed to back her in any votes on Brexit policy. But they are reported to be less keen on Mrs. May's mantra that "no deal is better than a bad deal" than some Conservatives, as that could close Northern Ireland's land border with the Republic of Ireland.

According to her own election message—when she urged people to vote for her to give her a bigger majority and more strength in the Brexit negotiations—Mrs. May's hand is now weakened and she is vulnerable to being pushed about by MPs on different sides of the debate, when they come to vote on any divorce deal. She has said she wants to remain as prime minister to provide stability and certainty.

Chapter 9 European Debt Crisis and Brexit

What About the Economy, So Far?

David Cameron, his Chancellor George Osborne and many other senior figures who wanted to stay in the E.U. predicted an immediate economic crisis if the U.K. voted to leave. House prices would fall, there would be a recession with a big rise in unemployment—and an emergency budget would be needed to bring in the large cuts in spending that would be needed.

The pound did slump the day after the referendum—and remains around 15% lower against the dollar and 10% down against the euro—but the predictions of immediate doom have not proved accurate with the U.K. economy estimated to have grown 1.8% in 2016, second only to Germany's 1.9% among the world's G7 leading industrialized nations.

Inflation has risen—to 2.6% in April—its highest rate for three and a half years, but unemployment has continued to fall, to stand at an 11 year low of 4.8%. Annual house price increases have fallen from 9.4% in June but were still at an inflation-beating 4.1% in March, according to official ONS figures.

What Is Article 50?

Article 50 is a plan for any country that wishes to exit the E.U. It was created as part of the Treaty of Lisbon—an agreement signed up to by all E.U. states which became law in 2009. Before that treaty, there was no formal mechanism for a country to leave the E.U.

It's pretty short—just five paragraphs—which spell out that any E.U. member state may decide to quit the E.U., that it must notify the European Council and negotiate its withdrawal with the E.U., that there are two years to reach an agreement—unless everyone agrees to extend it—and that the exiting state cannot take part in E.U. internal discussions about its departure.

When Will the U.K. Leave the E.U.?

For the U.K. to leave the E.U. it had to invoke Article 50 of the *Lisbon Treaty* which gives the two sides two years to agree the terms of the split. Theresa May triggered this process on 29 March, meaning the U.K. is scheduled to leave on Friday, 29 March 2019. It can be extended if all 28 E.U. members agree.

Who Is Going to Negotiate Britain's Exit from the E.U.?

Theresa May set up a government department, headed by veteran Conservative MP and Leave campaigner David Davis, to take responsibility for Brexit. Former defence secretary, Liam Fox, who also campaigned to leave the E.U., was given the new job of international trade secretary and Boris Johnson, who was a leader of the official Leave campaign, is foreign secretary. These three are each set to play roles in negotiations with the E.U. and seek out new international agreements, although it would be Mrs. May, as prime minister, who would have the final say.

How Long Will It Take for Britain to Leave the E.U.?

Once Article 50 is triggered, the U.K. has two years to negotiate its withdrawal. But no one really knows how the Brexit process will work—Article 50 was only created in late 2009 and it has never been used. Former Foreign Secretary Philip Hammond, who was appointed chancellor by Theresa May, wanted Britain to remain in the E.U. during the referendum campaign and suggested it could take up to six years for the U.K. to complete exit negotiations. The terms of Britain's exit will have to be agreed by 27 national parliaments, a process which could take some years, he has argued.

E.U. law still stands in the U.K. until it ceases being a member. The U.K. will continue to abide by E.U. treaties and laws, but not take part in any decision-making.

Why Will Brexit Take So Long?

Unpicking 43 years of treaties and agreements covering thousands of different subjects was never going to be a straightforward task. It is further complicated by the fact that it has never been done before and negotiators will, to some extent, be making it up as they go along. The post-Brexit trade deal is likely to be the most complex part of the negotiation because it needs the unanimous approval of more than 30 national and regional parliaments across Europe, some of whom may want to hold referendums.

The Likely Focus of Negotiations Between the U.K. and E.U.

Theresa May has made it clear that the U.K. will not seek to stay in the E.U. single market, but that strategy has now been put in doubt by the general election result, with some of her MPs—and the strengthened opposition Labour Party—thought to be against it. Labour has said it wants the U.K. to retain all the benefits of being in the single market, even though it does not necessarily have be a member. Staying in the single market mean the U.K. staying under the auspices of the European Court of Justice and having to allow unlimited E.U. immigration, under freedom of movement rules.

What Do "Soft" and "Hard" Brexit Mean?

These terms have increasingly been used as debate focused on the terms of the U.K.'s departure from the E.U. There is no strict definition of either, but they are used to refer to the closeness of the U.K.'s relationship with the E.U. post-Brexit.

So at one extreme, "hard" Brexit could involve the U.K. refusing to compromise on issues like the free movement of people even if it meant leaving the single market. At the other end of the scale, a "soft" Brexit might follow a similar path to Norway, which is a member of the single market and has to accept the free movement of people as a result of that.

What Happens if There Is No Deal with the E.U.?

Prime Minister Theresa May says leaving the E.U. with no deal whatsoever would be better than signing the U.K. up to a bad one. Without an agreement on trade, the U.K. would have to operate under World Trade Organization rules, which could mean customs checks and tariffs.

Labour says the idea of walking away with no deal must not be an option, and it would give MPs a say on the final Brexit deal—but it has ruled out a second referendum on the terms of that deal.

Some argue leaving the single market would make little difference because the U.K.'s trading partners in the E.U. would not want to start a trade war. Others say it will mean greater costs for U.K. businesses buying and selling goods abroad.

There are also questions about what would happen to Britain's position as global financial center, without access to the single market, and the land border between the U.K. and Ireland. There is also concern that Brits living abroad in the E.U. could lose residency rights and access to free emergency health care. Here is a full explanation of what "no deal" could mean.

Could There Be a Second Referendum?

It seems highly unlikely. Both the Conservatives and the Labour Party have ruled out another referendum, arguing that it would be an undemocratic breach of trust with the British people who clearly voted to leave.

❶ Summary Writing

Complete the following summary of the text in Chinese.

```
                英国脱欧后你需要知道的那些事儿
    脱欧公投结果如何：＿＿＿＿＿＿＿＿＿＿＿＿＿＿＿＿＿＿＿＿＿＿
    脱欧公投后英国政府出现了什么变化：＿＿＿＿＿＿＿＿＿＿＿＿＿
    特蕾莎·梅对脱欧的态度如何：＿＿＿＿＿＿＿＿＿＿＿＿＿＿＿＿
    特蕾莎·梅为何要提前选举：＿＿＿＿＿＿＿＿＿＿＿＿＿＿＿＿＿
    选举结果如何：＿＿＿＿＿＿＿＿＿＿＿＿＿＿＿＿＿＿＿＿＿＿＿
    公投后英国经济表现如何：＿＿＿＿＿＿＿＿＿＿＿＿＿＿＿＿＿
    什么是"第五十条"：＿＿＿＿＿＿＿＿＿＿＿＿＿＿＿＿＿＿＿＿
    脱欧的具体日期是在何时：＿＿＿＿＿＿＿＿＿＿＿＿＿＿＿＿＿
    谁会代表英国进行脱欧谈判：＿＿＿＿＿＿＿＿＿＿＿＿＿＿＿＿
    真正实现脱欧要多久：＿＿＿＿＿＿＿＿＿＿＿＿＿＿＿＿＿＿＿
    为何脱欧谈判要持续这么长时间：＿＿＿＿＿＿＿＿＿＿＿＿＿＿
    英国与欧盟脱欧谈判的焦点是：＿＿＿＿＿＿＿＿＿＿＿＿＿＿＿
    "软脱欧"与"硬脱欧"分别指什么：＿＿＿＿＿＿＿＿＿＿＿＿＿
    如果与欧盟无法就脱欧达成统一意见，怎么办：＿＿＿＿＿＿＿＿
    是否会举行二次脱欧公投
```

Chapter ⑨ European Debt Crisis and Brexit

❶ Reading Comprehension

Briefly answer the following questions about the text in English.

1) Why did Teresa May decide to call a snap election? What is the result of the election? Did it go as Prime Minster May had wished it to go?
2) What is the difference between "hard" exit and "soft" exit?
3) What is Article 50? What is *Lisbon Treaty*?
4) How long will negotiations last for Britain to leave the E.U.?
5) Why are negotiations between the U.K. and the E.U. fraught with difficulties? What are these thorny issues, if there are any?

❷ Language Exercises

Replace the expressions in bold in the following sentences/paragraphs without changing their meanings.

1) ...she **played only a very low-key role** in the campaign and was **never seen as much of an enthusiast** for the E.U.
2) Mrs. May's gamble **backfired** and she lost her overall majority and ended up with fewer MPs than before the campaign,...
3) But they are reported to be less **keen on Mrs. May's mantra** that "no deal is better than a bad deal" than some Conservatives, as that could close Northern Ireland's land border with the Republic of Ireland.
4) Mrs. May's hand is now weakened and she is vulnerable to being pushed about by MPs on different sides of the debate, when they come to vote on any **divorce deal**.
5) He has said MPs will get a decisive say on the final Brexit agreement with the E.U., which means the U.K. might try to **go back to the negotiating table** to push for a better deal.
6) Annual house price increases have fallen from 9.4% in June but were still at an **inflation-beating** 4.1% in March, according to official ONS figures.

287

7) This will end the **primacy** of E.U. law in the U.K.. This Repeal Bill is supposed to incorporate all E.U. legislation into U.K. law **in one lump**, after which the government will decide over a period of time which parts to keep, change or remove.

8) The post-Brexit trade deal is likely to be the most complex part of the negotiation because it needs the **unanimous approval** of more than 30 national and regional parliaments across Europe, some of whom may want to hold referendums.

9) Staying in the single market mean the U.K. staying **under the auspices of** the European Court of Justice and having to allow unlimited E.U. immigration, under freedom of movement rules.

10) But any deal on their future legal status and rights must be **reciprocal** and also give certainty to the 1.2 million British expats living on the continent after the U.K. leaves the E.U.

Ⅳ Translation

1. **Provide Chinese equivalents to the following terms and expressions.**

   1) turnout
   2) Home Secretary
   3) Foreign Secretary
   4) calling a snap election
   5) Downing Street
   6) Easter Bank Holiday
   7) opposition parties
   8) minority government
   9) Chancellor
   10) House of Lords
   11) House of Commons

2. **Translate the following text into English.**

关于英国脱欧协商 6 大重点

● 什么是第 50 条？

第 50 条是《里斯本条约》的一部分，2009 年由所有欧盟成员国签署成为法律，提供成员国脱离欧盟的正式机制。

Chapter 9　European Debt Crisis and Brexit

条文的重点是成员国一旦启动第 50 条，如果未就同意延长协商时间达成一致协议，则将在通知后两年内退出欧盟。这意味着英国将在 2019 年 4 月脱离欧盟。

● 目前进度如何？

欧洲理事会主席图斯克（Donald Tusk）表示，欧盟先提出脱欧协商指导方针草案。正式响应必须等到 4 月 29 日欧盟其他 27 国元首在高峰会议上的背书。

● 什么时候展开真正协商？

在欧盟成员国赋予欧洲执委会更详细、机密的协商授权前，还不能就英国脱欧事宜展开正式的协商。因此，英国和欧盟首次面对面协商要等到 5 月底之后。

英国希望在 2018 年 3 月前谈妥一切过渡措施。欧盟执委会的英国脱欧谈判代表巴尼耶（Michel Barnier）已经订下 2018 年 10 月为达成协议的最后期限，以允许成员国国会通过。

● 可能的协商焦点在哪里？

英国首相特蕾莎·梅于 2017 年 1 月发表脱欧演说后，各界了解到英国无意继续待在欧盟单一市场内。外界对这个议题已经揣测数月，原本以为英国会继续留在欧洲法院的管辖下，并必须根据自由迁徙原则，允许欧盟移民无限制入境。

双方希望英国脱欧后仍能维持贸易往来，其中英国寻求为希望继续从事商品劳务的贸易往来者，如伦敦金融城的从业者，争取到有利的结果，也希望谈成"全面的自由贸易协议"，赋予英国进入欧洲单一市场的"最大可能的渠道"。

特蕾莎·梅也说，希望英国和欧盟达成新的海关联盟协议。

● "软脱欧"与"硬脱欧"

事实上，所谓的软硬没有严格的定义，只是用来指英国和欧盟的关系紧密程度。

所谓"硬脱欧"可能是英国拒绝在人员自由流动等议题上让步，以保住进入欧洲单一市场的渠道。所谓的"软脱欧"可能是指英国步挪威的后尘，仍是欧洲单一市场的成员，所以必须接受人员自由流动。

● 英国和欧盟如未达协议会如何？

英国首相特蕾莎·梅说过，脱欧协商没达成协议，总比签下坏协议好。

英国如果未在贸易议题上达成协议，即必须遵守世界贸易组织（WTO）的规定，这就意味着会有海关检查和关税。

部分人士认为这样差别不大，因为英国的欧盟贸易伙伴无意启动贸易战争。其他人士则表示，这代表英国企业海外采购和销售成本将增加。

若失去进入欧洲单一市场的渠道，英国作为全球金融中心的前途如何也令人担忧。旅居欧盟的英国侨民也可能失去居住权或免费的紧急医疗救护。

Business Application

This chapter may have helped you understand the European Sovereign debt crisis and the Brexit. The changing political dynamics of recent years, particularly across Western countries, reflect a number of issues among voters, many of which come back to the structural economic transformation wrought by both technological change and globalization. Indeed, political analysts from across the world have voiced concerns on the specter of xenophobia and populism and their detrimental influence on globalization. It is even suspected that populism may become the trend of global politics in the coming years. First watch "Why Brexit Happened—and What to Do Next?" delivered by Alexander Betts on TED. Then find the evidence of "populism" in other parts of the world and write a report analyzing your stance on globalization. Do you think it is a force for good or a force for bad? Do you believe we should return to an age of isolation and self-protection?

Chapter 10
U.S. Tax Reform

Overview

Benjamin Franklin once said "in this world nothing can be said to be certain, except death and taxes". The importance of taxation is self-evident for every adult. At the end of 2017, Republican lawmakers joined President Donald Trump to push the most sweeping tax overhaul of the U.S. tax system in more than 30 years. What is this tax reform about? Why is it so difficult to reform the tax code? What are its impact on ordinary American people? Who are the winners and losers of the tax reform? How do Republicans and Democrats differ in their attitudes towards this tax reform? We will examine these interesting questions in this chapter.

Pre-reading Activities

1. What role does taxation play in a sovereign country?

2. In explaining the importance of taxation, Benjamin Franklin said "in this world nothing can be said to be certain, except death and taxes". Why does he make such a comment? Do you pay taxes even if you are not employed?

3. What are the major tax types in the U.S.?

4. What principle is used in tax collection?

5. Watch the video "The Tax System Explained in Beer" by Johnston Grocke from Youtube and describe the role of using progressive rates in tax collection.

6. Watch "Why Tax Reform Is So Hard" from CNN Money.

Part 1
How to Pay U.S. Individual Taxes

Read the following two texts, one in English and one in Chinese, and carry out your reading tasks as directed.

How to File Taxes—a Beginner's Guide

Tax season has arrived—again. That means once you have the appropriate paperwork you can e-file your tax return for 2015 income. You have until April 18 to file and pay. (That

Chapter 10 U.S. Tax Reform

is not a typo. As you probably learned in school, April 15 is generally Tax Day, but the deadline was pushed back this year in recognition of Emancipation Day, a holiday observed in Washington D.C. to commemorate the signing of the Compensated Emancipation Act. Who knew?)

If this is your first time filing, welcome to adulthood. You'll do this many times in your life, so take it slow and don't panic. That said, if you're an employee who has taxes withheld from your paycheck—as many first time filers are—you're likely to be getting a refund anyway. So, really, there's no reason not to tackle your 1040 ASAP. Paying taxes is not fun, but filing can be pretty painless.

If you're new to taxes they can be quite intimidating. Confusing language. Fear of getting in trouble with the IRS. Math. Don't worry, it's really not that hard. In our *Beginner's Guide to Taxes* we'll tell you everything you need to know to file your taxes and get a nice refund. This guide has 4 sections:

Do I Have to File?

The short answer—if you made any money, you should file a tax return even if you're not required to. Why? To get a refund! Most likely income tax is being withheld from your paycheck. Often too much. File a return and get some of your money back! Even if you only worked for a month and only made a few bucks, file a tax return. Besides the money in your pocket, better safe than sorry. The last thing you want is to get in hot water with the IRS. You may also be eligible for valuable tax credits even if you didn't have taxes withheld from your paycheck.

What Paperwork and Information Do I Need?

Besides basic information about yourself (name, address, date of birth, etc.), your spouse, and your kids, you'll receive tax forms in the mail from your employer and any banks you do business with. The most common of these forms are:

A W-2 from your job that reports the salary, wages, and tips you made. Your employer must mail your W-2 by February 1, 2016. Many employers offer electronic versions via the same website you can view your paycheck stubs. If you worked more than one job during the year, you'll receive a W-2 for each one.

If you received any unemployment income, you'll get a 1099-G from the state that paid you.

If you made $10 or more in interest from a checking or savings account, your bank will send you Form 1099-INT, otherwise you can use online banking or your account statements to determine the interest you made.

There are less common forms you may receive as well. They'll be mailed by early February at the latest.

How Do I Prepare and File My Tax Return?

You have three options:

1. Pen and paper

The old school way to do your taxes is with pen and paper. It takes a while and some tax knowledge, but you can't beat the price. Determine the forms and schedules you need, download them from the IRS, print them, and get cranking. Once you're done, mail your completed return to the IRS along with your W-2 and a check (if you owe additional taxes).

2. Pay someone else to do it for you

You can hire a CPA, EA, or go to a tax store and pay someone to do it for you. It's much less effort on your part, but it isn't cheap. Prices start at around $100, most people pay $200–$300. If you have complicated finances it can cost even more. They send your return and the needed paperwork to Uncle Sam for you.

3. Do it yourself with your phone or computer

Online tax software has revolutionized the tax preparation industry. Today's software has an "interview" format—it asks you a series of questions and creates the right tax forms based on your answers. It does all the math for you, puts the numbers in the right places, and checks for mistakes, ensuring you get the biggest refund possible. Once you're done, your return is filed electronically with IRS e-file. We believe TaxAct is the best software on the market. Try it for free and don't pay until you're happy.

Chapter 10 U.S. Tax Reform

How Do I Get My Refund?

Most taxpayers get a refund. A nice one, too. The average is around $2,700! As you're filing your return you'll chose to either have IRS cut you a check or direct deposit your refund into your bank account. Direct deposit is significantly faster, so we recommend it.

If you owe the IRS additional taxes, you can write them a check, or they can withdraw the money from your bank account electronically.

That's all there is to it. It's really not that bad.

Text 2

美国人为何期待报税的日子

4月15日是美国个人所得税报税的截止日。很多美国人都期待着这个报税的日子。个人所得税就是送钱给山姆大叔，为何美国人会期待报税的日子呢？

美国工薪阶层通常两个星期领一次工资，据说可以减少"月光族"痛苦的日子。工资单里有一项保留款（withheld），每次扣除的保留款是交给国税局的。自雇者则自己定期预交保留款。如果保留款预付不足，报税时就得补交，还可能要付利息和罚款。所以，通常大家都留有余地，也就是说预缴款多于应缴款。加上各种豁免扣税，比如：搬家、被窃、孩子送日托班、孩子上大学、炒股割肉、投资失败等，都可以抵税。如果报税了，就会收到国税局的退款。

大多数美国人没有什么存款，反正有吃有住，没有"丈母娘的刚性需求"，不用缴名目繁多的赞助费，生老病死靠社会保障体系，有保险，有政府，还有慈善机构。美国的穷人存款不会超过2千美元。政府给救济的时候，不看你的房子有多大，不看你的车子有多贵，就看你的存款，低于2千美元才合格。所以，若有穷人开着宝马、戴着钻戒去领救济，不是什么新闻。

报税后，最快两三个星期后，即可收到山姆大叔的退税，一下子退回几百、几千美元。拿到了钱，很多美国人就开始"活跃起来"了，情侣上高级餐厅，单身汉到酒吧泡妞，小家庭预定暑期全家欧洲游，或者装修房间，换新车……总之，赶快花掉这笔钱。

美国的个人所得税实际上叫作"个人收入退税"（individual income tax return）。Return，意思是归还，把多收的税归还给你。所以，大家自然期待报税日子啦。

美国个人所得税高不高呢？取决于你的收入。收入越高越"亏"，收入越低越"赚"。你的收入包括工资、小费、生意收入、租金收入、银行存款利息、投资收入等，甚至包括赌博收入（gambling winnings），所以，从理论上来说，打麻将赢的钱也应该算收入。这些钱加起来，是毛收入（gross income）。

政府会给你一些免税额。最大的一笔是标准减免(standard deduction)。2014年的标准减免是：夫妻合并报税或符合条件的寡妇鳏夫报税（married filing jointly or qualifying widow(er)），12 400美元。单身（或夫妻分开）报税，6 200美元。户主（head of household）报税，9100美元。如果你的"列举扣除额"（itemized deduction) 超过了标准减免额，那就用它来报税。列举扣除额包括：医疗支出、慈善捐赠、灾害损失、工作有关支出等。比如，你捐赠了2万美元，那当然报这个大的减免数字。

此外，还有政府给的个人免税额（personal exemption）和家属免税额（dependent exemptions），2014年都是3 950美元。

毛收入减去政府规定的免税额以及其他免税额，就是你的应纳税所得额（taxable income）。

以夫妻合报为例。夫妻加两个孩子，个人免税额和家属免税额可达15 800（3 950×4）美元，标准减免额是12 400美元。加上其他的免税额，若是低收入，比如3万美元，那基本上不用交什么税。但是收入高一些，就要缴税了，收入越高，税越多。此外，许多州还得交州税、地方税。你如果已经预付了一万几千，那就有几千美元的退税。

假如你是高薪打工达人，或有其他的收入，那么，山姆大叔宰你没商量。仍以夫妻合报为例，若应缴税收入是226 850至405 100美元之间，需缴税33%；405 100至457 600美元，需缴税35%；457 600美元以上，需缴税39.6%。你去炒房，你去赚外快，山姆大叔不管，到时间你要税，三成多以上都得交上来。

根据白宫公布的奥巴马2014年的报税资料，奥巴马夫妇捐善款约7万美元，约占收入的15%；奥巴马的年薪是40万美元，加上版税，调整后的净收入（adjusted gross income）是477 383美元；上缴美国政府的所得税是93 362美元；此外，他们属于伊利诺伊州居民，还得给州政府上缴22 640美元个人所得税。

Chapter 10 U.S. Tax Reform

据美国全国广播公司（NBC）4月14日报道，全美国个人所得税的一半是排名前1%的人上缴的（top 1% pay half of the income tax）。同时，全美大约半数人不用交一分钱个人所得税。低收入阶层还能获得政府住房、医疗、幼托、食品、大学学费等资助。美国政府的基本方针还是"劫富济贫"的。

Reading Tasks

I Summary Writing

1. Complete the following summary of the text in Chinese.

> **如何在美国报税**
>
> 报税的目的：_____
> 报税的人群包括：_____
> 如何报税：
> 方法一：_____（弊端及优点是：_____）
> 方法二：_____（弊端及优点是：_____）
> 方法三：_____（弊端及优点是：_____）
> 如何获得退税：_____

II Reading Comprehension

Briefly answer the following questions about the two texts in English.

1) What is tax day in the U.S.? Why isn't this year's day on April 15th?
2) For what purpose is Emancipation Day observed in Washington D.C.?
3) What is IRS?
4) What sort of trouble you may get yourself into if you don't honor your tax-paying duty before April 15th?
5) What does the sentence "you may also be eligible for valuable tax credits even if

297

you didn't have taxes withheld from your paycheck" mean in Text 1?

6) What is W-2 form? What is 1099-INT in Text 1?

7) Who are called CPA and EA in Text 1?

8) What are the benefits of filing for tax return according to Text 2?

9) Text 2 is ended with the conclusion "美国政府的基本方针还是'劫富济贫'的". What evidence is given to support such a conclusion?

III Language Exercises

Replace the expressions in bold in the following sentences/paragraphs without changing their meanings.

1) Besides the money in your pocket, **better safe than sorry**.

2) The last thing you want is to **get in hot water** with the IRS.

3) **The old school way** to do your taxes is with pen and paper. It takes a while and some tax knowledge, but you can't **beat the price**.

4) Determine the forms and schedules you need, download them from the IRS, print them, and **get cranking**.

5) As you're filing your return you'll chose to either have IRS **cut you a check** or directly deposit your refund into your bank account.

IV Translation

1. **Provide the Chinese equivalents to the following terms and expressions.**

   1) file tax returns
   2) tax refund
   3) tax credit
   4) taxes withheld
   5) paycheck stub
   6) checking account
   7) savings account
   8) account statement
   9) direct deposit
   10) write a check
   11) withdraw money

Chapter 10 U.S. Tax Reform

2. **The following is a post taken from an online forum by a Chinese student explaining his U.S. tax filing experience in Chinese. Translate it into English.**

无论你是美国公民，还是持有美国签证的工作者，甚至是学生，只要在美国有收入，你就需要报税，需要交州税和联邦税两种。（就算你只是在学校打工，你也需要交税！如果是在唐人街餐厅打工的话，只收现金工资就可以把税忽悠过去……但前提是你也不能把这笔钱存银行卡里，只能放在银行的保险箱里）。报税是每个人的义务，而且可以帮助你顺利退税。根据美国的政策，非公民在美国工作的前五年是可以退税的，当然也不是全额退税。美国报税表格有多种，比如1040EZ、1040A、1099、W-2等。根据每个纳税人的不同情况，比如说是否全职、是否结婚、是否有孩子等填的税单都是不一样的。如果实在搞不清的话，可以去看看《外国人报税指南》(*Publication 519*) 与《美国税收条约》(*Publication 901*) 这两本册子可以帮助你快速了解报税的基本知识。每年1月底前，纳税人会收到各工作岗位寄给你的薪资所得凭单。如果是全职工作者，收到的就是W-2表，上面记录有收入总额以及被扣除的个人所得税额和社会福利税额；如果你是在家工作的或者是 part time 的，单身没有孩子的话只需要要用 1040EZ 即可；有孩子的用 1040A；自己有房子，每月付贷款的，就必须要填最复杂的 1040 表了。1040 表只是总表，副表 (forms and schedules) 还有很多种。简单来说，每一个人都要填写基本报税单 1040 (或 1040EZ 或 1040A)，此外，还要填写其他的表格。虽然美国的报税表格五花八门，但是只要搞懂大方向与基本概念，第二次报税就不会有问题了。

下面再来跟大家说说怎么退税：楼主算是比较幸运的一个学生，每年到退税的时候，学校的国际办公室都会举办好几个纳税申报单工作坊 (tax return workshop)。所以建议大家到退税的时候去问问老师，你们学校是否有这样的一个工作坊。如果有的话，你可以不用看下文啦。如果需要自力更生的话，那就请接着看下去。此退税步骤适合的人群是：学生；留美时间短于5年；无配偶子女；有收入。你需要准备的有：一台联网的电脑并连接打印机；自己的 W-2 表格或者 1042S；一支笔 (铅笔只能打草稿，但是不能直接寄出铅笔填写的表格)，计算器 (如果你的数学差到那个份儿上的话)。符合上述条件的娃娃们，你需要填写 1040NR-EZ，步骤如下：一、用已联网的电脑进入官网打印表格，然后回到电脑前拿着自己的 W-2 或者 1042S。二、按照步骤和自己的真实情况，一步一步填写 1040NR-EZ 表。三、签字，然后附带你的 W-2 & 1042S & 8843 一起寄到美国国税局（Internal Revenue Service）。之后大家就可以等着收支票啦！

V Research and Discussion

Search the Internet for answers to the following questions and share your findings in class.

1) Do Chinese people file for tax returns in China?
2) How do Chinese people pay their taxes?
3) Compare similarities and differences of individual income tax between China and U.S. in both English and Chinese.

Part 2 Why Is Tax Reform Difficult?

Read the following two English texts and carry out your reading tasks as directed.

Text 1

Why Is It So Difficult to Agree on Tax Reform?

We see it today in the U.S. We saw it in India in 2010. In Mexico in 2007. And almost everywhere else in the past two decades. Around the world, comprehensive tax reform has been difficult—if not impossible. Rich or poor, countries have rarely managed to clean up their tax "codes"—the thousands of pages through which sales, income, property, value added, inheritance and many other taxes are imposed on all of us. At most, governments have added patches to what was already a patchwork of previous attempts at reform. Why? Don't we need taxes to pay for public schools, hospitals and roads? Can't we just agree on a system that is simple, fair and sufficient? Well, it's complicated. When you design a tax

Chapter 10 U.S. Tax Reform

system, you are trying to hit six—sometimes contradictory—objectives at the same time.

First, you want every tax to actually raise significant revenue. Why do you go through the administrative and political pain of having a tax if the money collected will be puny? Yes, you can put a tax on twelve-year-old whiskies or on twelve-cylinder luxury cars. But how good is it if so few people consume those goods that, at the end of the day, the revenue from the tax is spent chasing cheaters? You want taxes to be "broad-based", that is, to cover a wide range of consumptions or incomes.

Second, you do not want to alter people's behaviors too much. In technical parlance, you want your tax system to be "efficient", that is, not to push investors, savers, employers, workers and consumers to do things they would not do if there were no taxes. The typical case is the entrepreneur who opens a factory in the middle of nowhere just to benefit from a tax break that is only given there. But think also of the couple that gets married only because it is "better for tax purposes". Or the lone widow that trades up into a bigger house just to claim the "mortgage interest break". Seriously, taxes can make you do crazy things.

Third, equity. Notice that it does not say "equality"—it says "equity". You want those that have more to pay more, but not just dollar for dollar. You want them to pay proportionally more. If you earn a hundred thousand dollars, you pay 25 percent. If you earn a million dollars, you pay 40 percent. The tax rate goes up with your income. That is called progressivity and, of course, it is one of the most contentious aspects of any tax system. The left loves it, and the right hates it.

Fourth, administrative simplicity. This is the one condition everyone agrees on—and usually the one we fail to meet. Imagine a flat, 10 percent income tax for everybody on all sources of income—no thresholds, exceptions, discount, credits or loopholes of any sort. Such a tax would be very simple to calculate and collect. The corresponding law could fit onto a single page—not to mention the tax return. And being only 10 percent, there would be little incentive to dodge it. But, it would probably generate plenty of social tension and resistance. Why are the ultra-poor paying at the same rate as the ultra-rich? Why do you get the same deductions—that is, none—whether you have one child or five? In other words, simplicity and equity can clash.

Fifth, federal consistency. At any point in time, there are several governments trying to tax you. In addition to the federal taxman, you need to consider taxes paid to your state, your county, and even your city. The last thing you want is for them to all tax you for the same thing—"double" or "triple" taxation. So the various levels of government have learned to share "tax bases" according to their respective capacity to administer them. For example, it is easier for your municipality to know how much your house is worth and bill you for your property tax—the assessor probably lives close by—than for the federal government a thousand miles away. But only the federal government can track the income of a corporation that operates in many states, let alone many countries. You get the point.

Finally, a tax reform needs to pass through the legislature. Political feasibility is the minimum threshold. Here is where the economists' rubber meets the voters' road. At least in democracies, people's preferences and perceptions matter more than technical beauty. A crystal-clear example: It is technically preferable to apply the value added tax (VAT) to every good and service, without exemptions. This avoids "identification" problems—who says that a bottle of champagne is less "food" than a bottle of milk, or an injection of Botox is less "medicine" than an injection of antibiotics? But most politicians, especially in developing countries, would think twice before allowing food and medicine to be subject to VAT. They say that it would hurt the poor. They are right: Food takes up a higher portion of a poor family's budget. The theoretical solution is to compensate those in poverty through direct social assistance, and let the VAT be as "universal" as possible. In practice, food and medicine remain untaxed in many—if not most—countries.

So, there you have it: revenue generation, economic efficiency, social equity, administrative simplicity, federal consistency, and political feasibility—all need to be achieved at the same time. Is it possible? Yes, but it needs a lot of public education and communication to explain why everyone has to be inside the tax net and why some have to carry a heavier burden than others. It needs a strong civil service that can speak true to political power without fear. And, most importantly, it needs politicians who are not polarized, and who can negotiate tradeoffs. But don't blame politicians: They just reflect—or should reflect—the wishes of citizens. The real reason why comprehensive tax reforms are so rare is that not

Chapter 10 U.S. Tax Reform

many societies have come to agree on a vision of what they want from government—that is, which public services should be provided and who should pay for them.

How Does a Bill Become Law

Every Law Starts With an Idea

That idea can come from any American citizen. Contact the elected officials to share your idea. If they want to try to make a law, they write a bill.

Besides, the administration, American President and members of the cabinet, can also introduce legislation to the speaker of the House or the Senate. This approach is called executive communications.

The Bill Is Introduced

When Congress is in session, the Primary Sponsor introduces the bill by placing it in a wooden box called "the hopper". Here, the bill is assigned a legislative number before the Speaker of the House sends it to a committee.

The Bill Goes to Committee

Representatives or Senators meet in a small group to research, talk about, and make changes to the bill. They vote to accept or reject the bill and it changes before sending it to: the House or Senate floor for debate or to a subcommittee for further research.

Congress Debates and Votes

Members of the House or Senate can now debate the bill and propose changes or amendments before voting. If the majority vote for and pass the bill, it moves to the other house to go through a similar process of committees, debate, and voting. Both houses have to agree on the same version of the final bill before it goes to the President.

Presidential Action

If the majority of Congress votes in favor of the bill, they send it to the President for approval.

The President can:

1. Approve and pass

The President signs and approves the bill. The bill is law.

2. Veto

The President rejects the bill and returns it to Congress with the reasons for the veto. Congress can override the veto with 2/3 vote of those present in both the House and the Senate and the bill will become law.

3. Choose no action

The President can decide to do nothing.

If Congress is in session, after 10 days of no answer from the President, the bill then automatically becomes law.

4. Pocket veto

If Congress adjourns (goes out of session) within the 10 day period after giving the President the bill, the President can choose not to sign it and the bill will not become law.

Reading Tasks

Summary Writing

1. Complete the following summary of Text 1 in Chinese.

税法改革是件难事
税改一般需要实现六大目标 目标一：_____ 目标二：_____ 目标三：_____ 目标四：_____ 目标五：_____ 目标六：_____ 结论：_____

Chapter 10 U.S. Tax Reform

2. Complete the following summary of Text 2 in Chinese.

在美国如何让草案成为法律

法案源自想法：_____
提出草案：_____
草案移交国会委员会：_____
国会议员辩论与投票：_____
总统可以选择
通过：_____
否决：_____
不回复：_____

Reading Comprehension

Briefly answer the following questions about Text 1 in English.

1) What does it mean "taxes have to be broad-based in reforming tax code"?
2) What examples does Text 2 give to show taxes can make people do crazy things?
3) How does equality differ from equity?
4) Explain in your words why "simplicity and equity can clash" in designing tax reform?
5) What examples does Text 2 give to show tax reform has to achieve federal consistency?
6) Why does Text 1 use the example of levying VAT on drugs and food to show the legislative challenge in tax reform?

Research and Discussion

Search the Internet for answers to the following questions and share your findings in class.

1) What role does Congress play in U.S. politics?
2) What does the U.S. Congress consist of? What is the difference between the Senate

and House of Representatives? How are people elected to serve on the Congress?

3) When is the Congress in session and when does it adjourn?

4) Tell the differences between the following posts and committees in U.S. Congress.

GOP Senate Majority Leader	Senate Minority Leader
President of the Senate	Speaker of the House of Representatives
Senate Majority Whip	Senate Minority Whip
House Majority Leader	House Minority Leader
House Majority Whip	House Minority Whip
Standing Committee	Select/Special Committee
Joint Committee	Conference Committee
Sub-Committee	

IV Translation

Translate the following sentences/paragraphs into Chinese.

1) At most, governments have added patches to what was already a patchwork of previous attempts at reform.

2) But how good is it if so few people consume those goods that, at the end of the day, the revenue from the tax is spent chasing cheaters?

3) The typical case is the entrepreneur who opens a factory in the middle of nowhere just to benefit from a tax break that is only given there.

4) Notice that it does not say "equality"— it says "equity". You want those that have more, to pay more. But not just dollar for dollar.

5) ...of course, it is one of the most contentious aspects of any tax system. The left loves it, and the right hates it.

6) Imagine a flat, 10 percent income tax for everybody on all sources of income—no thresholds, exceptions, discount, credits or loopholes of any sort. Such a tax would be very simple to calculate and collect.

7) So the various levels of government have learned to share "tax bases" according to their respective capacity to administer them.

Chapter 10 U.S. Tax Reform

8) Political feasibility is the minimum threshold. Here is where the economists' rubber meets the voters' road. At least in democracies, people's preferences and perceptions matter more than technical beauty.

9) The theoretical solution is to compensate those in poverty through direct social assistance, and let the VAT be as "universal" as possible. In practice, food and medicine remain untaxed in many—if not most—countries.

10) ...it needs a lot of public education and communication to explain why everyone has to be inside the tax net and why some have to carry a heavier burden than others. It needs a strong civil service that can speak true to political power without fear. And, most importantly, it needs politicians who are not polarized, and who can negotiate tradeoffs.

11) The real reason why comprehensive tax reforms are so rare is that not many societies have come to agree on a vision of what they want from government—that is, which public services should be provided and who should pay for them.

12) The President rejects the bill and returns it to Congress with the reasons for the veto. Congress can override the veto with 2/3 vote of those present in both the House and the Senate and the bill will become law.

Part 3
U.S. Tax Reform at a Glance

Read the following English text and carry out your reading tasks as directed.

How to Make Sense of the Tax Reform?

Winners and Losers

On Nov. 2, 2017, House GOP leaders proposed legislation that would overhaul the U.S. tax code. Republicans unveiled their bill to overhaul the U.S. tax code on Thursday morning, and there were some major winners and losers. Here's a rundown of who is happy and who isn't as the details emerge regarding the *Tax Cuts and Jobs Act*, the centerpiece of President Trump's "MAGAnomics" agenda.

Winners

Big corporations

American mega-businesses would get a substantial tax reduction. The bill cuts the top rate that large corporations pay from 35 percent to 20 percent, the biggest one-time drop in the big-business tax rate ever. On top of that, companies would get some new tax breaks to help lower their bills, such as the ability to deduct all the costs of purchasing new equipment, as well as a special low rate on any money they bring back to the United States from low-tax countries such as Ireland. Many businesses have been holding cash overseas to avoid 35 percent U.S. taxes. Now they would get to bring the money home at a tax rate of 12 percent. The entire business tax system would also change from a worldwide system, in which money anywhere around the globe is taxed, to a territorial system in which it's mostly money made in the United States that is taxed. Businesses have long lobbied for this change.

The super-rich

The estate tax, often called the "death tax" by its critics, would go away by 2024, meaning wealthy families would be able to pass on lavish estates and trust funds to their heirs tax-free. At the moment, only estates worth over $5.49 million face the estate tax (the GOP plan doubles that amount immediately until the tax goes totally away). The mega-wealthy also would get to keep charitable deductions, a popular way to lower their tax bills, and they no longer would have to pay the alternative minimum tax (AMT), a safeguard against excessive tax dodging that's been in place since 1969.

People paying the AMT

The bill eliminates the alternative minimum tax, which forces people who earn more than about $130,000 to calculate their taxes twice, once with all the deductions they can find and once with the AMT method, which prevents most tax breaks. There is perhaps

Chapter 10 U.S. Tax Reform

no better example of how much this will benefit the rich than that fact that Donald Trump would have paid $31 million less in taxes in 2005 (the one year for which we have his tax returns) without the AMT.

"Pass through" companies

Some wealthy Americans who run businesses structured as sole proprietorships, partnerships or LLCs would get a sizable discount on their taxes. Under the GOP bill, these "pass through" companies would pay a tax rate of only 25 percent on 30 percent of their business income, a big reduction from the 39.6 percent rate some pay now. The bill tries to prevent "service firms" like law firms and accounting firms from being able to pay the lower 25 percent rate, but a good tax lawyer can probably make the case for these firms to qualify. Also, on the campaign trail, Trump said that hedge funds were "getting away with murder" on their taxes and that he would take away carried interest, the popular opening in the tax code these Wall Street titans use. But the bill does not change or eliminate carried interest, which is also used by some real estate developers.

Losers

Home builders

The legislation would cut in half the mortgage interest deduction used by millions of American homeowners, changing the deduction's rules for new mortgages. Presently, Americans can deduct interest payments made on their first $1 million worth of home loans. Under the bill, for new mortgages, they would be able to deduct interest payments made only on their first $500,000 worth of home loans.

Home-builder stocks are plummeting as a result, since many builders make a lot of their money from constructing high-end mansions. In addition to capping the mortgage deduction, the bill also caps the state-and-local-property-tax deduction to $10,000 a year, another hit to higher-end homeowners. That said, many economists and even some Democrats say these limits are a good idea because the housing incentives in the current tax code favor the wealthy. The National Low Income Housing Coalition says mortgages over $500,000 are rare: Only 5 percent of mortgages are more than that amount.

(Some) small-business owners

The National Federation of Independent Business, which represents 325,000 small businesses, said it would not support the GOP bill, because it "leaves too many small businesses behind". The original idea was to lower small businesses' taxes to 25 percent, but the language in the bill allows small-business owners to pay only 30 percent of their business income at the 25 percent rate. The rest would be paid at the business owner's individual tax rate. Any individuals earning over $200,000 a year (or couples earning more than $260,000) would pay the rest of their taxes at a rate of 35 percent.

People in high-tax blue states

Say goodbye to most of the state-and-local-tax deduction (SALT). Over a third of filers in many Democratic states such as California, New York, New Jersey and Connecticut claim the SALT deduction on their returns. Under the GOP plan, people would still be able to deduct up to $10,000 on the property taxes they pay locally, but they would no longer be able to deduct the other taxes they pay to state or local governments from their federal tax payments.

The working poor

While the bill includes lots of tax breaks for big businesses and the rich, the bottom 35 percent of Americans do not get any extra benefits, according to Lily Batchelder, who served on President Barack Obama's National Economic Council. They already have a $0 federal tax liability. Some argue a more equitable tax system would increase the credits (money back) that lower-income families get, especially those that work low-wage jobs. The GOP preserves the earned-income tax credit, a popular refundable credit for the working class, but the bill does not expand it.

Charities

The National Council of Nonprofits warns that charitable deductions are likely to go down under this bill. While the GOP enables the wealthy to continue deducting their charitable giving, many middle-class and upper-middle-class families would no longer get that tax break, because they probably would stop itemizing their deductions. At the moment about 30 percent of Americans itemize, but under the GOP bill, the standard deduction

Chapter 10 U.S. Tax Reform

roughly doubles from $6,350 to $12,000 for individuals and $12,700 to $24,000 for married couples, meaning fewer people would probably itemize. The GOP argues that middle-class people should end up giving more to charity since they will pay less in taxes.

Reading Tasks

I Summary Writing

Complete the following summary of the text in Chinese.

美国 2017 年税改方案影响	
获益者	原　因
大企业	
超级富豪	
纳替代性最低税的美国人	
由合伙人转缴企业税的公司	
受损者	原　因
房地产商	
部分小企业主	
蓝州居民	
底层工薪阶层	
慈善机构	

II Translation

1. Provide the Chinese equivalents to the following terms and expressions.

   1) tax code
   2) tax breaks
   3) worldwide system
   4) territorial system
   5) trust fund
   6) tax bill
   7) tax dodging
   8) alternative minimum tax
   9) proprietorship
   10) partnership

11) LLC
12) campaign trail
13) hedge fund
14) carried interest
15) blue states
16) tax liability

2. Translate the following table into English.

特朗普税改计划到底改了什么？			
收税类型	现行税法规定	税改计划	税改影响
企业所得税	35%	大企业最高 20%	企业税负大幅降低
导管企业所有者（为避税设立的公司）	按个人所得税税率征税	最高 25%	企业及富人没必要想方设法避税了
个人所得税	七档：10%、15%、25%、28%、33%、35%、39.6%	简化为四档，或维持七档，但低端税率将下降 3~4 个百分点	老百姓税负压力小了
替代性最低限额税	个人所得另一种计税方式，与一般所得独立存在，取高值交税	取消或大幅缩小纳税人群规模	中产阶级、富人交的税也少了
个税免征额	单独申报人：6 350 美元 共同申报人：12 700 美元	单独申报人：12 000 美元 共同申报人：24 000 美元	中产阶级家庭总体税负减少
遗产税	每人 543 万美元免税额，超出部分根据遗产价值的大小从 18%~48% 不等	取消或将免税额提高一倍至 1 100 万美元	富二代不要太高兴
净投资所得税	个人年收入超 20 万美元及家庭年收入超 25 万美元的投资者需缴纳 3.8%	取消或五年内逐渐取消	中产阶级、富人更愿意投资了
一次性利润汇回税	美国企业一旦将海外利润汇回美国，就要被征收 35% 的税	美国企业将留存海外的利润汇回美国，征税率将降至 7%~14.5%	跨国公司海外盈余可能大幅度回流美国

Chapter 10 U.S. Tax Reform

（续表）

收税类型	现行税法规定	税改计划	税改影响
全球所得税率	对美国大公司取得的全球所得征收所得税	对纳税人来自国外的收入不予征税	钱都往美国跑，美国可能成为最大的避税天堂
边境调节税	无	特朗普放弃对部分国家进口商品征税20%的"豪言"	墨西哥等邻国终于松了一口气

Language Exercises

Replace the expressions in bold in the following sentences/paragraphs without changing their meanings.

1) On Nov. 2, 2017, House GOP leaders proposed legislation that would **overhaul** the U.S. tax code.

2) Here's a **rundown** of who is happy and who isn't as the details emerge regarding the *Tax Cuts and Jobs Act*, the centerpiece of President Trump's "MAGAnomics" agenda.

3) Businesses have long **lobbied** for this change.

4) The bill tries to prevent "service firms" like law firms and accounting firms from being able to pay the lower 25 percent rate, but a good tax lawyer can probably **make the case** for these firms to qualify.

5) Also, on the campaign trail, Trump said that hedge funds were "**getting away with murder**" on their taxes and that he would take away carried interest, the popular opening in the tax code these Wall Street titans use.

6) Home-builder stocks are **plummeting** as a result,...

7) In addition to capping the mortgage deduction, the bill also **caps** the state-and-local-property-tax deduction to $10,000 a year, another **hit** to higher-end homeowners.

8) The National Council of Nonprofits warns that charitable deductions are likely to **go down** under this bill.

9) At the moment about 30 percent of Americans **itemize**, but under the GOP bill, the standard deduction roughly doubles from $6,350 to $12,000 for individuals and $12,700 to $24,000 for married couples, meaning fewer people would probably itemize.

Ⅳ Research and Discussion

Search the Internet for answers to the following questions and share your findings in class.

1) According to the text, the *Tax Cuts and Jobs Act* is regarded as the centerpiece of President Trump's "MAGAnomics" agenda. How do you understand "MAGAnomics"? What is the tenet of "MAGAnomics"?
2) What other controversial economic policies has President Trump put forward other than the tax reform plan?

Part ④
Republicans VS. Democrats on Tax Reform

Read the following two English texts and carry out your reading tasks as directed.

President Trump's Weekly Address
September 22, 2017

My fellow Americans,

The American Family has always been the heart of our great nation. In homes across this country, families teach their children to work hard, to love each other, and to make the most of their talents in pursuit of their dreams.

Yet for too long, American families have been hurt by Washington's policies that put the interests of other countries before the interests of our country.

Chapter 10 U.S. Tax Reform

That is why, in my Administration, we are pursuing tax cuts and reform that create jobs in America, for American workers—not foreign workers, but American workers.

Here are my four principles for tax reform:

First, we are going to make the tax code simple and fair so that families can spend more time with their children, and less time wading through pages of paperwork. A staggering ninety-four percent of families use professional help to do their taxes—and that's not fair, that's not right. That's why under our plan, ninety-five percent of Americans will be able to file their tax return on a single page without keeping receipts, tracking paperwork, or filling out extra schedules.

Second, we are going to cut taxes for the middle class so that hardworking Americans can finally save more for their future. We want to help families keep more of what they earn—and to be able to afford the costs of raising a family. Our tax code should recognize that the most important investment we can make is in our children.

Third, we are going to restore America's competitive edge by making our tax system more attractive for investment and job creation. Our business tax rate is the highest in the world—pushing jobs to foreign countries. That's not what we want, that's not what I've been talking about all these years—I've been talking about the exact opposite. We need to bring down our tax rate so we can create jobs, wealth, and opportunity right here, in the United States of America, so we can bring our jobs back and bring our businesses back. We want tax reform that puts America first. We want tax reform that makes America great again. Finally, we are going to bring back trillions of dollars in wealth parked overseas so that it can be invested in our country, where it belongs.

We have a once-in-a-generation opportunity to reform our tax code and pave the way to unprecedented prosperity. By doing what we're doing, we will see results like you've never seen before. It will be the largest tax cut in our country's history. I am asking members in both parties to come together, to put aside partisan differences, and to pass historic tax reform and tax cuts for the great citizens of our nation. That's how we will all succeed and thrive together—as one team, one people, and one American Family.

Thank you, God bless you, and God bless America.

Text 2

Weekly Democratic Address
November 3, 2017

Hello,

I am Congresswoman Rosa DeLauro, from the Third District of Connecticut.

The biggest economic challenge of our time is that so many people who play by the rules are in jobs that do not pay enough to live on. Wages are not keeping up with rising costs—for health care, child care, and housing—and too many families struggle to make ends meet, let alone put money in a college fund or go on vacation.

Meanwhile, big corporations, millionaires, and billionaires write the rules to make government work for them—and Republicans are their comrades in arms in rigging the game against the middle class. Enough is enough.

As Democrats, we will work for an economy that works for all, not just the very rich. We need to create good-paying jobs that cannot be outsourced—lower the cost of living for families by cracking down on corporate monopolies—and build an economy that enables more and more people to reach the middle class.

That is the America I believe in—and the one Democrats are fighting for.

Unfortunately, Republicans want to take our country further and further from this goal. On Thursday, they released their tax cut proposal—and frankly, it is a giveaway to corporations, millionaires, and billionaires. It leaves behind working people and the middle class. And worse, it will encourage companies who outsource American jobs. Congress must put middle-class families and jobs before corporations that have not been loyal to their employees and to our country.

The tax plan released by President Trump and Congressional Republicans is not real tax reform. Instead, it cuts taxes for the wealthiest Americans and raises taxes on middle-class families.

It slashes the tax rate for corporations, repeals the estate tax, and encourages multinational corporations to shift profits and jobs overseas. It also rewards those corporations that have outsourced jobs by allowing them to skip paying taxes on profits earned through their outsourcing.

When jobs are outsourced, it drives down wages and salaries here. The Republican plan is wrong—this plan encourages corporate excess at the expense of the middle class, who work hard and who have played by the rules their entire lives.

The Republican plan repeals the estate tax, giving America's wealthiest families over $171 billion in tax cuts. That is the same cost as the entire Pell grant program for nearly 5 years, which helps over 7 million low-income college students every year. Where are our priorities?

Instead of giving $1.5 trillion in tax cuts to the wealthiest Americans and corporations, we should be investing in the future of our country by rebuilding our crumbling infrastructure, expanding access to early childhood education, and equipping workers with the skills they need through job training and apprenticeship programs.

Where are the Republicans' values? Where is this Administration's commitment to the "forgotten men and women of our country?" They promised no more politics as usual, and this is a slap in the face that leaves people feeling betrayed. We need a tax policy that works for the middle class.

Turning to the Child Tax Credit, the Republican proposal leaves behind vulnerable families—shutting out military families, rural families, large families, minimum-wage earners, and those with the youngest children. Under the Republican tax plan, many families will not earn enough to benefit from the larger child tax credit. And Republicans have raised the income limit on the credit to an amount that will make Members of Congress eligible—while low-income families are excluded. This is unacceptable.

I came to Washington to fight for the hardworking people I represent—not those with the most lobbyists. It is time for a better deal for Americans—one that prioritizes job creation, rising incomes, and the 21st-century economy that levels the playing field for them. We must reject this misguided Republican proposal, and work to implement public policies that understand people's lives and the need for a big change in our country's direction.

Thank you.

 Reading Tasks

❶ Summary Writing

Complete the following summary of the two texts in Chinese.

> ### 共和党观点（以特朗普为代表）
>
> 税改计划应包括四个要点：
> 1. _____
> 2. _____
> 3. _____
> 4. _____

> ### 民主党观点（以 Rosa DeLauro 为代表）
>
> 税改：
> 1. 不应给大企业减税。原因：_____
> 2. 不应给富人减税。原因：_____
> 3. 政府应在 _____ 加大投资。
> 4. 不应将儿童税收抵免门槛提高。原因：_____

❷ Translation

Translate the following sentences/paragraphs into Chinese.

1) First, we are going to make the tax code simple and fair so that families can spend more time with their children, and less time wading through pages of paperwork.

2) That's why under our plan, ninety-five percent of Americans will be able to file their tax return on a single page without keeping receipts, tracking paperwork, or filling out extra schedules.

3) I am asking members in both parties to come together, to put aside partisan differences, and to pass historic tax reform and tax cuts for the great citizens of our nation.

4) Wages are not keeping up with rising costs—for health care, child care, and

Chapter 10 U.S. Tax Reform

housing—and too many families struggle to make ends meet, let alone put money in a college fund or go on vacation.

5) Republicans are their comrades in arms in rigging the game against the middle class. Enough is enough.

6) Frankly, it is a giveaway to corporations, millionaires, and billionaires.

7) It slashes the tax rate for corporations, repeals the estate tax, and encourages multinational corporations to shift profits and jobs overseas. It also rewards those corporations that have outsourced jobs by allowing them to skip paying taxes on profits earned through their outsourcing.

8) Where are our priorities?

9) Instead of giving $1.5 trillion in tax cuts to the wealthiest Americans and corporations, we should be investing in the future of our country by rebuilding our crumbling infrastructure, expanding access to early childhood education, and equipping workers with the skills they need through job training and apprenticeship programs.

10) They promised no more politics as usual, and this is a slap in the face that leaves people feeling betrayed.

11) It is time for a better deal for Americans—one that prioritizes job creation, rising incomes, and the 21st-century economy that levels the playing field for them. We must reject this misguided Republican proposal, and work to implement public policies that understand people's lives and the need for a big change in our country's direction.

III Research and Discussion

Search the Internet for answers that can be used to fill in the following table and share your findings in class.

Democrat vs Republican Comparison Chart		
Aspects	Democrats	Republicans
Economic Ideas		
Social and Human Ideas		

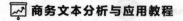

(Continued)

Aspects	Democrats	Republicans
Stance on Military Issues		
Stance on Gay Marriage		
Stance on Abortion		
Stance on Death Penalty		
Stance on Taxes		
Stance on Government Regulation		
Healthcare Policy		
Stance on Immigration		
Traditionally Strong in States		
Symbol		
Color		
Famous Presidents		

Business Application

You probably have some basic idea of the gist of the U.S. tax reform. It is time you apply what you have learned on U.S. tax system to review what is happening in China. The following is an overview of China's tax system. Describe in Chinese what these taxes are. And based on the news you have learned from the media in the past several years, describe what kind of tax reforms are currently under way in China.

Overview of PRC Taxation System

China is one of the biggest markets in the world and is attracting more and more global investors to move into the Chinese market. In order to run the business in the most cost-efficient way, it is necessary for the foreign investors to understand all the

Chapter 10 U.S. Tax Reform

potential relevant tax costs that would be incurred in China before making an investment decision. In addition, different type of investment activities will trigger different types of taxes. We provide below a brief introduction to the PRC taxation system.

Major Taxes in the PRC

The major taxes applicable to foreigners, foreign investment enterprises ("FIEs") and foreign enterprises ("FEs") doing business in China are as follows:

Category	Type of Tax
Tax on Income	• Corporateincome tax ("CIT")—standard tax rate is 25%, but the tax rate could be reduced to 15% for qualified enterprises which are engaged in industries encouraged by the China government (e.g. New/High Tech Enterprises and certain integrated circuit production enterprises). Tax holiday is also offered to enterprises engaged in encouraged industries. Other CIT incentives are also available for tax resident enterprises in China. • Individual income tax ("IIT")—progressive rates range from 3% to 45%.
Tax on Transactions (Turnover Tax)	• Value-added tax—applies to the sale of goods, except real estate properties, and the provision of labour services in relation to the processing of goods and repair and replacement services within China. The standard tax rate is 17% with certain necessities taxed at 13%. • Consumption tax—applies to 14 categories of consumable goods, including tobacco, alcoholic drinks, cosmetics, jewellery, fireworks, gasoline, diesel oil, tires, motorcycles, automobiles, golf equipment, yacht, luxury watch, disposable chopsticks and wooden floorboard. The tax is computed based on sales price and/or sales volume. • Business tax—applies to the provision of services (excluding processing services and repair and replacement services), the transfer of intangible properties and the sale of real estate properties in China. Tax rates range from 3% to 20%.

(Continued)

Category	Type of Tax
Tax on Specific Objective	• Land appreciation tax—a tax levied on the gains realized from real property transactions at progressive rates ranging from 30% to 60%. The gain is calculated based on the "land value appreciation amount", which is the excess of the consideration received from the transfer or sale over the "total deductible amount".
Tax on Resource	• Resources tax—a tax levied on natural resources, generally on a tonnage or volume basis at rates specified by the Ministry of Finance. Taxable national resources include crude oil, natural gas, coal, other raw non-metallic minerals, raw ferrous metals, nonferrous metallic minerals and salt (both solid and liquid).
Tax on Property	• Real estate tax—a tax imposed on the owners, users or custodians of houses and buildings at the rate at either 1.2% of the original value with certain deduction or 12% of the rental value.
Tax on Behaviour	• Vehicle and vessel tax—a tax levied at a fixed amount annually on the owners of vehicles and vessels used in the China. • Motor vehicle acquisition tax—10% of the taxable consideration will be levied on any purchase and importation of car, motorcycles, trams, trailer, electric buses, cart and certain types of trucks. • Stamp tax—a tax levied on enterprises or individuals who execute or receive "specified documentation" in China and the tax rates vary between 0.005% to 0.1%.
Tax Levied by the Customs	• Customs duties—duties are imposed on goods imported into China and are generally assessed on the CIF (cost, insurance and freight) value. The rate of duty depends on the nature and country of origin of the imported goods.
Tax Levied by Finance Department	• Deed tax—a tax levied on the transferees or assignees on the purchase, gift or exchange of ownership of land use rights or real properties, with the tax rates generally ranging from 3% to 5%.